THE
GRANDOLEOPRY®

THE
GRAND OLE OPRY®

THE MAKING OF AN
AMERICAN ICON

COLIN ESCOTT

BRENDA COLLADAY, PHOTO EDITOR

CENTER
STREET®

NEW YORK   BOSTON   NASHVILLE

Center Street
Hachette Book Group USA
1271 Avenue of the Americas
New York, NY 10020

Visit our Web site at www.centerstreet.com.

Center Street is a division of Hachette Book Group USA.
The Center Street name and logo are trademarks of Hachette Book Group USA.

Printed in the United States of America

First Edition: November 2006

10 9 8 7 6 5 4 3 2 1

Library of Congress Cataloging-in-Publication Data
Escott, Colin.
The Grand ole opry: the making of an American icon / Colin Escott.
— 1st ed. p. cm.
ISBN-13: 978-1-931722-86-5
ISBN-10: 1-931722-86-2
1. Country music—Tennessee—Nashville—History and criticism.
2. Country musicians—Tennessee—Nashville—Biography.
3. Grand ole opry (Radio program) I. Title.
ML3524.E6 2006
781.64209768'55—dc22   2006007796

A NOTE FROM THE GRAND OLE OPRY

The Grand Ole Opry has always had that special something that separates it from every other form of American entertainment: its people.

This book is dedicated to the dreamers who, for going on a century, have made their way to the Opry stage, aspiring to lend their voices to the Opry's song. Country music's home has been built upon their dreams, their performances, and their undying commitment.

This book is dedicated as well to those in the pews, cars, and living rooms around the world who have dropped by or tuned in over that same course of time, sharing in the Opry dream while laughing and clapping along.

Indeed, the Opry is set apart by its people. Good people.

CONTENTS

FOREWORD

by Vince Gill

People call the Grand Ole Opry a "family show," and that's exactly what it is. A lot of my deep appreciation and reverence for the Opry is attributable to my parents, and the generation of my family that came before me. My mom was born the year the Opry started, 1925. My dad taught me how to play guitar and my mom played the harmonica, and my grandmother played the piano in church. That was the generation that sat around the radio on Saturday night listening to the Grand Ole Opry. Even though that era was disappearing by the time I was born, all the records I heard were by Opry stars. Jim Reeves, Patsy Cline, Chet Atkins, and so on. Respect for the Opry and all it stood for was bred in me.

Thankfully, I got to know several of the performers who carried the show from the 1930s and '40s until quite recently: Minnie Pearl, Roy Acuff, Grandpa Jones, Bill Monroe, Jimmy Dickens, and Hank Snow. Every opportunity I got to sing with stars like Roy Acuff was a moment of pride for me because those were the heroes of my parents and my family. There's something so much deeper in my connection with those artists than the fact that we're all singers. I feel that I'm respected by the generation of Opry performers that came before me because I have reverence for them, and I back it up by being at the Opry every chance I can.

When you bring as many artists onto a stage every Saturday night as the Opry does, it'll never be right for everybody all the time. I hear people saying that the show isn't what it used to be, but you've got to take the long view. History alters what we think of as country music, and that's why the Grand Ole Opry is so important, because it's every era of country music together on one stage. You can even make a case for saying that "country music" as we know it didn't come along for maybe twenty years after the Opry was born. Before that, it was string bands, and those of us who love string band music and have some of that in our style—Alison Krauss, Ricky Skaggs,

Marty Stuart, myself—owe the Opry a debt of gratitude for keeping that music alive through some pretty lean years.

In these pages you'll find the story of the Grand Ole Opry in the words of those who were there. As you'll see, it wasn't always smooth sailing, but if the Opry had always been perfect and well-oiled, I don't think it would have lasted. The turmoil and struggles made people fight to keep it alive and keep it vibrant, and those struggles are the way in which every generation redefines what the Opry is.

There are so many lessons that every artist can learn from the Grand Ole Opry. I started out as a picker, and I already knew the backup musicians there, and I saw at once that it wasn't all about the stars. That's why you treat everyone the same. Artists, musicians, backstage people. It takes a village, and the Opry taught me that.

The Opry also helped me understand the difference between what's really important and what's trivial when it comes to making music. These days, our culture has become disposable. What's the hip, cool, and groovy thing right now? The engaging thing about the Opry is that it doesn't buy into that theory, and I don't think it ever will. You can go out there and see fifty years of what's truly important in country music history. What our music has been and what it is today. That's a great way to spend an evening. Then there's the unpredictability of the Opry. Jazz singer Diana Krall came out and sang with me, and no one expected it. Some nights there'll be giant train wrecks. Someone will say, "Hey, come out and do a number with me," and it just won't work, but then you'll get those moments that only happen at the Grand Ole Opry . . . and there have been so many. One night I remember in particular came toward the end of Roy Acuff's life. He couldn't see too well, so he'd get right up next to you while you were performing. He loved my song "When I Call Your Name," and asked me to sing that, and he had a big tear running down his cheek. I still choke up thinking about it.

It hurts me to see country artists who think they don't need the Grand Ole Opry. On one level, I get it. Things are different today than they were sixty years ago. But the Opry can and will stay relevant because enough people have reverence for it and care about its future as much as its past. I had an afternoon with Roy Acuff many years ago and he shared things with me that I'll probably never tell anybody, but he said, "I was a real big star back in the forties. Hollywood was after me, but the Opry *needed* me." That stuck with me. I thought, "That's what it takes sometimes. Somebody

willing to set aside their best interests, and do something for the good of the cause." When I do the Opry, they give me Mr. Acuff's dressing room. I think it's because I always leave the door open.

For the Grand Ole Opry's eightieth anniversary, we took it back to Carnegie Hall. The Opry had been there twice before, in 1947 and 1961, and people asked us how it felt to stage the Opry there. I've always found that people respond to great music wherever they are, but I was so proud to see our music in that venue. Carnegie Hall has an amazing weight to it. Even the few country LPs recorded at Carnegie Hall are landmark recordings. When you think how derided and looked down upon this music was at the time the Opry was born, it makes you realize how far we've come, and it makes you realize the Opry's role in getting us there.

Even today, the Grand Ole Opry is the first thing people think about

Vince Gill at the Grand Ole Opry.

when they think of country music. It conjures up the history of our music. In this book, you'll hear the words of those who went before us, and the words of those who make the Opry what it is today. When you step onto the Opry stage or sit in the audience, you feel the presence of those who went before and created the music that we're carrying on. I embrace the ghosts. If they're hanging out in the rafters, they're most welcome.

INTRODUCTION

There wasn't an empty seat at the Grand Ole Opry's eightieth birthday celebration in October 2005. Among the cast members onstage that night, there was one—Little Jimmy Dickens—who'd first appeared on the show in 1948. Back then, he'd mingled with veterans of the show's earliest days. At the eightieth, he stood backstage with Opry stars from the last fifty years. In the half-light, they formed a ragged, unbroken circle.

Today's Opry members coexist happily with the ghosts. No one who plays bluegrass can forget that Bill Monroe introduced the music from the Opry stage. Today's Opry members know that the torch has been passed to them, and that they in turn must pass it on. Away from the Opry, today's top stars can play to stadiums full of fans; at the Opry, they play to four thousand people, some of whom have little idea who they are. They have just a few minutes to win over the crowd while artists from the last fifty years watch from the wings. That's what makes the Grand Ole Opry one of the premier stages in American music.

Through the years, the legends of the Grand Ole Opry have become known by one name. Cash, Acuff, Hank, Patsy, and so on. At the eightieth anniversary, Garth was there. He emerged from a brief self-imposed retirement, and, in case he, or anyone else, was wondering, he's still the most powerfully iconic presence in country music. Before joining Steve Wariner for some duets, he went onstage as the fourth member of a quartet alongside Little Jimmy Dickens, Porter Wagoner, and Bill Anderson. Backstage, every hand was shaken and every photo taken. Old-timers used to call it "shake and howdy," and it's a tradition that has almost disappeared. Garth, though, seemed genuinely pleased to carry it on. Ernest Tubb, who personified shake and howdy, would have smiled his big benevolent smile and approved.

Country music venerates tradition, and the Grand Ole Opry embodies it. There is nothing remotely comparable elsewhere in music. No show covers all the bases, from street-corner blues to hip-hop or from rockabilly to heavy metal, but every night at the

Grand Ole Opry four thousand people of all ages can hear the broad sweep of country music from the back porch to the stadium. No one performs more than a few songs per segment, so the show isn't trapped in one time period. It's breathlessly varied and fast-paced, faster and more varied by far than the very first show when Uncle Jimmy Thompson played the fiddle for one hour to the sole accompaniment of his niece.

Brad Paisley, one of the current stars who has made a sustained commitment to the Opry, has a vision for the show. "Ideally," he said recently, "people will come hear Porter Wagoner or Bill Anderson on a night I'm singing and walk away saying, 'I like that new guy, too.' And maybe there'll be people who come to the show because they've heard my songs on the radio and they'll say, 'Boy, I didn't know Bill Anderson wrote "City Lights," or I didn't know Jimmy Dickens's "Bird of Paradise" is so funny. I need to go get their CDs.'"

The Opry came into a world with few entertainment options; now, of course, there are so many. Every era had its unique set of problems, though. In its earliest days, the Opry's managers had to contend with Nashville's old-money crowd, who believed that the show brought disgrace to their community. Today, as the interstates approach Nashville, the official road signs say "Metropolitan Nashville, Home of the Grand Ole Opry." The Opry has made Nashville synonymous with country music, and the country music business no longer has to trumpet how much it contributes to the city and its economy because the evidence is everywhere. Those entrusted with the future of the Grand Ole Opry contend with different problems, but the show will survive because too many people want it to survive. True, there are complaints that it isn't what it used to be, but it never was. If it was what it used to be, it would have been finished by 1930.

So much has happened in eighty years, and here for the first time the story is told in the words of those who witnessed it. Some were in front of the microphone, some behind the curtains, and some in the back office. Some observed and some participated. Everyone was there. Occasionally memories conflict, but that's as it should be. No two people have ever remembered the same event the same way.

For help in preparing this book, I'm deeply indebted to Brenda Colladay, curator of the Grand Ole Opry Museum and the vast archive that the Opry has accumulated along the way. The photo selection here is the tip of the iceberg. Brenda also compiled the list of Opry members by decade and assisted in many other ways. Thanks also to Melissa Fraley Agguini, vice president of Brand Development at the Opry's parent company, Gaylord Entertainment; to Gina Keltner, who helped arrange the interviews; and to Alex Smithline, whose idea this initially was. Finally, thanks to Steve Buchanan, president of the Grand Ole Opry Group, and Pete Fisher, manager of the Grand Ole Opry, who are steering the Opry into the twenty-first century with a vision that would appeal to those who originally conceived the show.

COLIN ESCOTT
Nashville, February 2006

THE

GRAND OLE OPRY®

1

THE AIR CASTLE OF THE SOUTH

One hundred years ago, country music as we know it today didn't exist. Depending on where you were, you'd hear Gaelic fiddle tunes, old English ballads, new American ballads, bawdy cowboy songs, hymns, or minstrel songs. Undocumented and ignored, it was called folk music because it was the music that the people of America sang and played for themselves. You'd hear it at weekend hoedowns and barn dances, when families who would rarely see another family all week would come together to share a meal and play music. The barn dance would be in someone's barn with hay bales for seating; the hoedown might be outside or in a church hall or in someone's front parlor. It would probably be on bath night, and the women would have curled their hair with curling tongs heated over the flame of the coal oil lamp.

As the nineteenth century ended, few could have foreseen the impact that two recent inventions, radio and records, would have upon the music played at rural get-togethers. When commercial radio became popular in the 1920s, local music suddenly wasn't local anymore. All the pieces of American folk music came together to make country music, and if there was one stage where it happened, it was the Grand Ole Opry.

Edwin Craig: "I just wanted everybody in this community to have access to this new medium."

The Grand Ole Opry was
one of the first *radio* barn
dances. An old idea in a new
era, the radio barn dance was a
Saturday night hoedown staged
in such a way that folks listening at home could share the
fun and excitement. A night at
the Grand Ole Opry has almost always included dancers,
older stars, new stars, traditional groups, and comedians.
That's the way it has been for
eighty years. Performers came
together on the Opry stage
from very different places and
very different backgrounds to create a new American art form, country
music, from traditional folk music. The Opry has not only come to define
country music but personify the values of the millions who listen to it.

Country music was first performed on radio in 1922; the first country
music recordings were made in 1923; and the Grand Ole Opry was
launched in 1925. The Opry began as just another show on Nashville's
WSM radio, but the station's owners, National Life and Accident Insurance Company, soon realized that it would help them reach a largely un-
tapped rural audience. When National Life Vice President Edwin Craig
launched WSM, it wasn't Nashville's first radio station, but, unlike the
earliest stations, it had solid financial backing and the steadfast commitment of its owners.

left: The National Life
Building. WSM was on the fifth
floor and called itself the "Air
Castle of the South."

right: Engineer Jack DeWitt
(second from left) with a group
of Scouts. DeWitt was later
awarded seven patents.

Once Edwin Craig had secured the funding to start WSM, he bought state-of-the-art equipment. His love of radio and belief in its potential had already led him to engineering genius John H. "Jack" DeWitt, who would become a key part of Opry history.

PETE MONTGOMERY, WSM *engineer:*

Even before WSM went on the air, Jack DeWitt and I experimented with radio in Nashville. We built a transmitter for Ward Belmont College, and they gave it to us when the dean decided that it used too much electricity. Then we set up in the parlor of the DeWitt home, and anybody could come and broadcast, but DeWitt's mother decided she didn't like all those strangers traipsing through her house. We moved to First Baptist Church, where they gave us studio space in exchange for broadcasting the Sunday sermon. We joined WSM when National Life bought a commercial transmitter. I met Edwin Craig, liked him, and decided to work for him.

JACK DeWITT, WSM *engineer:*

Edwin Craig was the son of one of the founders of National Life, Cornelius Craig, and got interested in radio just by listening to it. He had a good receiver and he loved to listen to distant radio stations. He wanted to leave the company and start a radio station. His father said, "You may not leave the company, but if you wish to put in a radio station, do it here." So he went ahead, and got the license for WSM, which was National Life's slogan, "We Shield Millions." Those

WSM Studio A. Jack DeWitt: "It was the only studio we had for a long time. There was a door from the studio to the hall and a door from the hall to the control room, and glass panels between the studio and control room."

call letters had already been assigned to a ship [the S.S. Fair Oaks], but Edwin Craig wanted "WSM" and pulled some strings. We went on air with a one-kilowatt Western Electric transmitter. It had a radius of maybe one hundred or one hundred-and-fifty miles. I think Craig's goal was to reach the states that National Life operated in.

WSM went on-air at 7:00 p.m. on October 5, 1925. It began with an announcement by Edwin Craig, followed by a prayer from Dr. George Stoves, pastor of the West End Methodist Church. The Shrine Band played the national anthem, and there was a dedication program that lasted until two o'clock in the morning. Craig didn't launch WSM with the idea of programming "folk" or country music (in fact, country music and blues were the only types of music unrepresented in the inaugural gala), but he hired a program director who'd already stumbled on the idea for the radio barn dance.

George D. Hay: November 1925

JACK DeWITT:

Edwin Craig and the people at National Life were first-class people, and they really understood the community. They wanted a radio station that reflected the community. That's why they brought in George Hay as station manager, and that was the middle of November 1925.

JUDGE HAY'S DAUGHTER, MARGARET:

George Hay was a Hoosier, born in Attica, Indiana, in 1895, son of a jeweler. His mother was widowed when he was ten and for the most part allowed him to grow

up on his own, never managing to overcome her depression over the loss of her husband. Unable to complete high school in Chicago, where they had moved, he turned to supporting himself by way of many jobs. . . . He was basically democratic. A gentle man with impeccable manners.

GRANT TURNER, *Opry announcer:*

He told me that he wrote a column for the Commercial Appeal *in Memphis called "Howdy, Judge." He'd write about all the people who'd been arrested over the weekend. Then the* Commercial Appeal *decided to build a radio station, and they told him, "You're the only one on staff who might be able to adapt himself to running this station." Judge knew nothing about radio, but he took it on.*

JUDGE HAY:

I was on from eight 'til nine o'clock every night. Just plain everyday talk, all ad-lib. Direct and simple and full of human interest. At first I signed off with my initials, then one day, on the spur of the moment, I decided to sign off with my childhood nickname. From that day, I closed every broadcast with "This is your Solemn Ol' Judge, George D. Hay." . . . I got the nickname "Judge" as a child. I was such a solemn kid, relatives would say, "He's solemn as a judge."

The Commercial Appeal *sent [me] to the Ozarks to cover the funeral of one of America's World War I heroes. We rode behind a mule team thirty miles up in the mountains from Mammoth Spring, leaving very early in the morning. The neighbors came from miles around in respect to the memory of this United States Marine, who gave his life to preserve their way of life. The young man's father welcomed them as he stood on the crude platform in the country churchyard, but*

closed his brief remarks in this manner: "Let all those who were against the government during the war pass on down the road." We didn't see anyone leave.

We lumbered back to Mammoth Spring and filed our story, and spent a day there. In the afternoon, we sauntered around town, at the edge of which there lived a truck farmer in an old railroad car. He had seven or eight children, and his wife seemed very tired with the tremendous job of caring for them. We chatted for a few minutes and the man went to his place of abode and brought forth a fiddle and bow. He invited me to attend a hoedown the neighbors were going to put on that night until the crack of dawn in a log cabin about a mile up a muddy road. He and two other old-time musicians furnished the earthy rhythm. About twenty people came. There was a coal oil lamp in one corner of the cabin and another in the "kitty" corner. No one in the world has ever had more fun than those Ozark mountaineers did that night. It stuck with me until the idea became the Grand Ole Opry.

I never would have left the South if a Chicago station, WLS, had not offered so much more money. They asked me my price and I said, "Seventy-five dollars a week." It was so much more than I'd ever made in Memphis. That was 1924. Several weeks after the WSM launch, I was in Dallas, and [WSM treasurer] Mr. Runcie Clements and Mr. Craig asked me to come to their new station. Within a few weeks after it started, I came to WSM as director.

Edwin Craig's old-money background didn't prevent him from enjoying country music, and he shared Judge Hay's enthusiasm for preserving the old ballads. As a student at Branham-Hughes Military Academy in Spring Hill, Tennessee, Craig had played mandolin in a string band, together with several classmates and, he said later, "a young Negro boy who was the janitor in our dorm."

Uncle Jimmy Thompson: November 1925

JUDGE HAY:

The Grand Ole Opry is a very simple program, [and] it started in a very simple way. WSM discovered something very fundamental when it tapped the vein of American folk music, which lay smoldering in small flames for about three hundred years. Realizing the wealth of folk music material and performers in the Tennessee Hills, [I] welcomed the appearance of Uncle Jimmy Thompson, who went on the air at eight o'clock Saturday night, November 28, 1925. Uncle Jimmy told us that he had a thousand tunes. He was given a comfortable chair in front of an old carbon microphone, while his niece, Miss Eva Thompson, played his piano accompaniment.

Uncle Jimmy was about eighty years of age. He told us that he had recently come out with a blue ribbon in a big fiddlers' contest and shindig in Dallas, which had lasted about a week. WSM's studio was rather small and beautifully decorated in a quiet way with red drapes, suggesting a very dignified type of

George D. Hay introduces Uncle Jimmy Thompson.

music. Uncle Jimmy was somewhat amazed, but by no means rattled or thrown for a loss. He was the extrovert type and nothing about the radio seemed to bother him, not even the fact that it was a new proposition. After he had played for about an hour, we suggested very softly on account of the microphone that perhaps he had played enough. His reply came back not so softly: "Why shucks, a man don't get warmed up in an hour."

Uncle Jimmy was cantankerous and hard-drinking, and although he wasn't quite as old as Hay thought (seventy-seven, not eighty), he'd begun fiddling before the Civil War. He claimed that his fiddle, "Old Betsy," had come with his ancestors from Scotland. Despite his advanced years, he immediately saw the potential of radio. "I want to throw my music out all over the Americee," he told his niece. Seated in front of WSM's microphone, he'd yell out, "Tell the neighbors to send in their requests, and I'll play 'em if it takes me all night."

Like Judge Hay, Uncle Jimmy believed his music needed no more sophistication than it already had.

JACK DeWITT:

A guard at the National Life building said, "Hey, Uncle Jimmy, [classical violinist] Fritz Kreisler is in town. Would you like to hear him perform?" They gave him a ticket, and Uncle Jimmy went down to where Fritz Kreisler was performing. Anyway, Uncle Jimmy stayed down there about thirty or forty minutes, and the guard said, "How'd you like Fritz Kreisler?" Uncle Jimmy said, "Aw, he just kept practicin' and practicin'. He never did strike up a tune, so I left."

But as Hay's new barn-dance show became popular, Uncle Jimmy became more of a liability than an asset, and by 1928, he'd almost stopped appearing.

SAM KIRKPATRICK, *Uncle Jimmy's neighbor:*

I'll never forget the last night Uncle Jimmy played. He kinda liked his bottle pretty well. He was playin', and before he finished, there was this stopping, and we didn't hear nothin' for a minute. Then George Hay come on, and said Uncle Jimmy was sick tonight. Come to find out he'd just keeled over and passed out.

The unpolished performers led to unrelenting criticism of Hay's Barn Dance, and the fact that it stayed on the air infuriated Craig's country club friends. WSM, they argued, should enhance Nashville's reputation as the "Athens of the South," a place of commerce, culture, and learning. If anything, WSM should try to educate the "hillbillies," not pander to them. Craig, though, stood his ground.

JUDGE HAY:

Edwin Craig saved the Opry. He's the man who kept me from being run out of town and the Opry with me during those early days when we didn't know from week to week whether this community would let the Opry live. Every Monday morning brought a crisis. Conservative elements of Nashville's population railed against hillbilly music taking such a prominent place in the programming of this new station. Every week, I'd take my troubles to Mr. Edwin Craig, and he handled them in some way unknown to me. All I know is that the Barn Dance, as it was called then, stayed on the air.

Dr. Humphrey Bate: 1925

Almost as soon as it went on the air, WSM's Barn Dance attracted performers from in and around Nashville. They weren't paid, but didn't care

Dr. Humphrey Bate (left) led his band on WSM *before the Opry started and was on one of Nashville's first stations, WDAD, before that.*

because music was a pastime, not a profession. One of the show's early mainstays was a genial country physician from Sumner County, Tennessee, Dr. Humphrey Bate.

Just a dozen or so long-unavailable recordings are the only tangible reminders of Dr. Bate, but his importance to the Opry in its early days was inestimable. He traveled widely and had a good ear. If he heard someone he liked, he'd recommend them to Judge Hay. Bate himself played the harmonica, and, as soon as he heard DeFord Bailey, he knew he'd found one of the instrument's finest practitioners.

DeFord Bailey: 1925

DeFORD BAILEY:

Dr. Bate wouldn't take no for an answer. They had a hard time getting me to go down there. I was ashamed of my little cheap harp and them with all them fine, expensive guitars, fiddles, and banjos. But Dr. Bate told me, "We're going to take you with us if we have to tote you." He told the Judge, "I will stake my reputation on the ability of this boy." The Judge knew at once he wanted me. He give me two dollars and told me to come back next week.

You can't x-ray it or do blueprints like a doctor or engineer to understand my style. It's just in me. I can't help it. I don't ask nobody to help me or show me how to do it. I just do it. You hear something all the time with my music. Other people's music is good, but it's missing something. I add time to vacant space.

DeFord Bailey had two showstoppers: an imitation of a railroad train and "The Fox Chase."

DeFord Bailey. Hay dubbed him "the harmonica wizard." On show dates, few of which had amplification, he played through the megaphone seen here. To his right is a rack to create train effects.

A letter to WSM's magazine, Our Shield, *dated February 7, 1928, from*
MR. AND MRS. HOLLOWAY SMITH *in Jefferson City, Missouri:*

*Needless to say, we thoroughly enjoy your Saturday night program. I have one
request to make, and that is when your harmonica artist puts on the "Fox Hunt,"
that we are given some advance notice as to what to expect. Last night my old
Irish Setter bird dog was laying in front of the fireplace when your artist reached
the point in his playing where he repeated the words, "Get him, sic him," before
anyone could interfere my old dog had turned over two floor lamps and a
smoking stand.*

Even with the beginning of a regular cast and steadily growing listenership, the future of WSM's Barn Dance remained uncertain. It was moved
around various time slots until it became a fixture on Saturday night.
Then, in 1927, it faced another threat when WSM joined the newly
launched NBC network. NBC supplied networked shows from New York
and Chicago during prime time, and the understanding was that its affili-
ates would fill in with locally produced shows at other times. Once again,
Edwin Craig stepped in to defend the Barn Dance.

EDWIN CRAIG:

*We almost lost our NBC affiliation at one point. The network reserved the right
to preempt Saturday night time on all its stations, but we refused to go along
with this. We felt that we were acting in the public interest by bringing good
entertainment to people in our own community, so we took a firm stand. We
became the only station in the whole network not obligated to give the network
prime Saturday time.*

Although Judge Hay was in charge of all local programming on WSM,
the Barn Dance was the show closest to his heart. From its inception, he'd
been on the lookout for a new name.

JUDGE HAY:

*For the first two years, our Saturday night show was called the WSM Barn
Dance, which, as a name, was a "dead head," as we would say in the newspaper
game. But with the organization of NBC, and WSM's association with it, we
carried practically full network service. It so happened that on Saturday nights*

from seven to eight o'clock WSM carried the Music Appreciation Hour, under the direction of the eminent composer and conductor Dr. Walter Damrosch. Dr. Damrosch always signed off his concert a minute or so before eight o'clock, just before we hit the air with our mountain minstrels. The change in pace and quality was immense, but that is part of America. The members of our radio audience who loved Dr. Damrosch and his symphony orchestra thought we should be shot at sunrise and did not hesitate to tell us so.

The monitor in our Studio B was turned on so that we would have a rough idea of the time which was fast approaching. At about five minutes to eight, [I] called for silence in the studio. Out of the loudspeaker came the very correct but accented voice of Dr. Damrosch: "While most artists realize that there is no place in the classics for realism, nevertheless I am going to break one of my own rules and present a composition by a young composer from 'Ioway,' who sent us his latest number, which depicts the onrush of a locomotive. . . ." After which, the good doctor directed his symphony orchestra through the number, which carried many "shooses," depicting an engine trying to come to a full stop. Then he closed his program with his usual sign-off.

Our control operator gave us the signal which indicated we were on the air. [I] said something like this, "Friends, the program which has just come to a close was devoted to the classics. Dr. Damrosch told us that there is no place for realism in classical music. However, for the next three hours we will present nothing but realism. It will be down to earth for the earthy. In respectful contrast to Dr. Damrosch's presentation which presents the onrush of a locomotive, we will call on one of our performers, DeFord Bailey, to give us his version of his 'Pan American Blues.' " At the close of it, [I] said, "For the past hour, we have been listening to music taken largely from grand opera. From now on, we will present the Grand Ole Opry."

The earliest Grand Ole Opry souvenir folio, circa 1928.

No one is completely sure when the name change took place. National Life's in-house magazine, *Our Shield*, is the best guide. On December 27, 1927, the show was still billed as "Regular barn-dance program," but it was "The Grand Old Op'ry" one week later. According to Judge Hay's daughter, Margaret, he renamed it on December 10, 1927.

In later years, many artists would claim that they were there the night that WSM's Barn Dance became the Grand Ole Opry, but the lineup wasn't published. In fact, the casting was so informal that Judge Hay probably didn't have a good idea of who would be on the show until Saturday evening came around.

FIDDLIN' SID HARKREADER,
early Opry performer:

I played two tunes on my fiddle the night the Opry was named. The others who were in the studio that night were Dr. Humphrey Bate and his Possum Hunters, Burt Hutcherson, and DeFord Bailey, George Wilkerson and his Fruit Jar Drinkers, and the Binkley Brothers. [But at that time] everyone who could play an instrument or sing old-time country music was welcome. No one at any particular time. All they needed to do was just go by the station, and it was almost certain that they would get on the air.

Fiddlin' Sid Harkreader.

Grand Ole Opry cast, circa 1928.

The Air Castle of the South

Sam and Kirk McGee from Sunny Tennessee. Sam McGee: "Just as soon as word circulated about the Opry, the Barn Dance it was then, everybody got excited about it. Uncle Dave Macon and me were down in Alabama. He says, 'Let's go and play on that Barn Dance.' It wasn't any trouble to get on then because it was so new and they didn't have the people they needed."

SAM McGEE, *early Opry performer:*

The Opry came down here and said they wanted players who were outstanding in the field—and that's where they found us, out standing in the field.

Although the Opry claims to have been on-air every Saturday night since November 28, 1925, the station itself was off the air from some point in December 1926 until January 7, 1927, as the wattage was increased. Then, in September 1928, the Opry was preempted by a political debate.

In its earliest years, WSM was a single-advertiser station, and that advertiser was its owner, National Life and Accident Insurance Company.

Paul Warmack (right) with the Gully Jumpers made the first record by a Nashville artist to be released. Jack DeWitt: "No one remembers him today, but Paul Warmack was very popular. He had a big belly. I touched him on his belly, and said, 'You've done pretty well by yourself, haven't you?' He said, 'It's a mighty poor man won't build a shed over his best tool.'"

Edwin Craig's enthusiasm for the Opry stemmed in part from his realization that the show enabled him to write more business in rural areas. Already, it touched people in rural America in a way that no other radio program ever had or would.

National Life's *Our Shield* ran testimonials from WSM's listeners. Atmospheric conditions permitting, the station could be picked up across the eastern United States.

Letter from WILL PRENTIS, *Lincoln Avenue, Detroit, 1928:*

Mrs. Prentis and I, together with our two good friends and neighbors, Mr. and Mrs. Parker, all true and loyal Southerners, wish to extend to you our hearty appreciation of your splendid barn-dance program, which came in perfectly last night on our set. The music has the true ring and swing of the Old South, than which no higher compliment can be paid.

WSM reception verification stamp. Early radio buffs collected stamps from the various stations they were able to pick up with their receivers. "Distance hounds," as they were known, sent letters requesting proof of their "DXing" (long-distance receiving) prowess, and the stations could then determine the reach of their signal.

TUNING IN

When radio became popular in the 1920s, almost anyone could afford a primitive "crystal" receiver. The tuner inductor coil would be wound onto a cylindrical oatmeal box or drinking glass, and a detector to pick up the stations was attached to a makeshift antenna (steel bedsprings were popular), but without an amplifier only one person at a time could listen in. Electronic amplifiers and oscillators made crystal sets obsolete, but required more power, and that was often a problem in rural areas.

FIDDLIN' SID HARKREADER, *early Opry performer:*

The old crystal radio set was attached to a window sill and had earphones. Only one person could listen to the broadcast. The crystal set was replaced by an upright cabinet battery radio, which could be heard all over a room. It had a volume control and people thought it was the grandest thing in the whole world, but the batteries didn't last long. Country people would gather at the country store or at a neighbor's house to listen. Large crowds would gather on Saturday night to hear the Grand Ole Opry.

Letter from W. A. TEASLEY, *Bowman, Georgia, 1928*:

I was talking to a fellow six miles out in the country who some two or three weeks ago installed a set, and he told me that his house would not hold the crowd last Saturday night. They wanted to hear nothing but [the Grand Ole Opry], and some had walked as much as five miles in the cold so that they might hear the Gully Jumpers, the Possum Hunters, the Clod Hoppers, the Fruit Jar Drinkers, and other stars who are unmatched. Long live these saints to scatter sunshine and fetch the memories of old back.

Our Shield *was the internal company magazine for National Life and Accident Insurance Company, "for the education and inspiration of its home office and field force." The fact that the magazine printed a WSM lineup and letters from listeners was a testament to the importance of the station as a sales tool for the company.*

17

The Air Castle of the South

CAST OF CHARACTERS

DR. HUMPHREY BATE AND HIS
POSSUM HUNTERS

PAUL WOMACK AND HIS
GULLY JUMPERS

THERON HALE AND DAUGHTERS

CROOK BROTHERS AND THEIR BAND

ED POPLIN AND HIS BAND

ARTHUR AND HOMER SMITH,
FIDDLE AND GUITAR

G. W. WILKERSON AND HIS
FRUIT JAR DRINKERS
UNCLE JOE MANGRUM WITH HIS FIDDLE
FRED SHRIVER WITH HIS ACCORDIAN

UNCLE DAVE MACON AND SID HARKREADER
(THE DIXIE DEW DROP AND FIDDLIN' SID)

DEFORD BAILEY, HARMONICA WIZARD

THE ORIGINAL GRAND OL' OP'RY MADE ITS DEBUT ON
THE AIR FROM WSM IN NOVEMBER, 1925, CHARACTER-
IZING THE HOMESPUN TUNES OF THE TENNESSEE
HILLS. EACH SATURDAY NIGHT FROM EIGHT O'CLOCK
UNTIL MIDNIGHT, WINTER AND SUMMER, SPRING AND
FALL, RAIN OR SHINE, THESE PERFORMERS PRESENT
A PROGRAM WHICH BRINGS MEMORIES OF DAYS GONE BY.

GEORGE D. HAY	HARRY STONE
"THE SOLEMN OLD JUDGE"	ASSOCIATE
DIRECTOR	DIRECTOR

"GRAND OLD OP'RY" ENTERTAINERS AT
WSM, NASHVILLE, TENN.

GRAND OLE OPRY®

MEMBERS: 1920s

DeFord Bailey

Henry Bandy

The Binkley Brothers and
Their Dixie Clodhoppers

The Crook Brothers

Kitty Cora Cline

The Fruit Jar Drinkers

The Gully Jumpers

Theron Hale and
His Daughters

Fiddlin' Sid Harkreader

Uncle Dave Macon

Uncle Joe Mangrum and
Fred Shriver

The Pickard Family

W. Ed Poplin and
His Barn Dance Orchestra

Dr. Humphrey Bate and
His Possum Hunters

Arthur Smith

Uncle Jimmy Thompson

Mazy Todd

My Life and Experience

written especially for
BRUNSWICK TOPICS

By

Uncle Dave Macon

ON A FARM in Warren County, Tennessee, near the city of McMinnville overshadowed by the blue skies of Ben Lomond Mountain so near Heaven that the angels' feet could be easily touched—was borned on October 7, 1870— Uncle Dave Macon the eighth child of a family of eleven children belonging to Captain John Macon and his wife Martha Ann Ramsey.

When a boy of thirteen years David Harrison Macon's family removed to Nashville, Tenn. and on the same spot where the Illustrious Sam Jones held his first noted revival in that city for two weeks. On the same spot for the next two weeks was shown the famous Sam McFlins circus show composed of twenty-four men and four ladies, all stopping at the Broadway Hotel on Broadway, Nashville, Tenn. Captain John Macon was Proprietor of that hotel at that time the home of the family. David Harrison and a younger brother, R. G. Macon now a prominent farmer in Oklahoma, were given free passes to all the performances and it was there that his childhood dreams of stage life began developing. After this company filled their engagement and went away, the spirits of this boy banjoist began to lag and pine and one day in the early spring of 1885, he went to his Dear Beloved old Mother and asked her to buy him a banjo so that he could try to learn to play it. She willingly complied with this childhood request and he brought home the banjo. For many days and months she listened to the many discords of many hours of practice.

On October 16th, 1886, Captain John Macon died at the Broadway Hotel from Nashville, Tenn. The family removed from Nashville, Tenn. to Readyville, Rutherford County, Tenn., buying a large, fertile farm situated on Stones River containing 423 acres, being the old home of Colo. Chas. Ready from whom the Village took its name. Many hard years and days of plowing, sowing and reaping overtook this boy Banjoist on this big farm, yet he found time on rainy days and nights to build up his spirits with his favorite old banjo. Ten years passed by very much the same—farm life and practice continued. At the age of 27 years Cupid came on the scene, the practice was easier, the songs were sweeter, the chords were more harmonious as he played the songs for the girl of his choice. On November 28th David Harrison Macon and Mary Matilda Richardson were married by Rev. D. B. Vance, then of Woodbury, Tennessee. To this union 7 sons were borned, all being boys. In 1900 they removed from Readyville to the farm where they now own and reside 8¼ miles E. Main Street, Murfreesboro, Tenn. He entered the transfer business in 1901, attending to that and farming for 20 years, making these midway trips with four Mitchell wagons drawn by large mules from Murfreesboro to Woodbury, a distance of 19 miles, every morning at 4 o'clock winter and summer. These teams were fed by Uncle Dave his faithful wife prepared the early morning breakfast and wrapped the road wagon lunch. R. H. Sanford, Uncle Dave's close neighbor now, being his faithful Superintendant of the wagons at all times and when Uncle Dave was compelled to stay and work on his farm, he, R. H. Sanford, missed no trip with the wagons for 20 years. Only 1 day off and that was to get married and, of course, he has had to work every day since.

In the early summer of 1920 the ill health of a favorite nephew that was compelled to go to a higher climate caused Uncle Dave to go along with him and his mother, Uncle Dave's sister. On arriving at Pensacola, Okla. the home of his Brother R. G. Macon, many friends and neighbors of this family gathered to greet them while there it was suggested that Uncle Dave play some of his favorite songs. He did so and a lady present asked if he would play at the School House for the benefit of furnishing the Preacher's home. Uncle

Dave replied yes. So in July 1920 was his first performance with pay. The night came on, a large crowd assembled, and she was well pleased with the entertainment and proceeds. After that he began being invited to other places in the West and continued playing for the public there for 3 months when we all returned to our old homes in Sunny Tennessee. One day while playing and singing in Public in Nashville, a fine looking gentleman by the name of Bob Smith, who claims he put me on the map, came to me for a performance of 15 minutes at his Club. Asking my price, I asked what he would give me. I said $15 and your dinner—overjoyed at these figures I gladly accepted and was promptly on time and went over fine. While at this Club, another gentleman offered him $30.00 for 3 nights' work of 10 minutes each—he accepted this offer and it was at this engagement that Mr. E. A. Vinson, Marcus Leow's Manager of the Vendome in Nashville saw my performance and he gave me an engagement for 1 week salary $50.00 to drive two little mules to a wagon across the stage in a play called "Whoa Mule". So as I was accustomed to driving mules and playing my Banjo at the same time he said I went over good.

The next year Mr. Vinson engaged me to play for 5 consecutive weeks at Leow's Bijou Theatre, Birmingham, Ala. $100.00 per week to packed houses. Then he sent me on Leow's Southern circuit via Memphis, Atlanta and New Orleans as an extra added attraction and there it was he gave me the name of the Dixie Dew Drop. After this engagement I turned my face homeward remaining a few days I was urged by many calls I had to pack up my few belongings and my faithful old Banjo and hit the trail again. On stopping at a hotel in Nashville I met an old friend and neighbor, Bill Jones. He insisted on me going to his home in a mining town in Kentucky. I replied "I don't think I can go." He said "Uncle Dave I will buy your ticket and board you while you are there if you will go." I replied, in fun, "Well, Bill, get the ticket." He soon came with the ticket and remembering my early training that my word

Uncle Dave and Sam McGee

a guitar but I believe I can beat it with my own. He said, "let me hear you." Unstrapping my up parcels I began playing and singing for you to go to New York to make records for me. When my concert was over he asked. When replied, "I don't reckon I can go that far away." that moment a fine looking, middle-aged gentleman from my audience came to me and said, "I in Memphis, Tenn." Introduced himself to me He said, "Now Mr. Macon, give God the credit for that talent he gave you. He is just letting you and I closely watched and saw you the other night deliver it. I heard and listened with wide eyes and mouth. Now Mr. Macon, the world is clamoring for what you possess. So don't forsake this opportunity of letting them have it. Don't say 'I may go,' say 'I'm going.'" So for four years I have labored on the Brunswick Vocalion records made by the Brunswick people. That contract having expired on May the 4th, 1928, I have accepted a contract now with the Brunswick Company, beginning June 28, 1928, for one year. I have received numbers after numbers of letters from playing and singing over different Radio Stations. I received one at Dallas, Texas from an old lady down in Arkansas which read as follows:

We certainly did enjoy you over our Radiator last night, and from the way you talk, laugh and sing, you must be one of the most wonderful old negroes in the South."

Now the good old sister just could not see me over the air.

should
felt he
and s
Jones'
treated
taining
home a
ahead for
On re
Bill Jones'
them Goo
to the depo
On the way
I passed a la
front of a r
Thinking som
had occurred I
inquire because
listening to reco
by a Kentucky r
Renau, playing a
ing on his guitar
asked me how I l
I replied "very go

2

EARLY DAYS . . . EARLY STARS

The Grand Ole Opry's first major star, Uncle Dave Macon, was a sprightly fifty-five at the time of his first appearance, and celebrated his eightieth birthday on the Opry stage. When Uncle Dave joined the Opry, he was already a star on the southern vaudeville circuit, and was the first Opry performer to make his livelihood from music. Although he lived into the atomic age, his roots were in the rural South of the Reconstruction era. Some of his songs were from minstrel shows, some were folk ballads and hymns, but many were drawn from his long, colorful life.

GRANT TURNER, *Opry announcer:*

Uncle Dave grew up on the streets of Nashville. Later, during the Second World War, he'd go out and sing for the troops lined up to eat at Gus & George's restaurant. That's the kind of fella he was. When he was onstage, he'd lean back on an old cane-bottom chair. God knows

Interviewed in this record company newsletter, Uncle Dave served up an anecdote that harked back to minstrel-era routines. "I have received number after number of letters from singing and playing over the radio. I received one from an old lady down in Arkansas, which read, 'Uncle Dave Makins: We certainly did enjoy you over our radiator last night. From the way you talk, laugh, and sing, you must be one of the most wonderful old negroes of the South.' "

how he balanced himself. He played the banjo. He had a gates-ajar collar, gold teeth, and his shirt pockets were a different color from the shirt. I asked him where he got those shirts, and he said he had a "worman," that's how he pronounced it, a "worman" who made them for him.

RUFUS JARMAN, *journalist, in* Nation's Business:

He used to play for quarters in a hat at a country school in Lascassas, Tennessee. He did wonderful things on a variety of banjos and he sang in a voice you could hear a mile up the road on a clear night. Mules used to stir in their stalls halfway up the valley when they heard Uncle Dave sing. "As long as bacon stays at thutty cents a pound, I'm a-gonna eat a rabbit if I hafta run him down." I remember the first Saturday night in 1926 when Uncle Dave made his debut on WSM. We had read about it in the paper but we didn't mention it around Lascassas. We had one of the two radio sets in the community, and we were afraid everybody in that end of the county would swarm into our house and trample us. Nevertheless, word got around and just about everybody did swarm into our house.

Recording of "Uncle Dave's Travels, Part 4": "People, when Columbus discovered this country, it was plum full of nuts and berries, but I'm right here to tell you, the berries is just about all gone."

Before Uncle Dave became a professional musician, he'd owned a mule freight company southwest of Nashville. He blamed cars and trucks for the failure of his business and for most modern vices, but that didn't prevent him from hiring support acts who'd drive him to shows. As work on the vaudeville circuits diminished, he played schoolhouse dates. During the Depression, school principals would often book shows for the community to raise money for their schools. They'd split the proceeds with the performer, who in turn, would split it with the supporting act.

ALTON DELMORE *of the Delmore Brothers, 1930s Opry stars:*

Now Uncle Dave Macon had people all over the country that knew him personally before there ever was a radio station in Tennessee or, for that matter, anywhere. He had been playing for tobacco auctioneers, political rallies, and various other events for years and years. He knew how to operate and he was as honest as the day is long. He didn't want a penny that wasn't his, and he didn't want you to have a penny that belonged to him. Very often when we counted out the money at the end of a show, there would be an odd penny. Now you can't divide a penny, and Uncle Dave would put it down in his little book, and remember every time who the odd penny belonged to.

MINNIE PEARL, *Opry star:*

He used to carry a black satchel with him when he went out on tour. It had a pillow, a nightcap, his bottle of Jack Daniel's, and a checkered bib. He'd often talk of religion. He complained about preachers departing from the Bible. He could quote at length from scripture and use it to solve all the problems of the world.

Judge Hay visits with Uncle Dave at home. Uncle Dave told friends that he preferred singing at home because he could spit into his fireplace.

Like most performers with roots in the nineteenth century, Uncle Dave was a visual act, but his personality shone through so forcefully in his banter and songs that several generations of Opry listeners came to regard him as an endearingly eccentric family member. His ability to hold a crowd was the envy of every Opry performer, and his refusal to change meant that, in later years, his songs and patter became a window onto a lost world.

DAVID STONE,
WSM *announcer:*

If I remember right, he had seven sons, and he didn't call any one of them by name. He'd say, "the one-eyed boy that lives over the hill" or "the one that has the basement full of home-cured hams" or "the

Uncle Dave's recording of "Comin' Round the Mountain": "I'm gonna play with more heterogeneous constapolicy, double flavor 'n' unknown quality than usual."

preacher they didn't see anytime on Sunday." He knew who he was talking about, I guess. People accused him of coming on the air drunk, but he did not. It was his way of entertaining, playing the banjo as he did it. Swinging it over his head and spinning it around. But a lot of people didn't understand, and we had critical letters about it.

BASHFUL BROTHER OSWALD,
Roy Acuff's Dobro player:

Uncle Dave would come out onstage, look into the audience and say, "I may be old and ugly, but I don't feel a damn bit lonesome here tonight." When he was staying at a hotel, he would still rise about five a.m. He enjoyed going down and talking to the night clerk, who'd be tired and wasn't really interested in hearing Uncle Dave's jokes, but Uncle Dave went ahead and laughed enough at his jokes for both of 'em.

Uncle Dave's last recording, January 26, 1938:

With laughter and good humor just to pass the time away

So while I'm here I'll do my best to please you while I say

So come along and join my song and raise a merry shout

For in fact, I am, and always was, the gayest dude that's out

WSM press release, August 1937:

To show how close the Grand Ole Opry comes to the hearts of its listeners, it's interesting to know that Fred Ritchie, who died in the electric chair at the state prison this summer for slaying his wife had warden Joe Pope call up on his last Saturday night and request Uncle Dave Macon to play "When I Take My Vacation in Heaven."

Uncle Dave Macon helped Judge Hay define the Opry's image. In pursuit of his vision, Hay famously named or renamed many of his regular groups. Dr. Bate & His Augmented Orchestra became the Possum Hunters, while the Binkley Brothers Barn Dance Orchestra became the Dixie Clodhoppers. Hay also named the Fruit Jar Drinkers and the Gully Jumpers, and insisted that his acts dress the part, despite the fact that many of them were city dwellers.

Very quickly, Judge Hay came to see the Grand Ole Opry more as a

Before and after the Judge Hay makeover. Left: **Ed Poplin's band.** *Right:* **The Poplin Woods Tennessee String Band.**

calling than a job. His early life had been rootless, but the show helped him arrive at a sense of who he was and where he should be. He believed that he was preserving something of importance, and was entertaining people otherwise ignored by the entertainment media. His sign-on and sign-off, his catchphrases and heavily stylized delivery became familiar throughout the Opry's increasingly large listening area.

GRANT TURNER:

I can see Judge Hay now, walking into the studio with his script in one hand, and a glass of water in the other, going "mi-mi-mi," testing out his voice to see if it was clear. Before each performance, he would turn to the entertainers and say, "Let's keep 'er close to the ground, boys." [He] would take that old steamboat whistle out of a black storage box. He tucked it under his arm, neatly under one elbow. When he got to the center of the stage, he'd take out that old whistle and blow two long mournful notes, adding a little postscript. Toot-toot. The station break would follow. "WSM. The National Life and Accident Company in Nashville, Tennessee, pre-sent-ing the Grand Ole Opry."

CHET ATKINS, *producer and guitarist:*

Yeah, the Judge would say, "Keep it close to the ground, boys," which meant don't get too fancy. Play the melody. Other barn dances tried to appeal to Madison Avenue and the big-city audiences, but they lost the country audience.

GRANT TURNER:

After the fiddlers fiddled their last tune, and the comedians had started rubbing off the greasepaint and wiping down with cold cream, Judge Hay was standing at the microphone, and he'd intone these words in a singsong voice. "That's all for now, folks, because the tall pines pine, the pawpaws pause, and the bumblebee bumbles all day; the grasshoppers hop and the eavesdroppers drop, while gently the old cow slips away. George D. Hay—the Solemn Ol' Judge—saying so long for now."

This 1930s postcard from Opry sponsor O'Bryan Brothers shows Judge Hay surrounded by the cast of the show he created.

Grand Ole Opry cast, 1934. The image that Judge Hay envisioned for the show is fully realized. David Stone, announcer and later manager of the WSM Artists Service Bureau, is third row from the bottom, far left.

Although he'd been hired as WSM's station manager, Judge Hay began concentrating solely upon the Opry. As WSM's listenership grew, Edwin Craig realized that Hay didn't have the skills to manage the entire station, and, in 1928, he hired Harry Stone away from a rival Nashville station, WBAW. In 1932, Stone became WSM station manager, leaving Judge Hay in charge of the Opry. Harry Stone brought in his brother, David, as an announcer.

JACK DeWITT:

George Hay had an illness. It was mental. I don't know what you'd call it medically. Barmy is not a good word, but that's it. He was flaky. Really a very nice man, and it was a shame that it turned out the way it did. Harry Stone was very cantankerous. Very rude. He'd refer to Edwin Craig as "that son of a bitch." Stone and I didn't get along very well, either. He hated me.

IRVING WAUGH, WSM *executive:*

Harry Stone and Mr. Craig really fought. Mr. Craig felt very close to the Opry, and his position was that it was being endangered. He wanted to keep it the way that it had been in 1935 with a cast made up primarily of instrumental string bands. He believed the Elizabethan folk songs would survive, and he disagreed with the star system as it evolved. Harry was very near the same age as Mr. Craig, and would sometimes raise his voice in disagreement with Mr. Craig, which none of the rest of us would do.

DAVID STONE, WSM *announcer:*

George Hay was a lot of fun, but he never wanted to settle down to the details of running a big enterprise. He just walked around all day with his hat on. He had a habit of visiting some relatives up in Indiana, and would disappear suddenly without telling anybody where he was going. We'd just come to find out he wasn't available.

One of the problems bedeviling Judge Hay and Harry Stone was finding a permanent home for the Grand Ole Opry. Initially, the show was broadcast from WSM's studio on Seventh Avenue North in Nashville, but the studio was in National Life's office building.

As soon as Harry Stone (left) took over from Judge Hay, he signaled his intention by hiring a smooth vocal trio, the Vagabonds (right). Trying to appeal to the Opry's audience, the Vagabonds wrote a song that became a sentimental standard, "When It's Lamplighting Time in the Valley."

AARON SHELTON, *WSM engineer:*

The Opry started in WSM's Studio "A," which was not really made for that sort of thing. The heavy velour drapes ensured that it was very dead technically. By "dead," I mean that there was no reverberation. Then, around 1926 or '27, they built Studio B, which had a large plate-glass window all the way across one side of it. Studio B didn't have all those drapes. It had normal walls, and the resonance and reverberation time was much longer so that it held music pretty well for a small studio. We set up chairs in front of this big window, and people could look in and see the artists performing. Two or three hundred chairs would be set up each Saturday night. People would start lining up outside the building at six o'clock, and the show didn't start until eight. [WSM] tried to discourage the people coming because it wasn't long before they were overflowing and interfering with National Life's normal thing. We'd have the Anglo-Saxon type of descendants from around the area coming in, and they wouldn't applaud or cheer or anything. Then the artists changed to a younger group, and the younger group had a younger following. Next thing you know they were throwing cigarettes everywhere, and it got to be a problem.

An even larger, auditorium-style space, Studio C was completed in February 1934, and could seat about five hundred audience members. But even that larger capacity wasn't enough to accommodate the Opry crowds.

JUDGE HAY:

The crowds stormed the wrought-iron doors of the home office building to such an extent that our own officials could not get into their offices when they felt it necessary to do so on Saturday nights. The payoff came one Saturday night when our two top officials were refused admission to their own offices. Our audience was very politely invited to leave the building, and for some time we did not know if the Grand Ole Opry would be taken off the air. We broadcast for some time without any audience, but something was lacking. It seemed that a visible audience was part of our shindig.

But that wasn't quite the way WSM's news service reported it.

WSM press release, October 21, 1934:

The Grand Ole Opry has outgrown its old clothes. Last February [1934] when the new WSM auditorium-studio was completed, WSM officials felt they had solved the problem of accommodating the crowds which assemble every Saturday night. From February to July, the audience was admitted to the Opry in the new auditorium-studio, which has a capacity of 500. Three color tickets were issued, each admitting a person to one hour of the Opry. Thus 1,500 were taken care of on Saturday night. After a summer of no audiences, the Opry again opened its

left: **WSM's Studio B. The instruments show that WSM was programming pop music in addition to country.**

right: **WSM's Studio C. The attractively decorated studio prompted Armstrong Flooring to feature this colorized photograph in an ad campaign. Jack DeWitt: "[Studio C] was a big conference room. They put chairs in it for the Opry, but the National Life officials didn't like that at all."**

Early Days . . . Early Stars

The Opry cast on the stage of the Hillsboro Theater, 1935.

doors and this time even the large auditorium studio of WSM proved inadequate.

GRANT TURNER:

Scouts were sent out to find an auditorium that would accommodate a few hundred to one thousand people. The struggling Nashville community playhouse at Hillsboro and Belcourt rented out their quarters [October 3, 1934]. A makeshift control room was constructed in one corner of the stage. The bands could never keep to the time slots. They would perform a song, and all of a sudden, before the Judge could thank them and get them off, they'd burst into another song. Judge told Harry Stone of his trouble, so Harry suggested that they get a musical contractor to come assist the Judge and put some muscle into the show. Vito Pellettieri was that man.

VITO PELLETTIERI, *Opry stage manager:*

I don't think there will ever be a man who could go in front of a microphone like Mr. Hay. Never, never will be another one. I went to see Mr. Hay, and he laughed. "What are you doing out here?" I said, "I want to help you on the Opry tonight." He said, "What are you going to do?" I said, "Your guess is as good as mine."

I'd told Harry Stone I didn't know a thing about those damn hillbillies. That first night, I saw all these open, horse-drawn wagons. The beds were filled with hay to

make it easier on the backside. There were only a few cars and most of them were Fords. The acts were string bands. Fiddles, banjos, and basses. They would come in off the road and half of them were full of mountain dew. They'd show up when they felt like it. I'd take four numbers from them, which would be about ten minutes, then I would pass it over to Mr. Hay, and he'd announce the numbers, and we tried to keep it up until twelve midnight.

I got out of there. I went home, took me a big drink, and told my wife there weren't enough devils in hell to ever drag me back. She says, "You stay with it. That's your job. You stay with it." So I went to Harry, and I says, "Harry, I can't do it the way you've got it. I want to block that show off in fifteen-minute blocks. I want to tell each one of the fellows when they're supposed to be here, and if they're not here . . . that's it." Next Saturday night, why, I blocked them off in fifteen-minute blocks and put them on. I told each one of them, "Next Saturday night, you're on at a certain time."

It wasn't unknown for Vito Pellettieri to phone a top Opry entertainer and say, "Hey, you no-good hillbilly. What kind of garbage are you going to dish up this week?"

JEANNIE SEELY, *Opry star:*

Vito was a wonderful dirty old man. He loved it when I said suggestive things to him. But he was full of good advice. Little things, like he told me, "Never turn your back on the audience, even if you're taking a bow." He taught us all like that.

Until Vito Pellettieri came into the picture, the Opry's only advertiser (or sponsor) was National Life, but after Vito divided the show into segments, he came up with another idea.

VITO PELLETTIERI:

After I guess maybe three or four months, I told Harry, "Now, it's all right, but I'm very commercial. Why can't we sell this stuff?" He said, "Well, if you feel we can do it, why, we'll just sell it." So he sold fifteen minutes, then thirty minutes to the Crazy Water Crystals. So I got a format up. The fact of the matter is that the show that's on the Opry right now is the same format I gave 'em.

Vito Pellettieri with the La Dells. Bill Anderson, Opry star: "He was the dirty-talkingest, filthy-mouthed old man I ever was around in my life, and I say that with more love and respect than you could ever imagine."

Crazy Water Crystals was a Texas company that claimed its product could cure an unlikely number of ailments. Analysis revealed that the crystals were mostly horse salt and laxative, and the Federal Communications Commission eventually closed the airwaves to them, but by then Vito Pellettieri had established the Opry's "sponsored segment" format. In the late 1930s, thirty-minute segments could be had for $350. And Pellettieri, the son of Italian immigrants and a former "sweet" band leader, came to appreciate both the Opry and its performers.

VITO PELLETTIERI:

When I was in the bands, somebody would get sick or be in financial trouble. I'd go around to the other musicians and they'd say, "Hell, no, I work as hard for my money as he does for his. He didn't have to go out and blow it all 'til he was broke." But then I got with the hillbillies. One of them would get sick and you'd go tell the others, and they'd say, "Damn, is that right?" And they'd haul out

Vito Pellettieri and his saxophone orchestra . . . in business until the Depression.

their fifties and hundreds. I never saw any of them back away from one of their own people in trouble. When I saw that, I said to myself, "Well, from now on, I'm going to be a hillbilly."

With Harry Stone in the front office, Vito Pellettieri backstage, and Judge Hay auditioning the artists and emceeing the show, the Grand Ole Opry was poised to become radio's leading barn dance.

3

"GREATEST SHOW ON EARTH FOR THE MONEY"— THE OPRY HITS THE ROAD

The Grand Ole Opry's home turf, the South and Southeast, was especially hard hit by the Depression. As personal incomes fell, the country music record business almost disappeared, and records by top artists sold as few as five hundred copies. Offering free entertainment, the Opry prospered, but faced stiffer competition as an increasing number of stations devoted airtime to hillbilly music. Meanwhile, the music itself was changing. The first nationwide country star, Jimmie Rodgers, died in 1933 without once playing the Opry, and his success made it clear that Judge Hay's concept of amateur string bands was out-of-date. The Opry needed stars, but stars wanted to make a living from their music. With that in mind, Hay organized the Artists Service Bureau to book and coordinate shows around the mid-South.

PEE WEE KING, *Opry star:*

We had to be on the Opry for the prestige and the publicity, and on the road for our income.

The idea for the Artists Service Bureau began with a trip to west Tennessee for a show over the Independence Day weekend, 1934. The turnout surprised Judge Hay,

Grand Ole Opry tent show, "The Greatest Show on Earth for the Money."

who brought along Uncle Dave Macon and several other Opry acts. Almost eight thousand people showed up for the all-day show, and Hay's eyes were opened to the potential of the Opry on the road. Open-air picnics were an especially big draw because admission was sufficiently low to attract Depression-weary farm families.

JUDGE HAY:

The Opry was pretty solid after about ten years, and so was the Artist Service Bureau. The Artist Service Bureau was started during the last part of 1934, but we didn't get underway to any appreciable extent until the first part of 1935. Very soon, it was no longer a case of groping in the dark. We had records of the dates played; which act had played it; the amount taken in at the box office; how large the attendance, etc. Theatre managers, high school principals, promoters of fairs and picnics called WSM frequently for acts, whereas in the first years we had a selling job to do.

Judge Hay's role at the Opry and the Artists Service Bureau could have made him into one of the most powerful men in the young country music business, but personal problems sidelined him, and he took a leave of absence between December 1936 and March 1938. Harry Stone's brother, David, took over the Artists Service Bureau and assumed responsibility for the Opry's newest stars, the Delmore Brothers. The Delmores had come to the Opry in 1933 and were instantly popular. Their two guitars and haunting sibling harmony wove delicate patterns, quite unlike the boisterous string bands. The earlier Opry acts had come of age in the pre-microphone era, but the Delmores, like Bing Crosby and the pop crooners, used microphones to produce a much subtler, nuanced sound. Their musical harmony didn't spill over into their personal lives, however, and they fought each other and the Opry management.

ALTON DELMORE *of the Delmore Brothers:*

We had pulled for David Stone to take Judge Hay's place as Artists Service manager when Mr. Hay got sick. We thought David would help us to get someone to play with we could depend on, but we couldn't get the good ones from the Opry. We had to take the drunkards and troublemakers and it nearly drove us nuts. We had pulled for David to get the job, but when he got in he

The Delmore Brothers, Rabon and Alton.

forgot about us, and I learned another lesson in human personality. We'd gotten along real well together until he got the big job of being our big boss.

Trying to keep the Delmores employed, David Stone put them on the road with the Opry's African American "harmonica wizard," DeFord Bailey.

DeFORD BAILEY:

They'd stick by me through thick and thin. They was one hundred percent. They watched out for me. "If you can't feed DeFord, we can't eat here, either," I remember them saying many a time. I usually had to eat in the kitchen, but at least they saw to it that I got to come in and eat, and not have to set out in the car. If the place wouldn't let me come in at all, they'd drive on down the road fifty miles or more to find another place that would. Most of the other performers would bring me a sandwich to eat in the car, but not them boys.

Judge Hay wrote several booklets and many articles about the Grand Ole Opry, almost never mentioning rival radio barn dances, like the WLS

Barn Dance in Chicago, or competition from hugely powerful American-owned stations just across the Mexican border. WSM had a five-thousand-watt signal, but the border stations' five-hundred-thousand-watt signals were so powerful that wire fences could pick up their transmissions. David and Harry Stone, however, were very much aware of the competition, and fought it ruthlessly.

ALTON DELMORE *of the Delmore Brothers:*

One Saturday night, Harry Stone called us off and whispered to us confidentially, "Boys, I understand that some WLS big shots [program directors from WLS, Chicago, which hosted the WLS Barn Dance] are coming down next week to make you a lot of promises and tell you a lot of lies. They will be trying to get you to come work on WLS. You have a good future here on the Opry, [and] I'm raising your pay. You, Alton, will get twenty dollars a week and Rabon will get fifteen. Now don't have anything to do with those sons of bitches when they come here next week. They just want to pull you away from us because you are so popular. If you leave, I will never take you on the Opry again. Your career will be ruined." Four or five weeks later, we were called into Mr. Stone's office. "Boys, I have bad news for you. We're gonna have to cut you back to the regular rate for Opry entertainers." That was five dollars a week each.

Edwin Craig and Harry Stone were sufficiently concerned about the five-hundred-thousand-watt border stations and fifty-thousand-watt American stations to lobby the Federal Communications Commission for an increase in WSM's wattage. Most fifty-thousand-watt stations were allocated a "clear channel," so that no other stations could broadcast on their frequency.

JACK DeWITT, *WSM's chief engineer:*

In 1931, WSM got permission to go to fifty kilowatts [fifty thousand watts]. In the daytime, the fifty kilowatt is a ground wave and it's steady. It reached about two hundred miles. At night, the ionosphere reflects the skywaves to great distance, so WSM could be heard eight hundred to a thousand miles away, but it's always a fading signal, slightly intermittent due to the ionosphere moving around. I'd been a part-time engineer [at WSM in 1925–1926] and I rejoined the station in March 1932 as chief engineer. We went to fifty thousand watts in November that year.

J. H. DeWitt, Jr., is WSM's Chief Engineer and what he doesn't know about technical radio you can put in your left eye and still cry.

Jack DeWitt: "Originally, we had a five-hundred-foot tower that a bridge company built, and that had trouble, so we made a contract with Blaw-Knox to build a transmitter in Brentwood. It was designed by a Chinaman at MIT. I couldn't get him to let me pay him for it. I finally sent him a check for fifteen hundred dollars, and he told me it made an alcoholic out of him." The new tower was completed in 1932, the year WSM went to fifty thousand watts.

Old Colonial Style Transmitter Of Shield Station Attractive

Rapid Completion of Construction Work Enables Engineers to Start Installation of New 50,000 Watt Equipment

8—WSM—AMERICA'S TALLEST RADIO TOWER, 878 FEET, NASHVILLE, TENN.

323 FEET HIGHER THAN THE WASHINGTON MONUMENT

The increased wattage took the Opry from the Rockies to the Caribbean, and that in turn brought many more people to Nashville to see the show. After less than two years at what is now the Belcourt Theatre, a larger venue was required, and, in mid-June 1936, the Opry moved across the Cumberland River to the Dixie Tabernacle in East Nashville. Even in the larger venue, the show was still full to overflowing every Saturday night.

AARON SHELTON:

The Dixie Tabernacle was a tent operation. It was a big tent set up where they had revival services during the week and on Sunday, but on Saturday night they'd rent it out to the Grand Ole Opry.

left: **WSM's Tower under construction.**

right: **A souvenir postcard of the completed WSM tower.**

39

"Greatest Show on Earth for the Money"

Very few photos were taken of the Opry during the years 1936–1939, when it was staged at the Dixie Tabernacle.

BASHFUL BROTHER OSWALD, *Roy Acuff's Dobro player:*

The Tabernacle had a dirt floor. Wooden benches on a concrete block, and it was free. They gave us tickets to hand out to people on the road when we'd play a job.

DAVID STONE, *Artists Service Bureau manager:*

It was like carnival days. Sawdust on the floor. Old hinged lighting along the side. You'd have to go along on a hot night and put broomsticks under the lights

Judge Hay is seen with Texas announcer Byron Parker, aka the Old Hired Hand.

to hold them up. There was no room to do anything. It held maybe six hundred or eight hundred people.

WSM's *Home Office Shield* magazine had a much higher estimate of the weekly attendance. The Tabernacle probably held less than one thousand people, but some would leave during the show to be replaced by others.

WSM's Home Office Shield *magazine, October 1936:*

About twenty-five percent of the capacity crowd, which runs well over three thousand people, are from other states. The boys on the door look at the license plates on cars which line up the streets within a half-mile radius of the Grand Ole Opry House. They report licenses from ten to fifteen states on average. Believe it or not, thousand mile trips are made with the sole purpose of visiting the Grand Ole Opry. The audiences are the most friendly to work for, and WSM has no trouble whatever. Once in a while, some of the youngsters get a little frisky outside the building, but two uniformed policemen take care of them in short order and in a nice way.

Free tickets to the show were handed out by National Life "Shield Men."

In fact, there was often unruly behavior, and WSM's mail-room employee, Jim Denny, made a little weekend money as a bouncer.

JIM DENNY:

If someone was acting up and disturbing people, I would ask him very sweetly to leave. If he gave me any backtalk at all, it was WHAM! Right then! A right to the head. Usually by the time they got over their surprise, they were outside.

But Jim Denny had ambition. He watched and learned as Harry and David Stone recruited the stars who would ensure the Opry's future. Denny would eventually take over the Artists Service Bureau from David Stone, and make the position into one of the most powerful in country music.

SATURDAY, DEC. 24
W L A C

7:00	Sunrise Serenaders.
8:00	Little Jack Little, CBS.
8:15	The Commuters, CBS.
8:30	Tony's Scrap Book, CBS.
8:45	Reis and Dunn, CBS.
9:00	Melody Parade, CBS.
9:15	1001 Kiddie Club.
10:00	The Gift Shopper.
10:05	Adventures of Helen and Mary, CBS.
10:30	Concert Miniatures, CBS.
11:00	Buddy Harrod's orchestra, CBS.
12:00	Luncheon Program.
12:25	Services from Central Church of Christ.
12:55	Madison Ensemble, CBS.
1:00	Saturday Syncopators, CBS.
1:30	Columbia Salon Orchestra, CBS.
2:00	Round Towners, CBS.
2:30	Rhythm Kings, CBS.
3:00	Spanish Serenaders, CBS.
3:30	George Hall's Orchestra, CBS.
4:00	Eddie Duchin's Orchestra, CBS.
4:30	Bob White.
4:45	Tito Guizar, CBS.
5:00	Funny Boners, CBS.
5:15	What Congress Did Today, CBS.
5:20	Mike Ryan's Melody Men.
5:45	Do Re Mi, CBS.
6:00	Services from Central Church of Christ.
6:30	Secret "3" (E. T.)
6:45	Santa Claus.
7:00	Frances Hill and orchestra.
7:15	Bob White.
7:30	Mike Ryan's orchestra.
7:45	Isham Jones' orchestra, CBS.
8:15	Hymn Singers from First Baptist Church.
8:45	Vito's Vagabonds.
9:00	"A Christmas Carol," CBS.
10:00	Dancing Christmas Memories, CBS.
11:00	Carol Service, CBS.

EVANS MOTORS—AUSTINS
On the Air Every Saturday
WLAC   -   -   7:30 P.M.

NASHVILLE ARTIST HONORED

Nellie Gee Erwin, whose violin playing we have enjoyed over WSM for several years, broadcast on Nov. 25 in Atlanta over WSB, and was accorded a cordial welcome. Lambdin Kay, in introducing her, mentioned his presence at the opening of our new 50,000-watt station and ended by saying, "Now I find everybody in Atlanta listening to WSM instead of their local station."

Mrs. Erwin is a musician of more than passing note, and her oft appearance over our local stations has always been a feature of great enjoyment to listeners here and elsewhere.

On the Screen

BELMONT
December 19 and 20
"Mouthpiece"
December 21 and 22
"Rainbow Trail"
December 23 and 24
"World and Flesh"
News and Comedy

FIFTH AVENUE
December 19, 20 and 21
"Man Who Played God"
December 22, 23 and 24
"Flaming Guns"

KNICKERBOCKER
December 16 to 22
Mitzi Green in
"Little Orphan Annie"
McNamee News
Cartoon and Comedy

L O E W ' S
3-Feature Frolic
1—"Fast Life"
2—"Isle of Desire"
3—Laurel and Hardy
Week Starting Friday, Dec. 16

PARAMOUNT
Monday, Tuesday and Wednesday
Geo. Raft and Nancy Carroll in
"Undercover Man"
Thursday, Friday and Saturday
Zane Grey's
"Wild Horse Mesa"

PRINCESS
"Maxine's Ballyhoo Revue"
A Big Unit Show—27 People
News—Cartoons—Comedy
On the Screen
John Boles and Linda Watkins in
"Good Sports"

R E X
December 19, 20 and 21
"Hell-Fire Austin"
December 22, 23 and 24
"A Man's Land"

SATURDAY, DEC. 24
W S M

7:00	Paul and Bert, NBC.
7:15	Laymen's Morning Devotion.
7:30	Cheerio, NBC.
8:00	The Pepper Pot, NBC.
8:30	Vic and Sade, NBC.
8:45	Nothing but the Truth, NBC.
9:00	The Vass Family, NBC.
9:15	John Fogarty, tenor, NBC.
9:30	Carol Services from King's College, NBC.
9:45	Breen and De Rose, NBC.
10:00	Melodies of the South, NBC.
10:15	Radio Household Institute, NBC.
10:30	Swen Swensen and his Swedehearts, NBC.
11:00	John Marvin, tenor, NBC.
11:15	American Legion National Trade Revival Campaign, NBC.
11:30	The Farmers' Union Program, NBC.
12:30	National Press Club Christmas Eve Party, NBC.
1:00	Opera, "Rigoletto," by Verdi, NBC.
3:45	Concert Favorites, NBC.
4:00	Lighting of National Community Christmas Tree, NBC.
4:30	Beau Balladeer, NBC.
4:45	Easyway Piano Time.
5:00	Fannie Battle Day Home speaker.
5:05	NBC Santa Claus, NBC.
5:30	Lee Sims and Orchestra, NBC.
5:45	Tuneful Tales.
6:00	International Sunday School Lesson.
6:15	Banner Bulletins.
6:30	Cuckoo, NBC.
7:00	WSM Dance Orchestra.
7:30	Morton Salt Program (The Vagabonds.)
7:45	Aladdin Lamp Program (Ed McConnell, E. T.)
8:00	Dr. Humphrey Bate and his "Possum Hunters."
8:25	Uncle Dave Macon and Dorris.
8:50	DeFord Bailey.
9:00	Obed Pickard.
9:15	Asher and Little Jimmie.
9:30	Arthur Smith and his "Dixie Liners."
9:50	Paul Warmack and his "Gully Jumpers."
10:15	The Vagabonds.
10:30	Theron Hale's Band.
10:45	Obed Pickard.
10:55	Trinity Church Chimes, NBC.
11:05	DeFord Bailey.
11:15	Binkley Bros. "Dixie Clodhoppers."
11:35	G. W. Wilkerson and his "Fruit Jar Drinkers."

GRAND OLE OPRY®

NEW MEMBERS: 1930S

ROY ACUFF AND
HIS SMOKY MOUNTAIN BOYS

ZEKE CLEMENTS

THE DELMORE BROTHERS

CURLY FOX AND TEXAS RUBY

HILLTOP HARMONIZERS

JAMUP AND HONEY

PEE WEE KING AND
HIS GOLDEN WEST COWBOYS

THE LAKELAND SISTERS

LASSES AND HONEY

ROBERT LUNN

SAM AND KIRK MCGEE

BILL MONROE AND
HIS BLUE GRASS BOYS

NAP AND DEE

FORD RUSH

SARIE AND SALLY

JACK SHOOK AND
HIS MISSOURI MOUNTAINEERS

ASHER AND LITTLE JIMMIE
SIZEMORE

THE VAGABONDS

WSM schedule from Broadcast News, *December 1932.*

4

THE STAR SYSTEM

U ncle Dave Macon, Sam and Kirk McGee, and others in the Opry cast provided a link to the show's earliest and rowdiest days, but several stars who'd
broadened the Opry's popularity in the 1930s, including the Delmore Brothers and the Vagabonds, left within a few months of each other in 1938. And DeFord
Bailey's days were numbered.

DeFord Bailey's dismissal in 1941 remains controversial, but the likeliest reason is
that his songs were licensed for performance through the American Society of Com-
posers, Authors and Publishers (ASCAP). In 1941, the National Association of Broadcasters felt that ASCAP was holding radio to ransom and decreed that no one would
perform ASCAP-protected songs on-air. The broadcasters set up a rival performing
rights society, Broadcast Music Inc. (BMI), and DeFord Bailey probably refused to
learn BMI-protected songs. Bailey, though, believed that the Opry had other reasons
for dismissing him.

Ernest Tubb.

JUDGE HAY:

DeFord was a bright feature of our show for fifteen years. Like some members of his race and other races, DeFord was lazy. He knew about a dozen numbers which he put on the air and recorded for a major company, but he refused to learn any more, even though the reward was great. He was our mascot and still loved by the entire company. We gave him a whole year's notice to learn some more tunes, but he would not. When we were forced to give him his final notice, DeFord said without malice, "I knowed it wuz comin', Judge, I knowed it wuz comin'."

DeFORD BAILEY:

[Judge Hay] had a boss, too. It was the company. It's terrible for a company to say things like that about me. That I didn't know no songs. I reads between the lines. They seen the day was coming when they'd have to pay me right, and they used the excuse about me playing the same old tunes. I walked out of WSM with a smile. I told myself, "God gave every man five senses and I'm going to use them. I ain't gonna work for another man as long as I live." I made the back room of my house on Thirteenth Street into a shoe shine parlor, and I cooked dinners and sold 'em to workmen.

What's certain is that DeFord Bailey was not replaced by another harmonica soloist, black or white. The day of the instrumental soloist on the Opry had gone. The departed stars were replaced by Pee Wee King, Roy Acuff, Bill Monroe, Minnie Pearl, and Ernest Tubb. There was no master plan behind their hiring, but these new stars would create a fanatically loyal audience numbered in the millions. They not only broadened the show's appeal but (with the exception of Pee Wee King) stayed into the 1980s or beyond, thereby creating the continuity for which the Opry became renowned. The Grand Ole Opry would make them household names, and they in turn would become its mainstays.

Pee Wee King: June 1937

Born Julius Frank Kuczynski in Milwaukee, Wisconsin, Pee Wee King was in some ways a more unlikely Opry star than DeFord Bailey. An accordionist, his earliest appearances were at polka dances in Polish community centers around the upper Great Lakes. Pee Wee not only brought Eddy Arnold, Cowboy Copas, and Grandpa Jones to the Opry, he brought his father-in-law, J. L. Frank, who booked many Opry touring packages, and played a role in the Opry's acquisition of Roy Acuff and Ernest Tubb.

PEE WEE KING:

Mr. Frank had gotten Gene Autry his movie contract, but he decided not to go out there himself. Gene gave me a sense of what I wanted to do musically, but Joe Frank showed me how to do it. I married [Frank's stepdaughter] Lydia, and I formed the Golden West Cowboys. We tried to make the Cowboys a unique band. We were a dance band and more. By the time we got to the Opry, we were a well-rehearsed, versatile band. We could play single-note violin, an accordion playing two-part harmony, waltzes, two-steps, polkas, ballads. My boys could all read music. One of Mr. Frank's main goals was to get one of his acts on the Opry, and we were the first one to make it. We went down for an audition on Easter weekend of 1937, and we were asked to stay for the Saturday night shows.

If Judge Hay had not been on extended sick leave, it's doubtful if Pee Wee King would have been hired. Pee Wee's music was too slick and up-town for the Judge, but Hay wasn't there and Harry and David Stone heard an artist who would professionalize the show.

Elected to the Country Music Hall of Fame in 1967, J. L. Frank was known as the "Flo Ziegfeld of country music," and was the first promoter to see the nationwide potential of Opry acts in touring packages.

47

DAVID STONE:

It was one stormy, snowing afternoon. Almost everyone in the office had gone home. Vito Pellettieri and I were in the studio, and J. L. Frank came in with his group, the Golden West Cowboys. They did a very short audition, fifteen or twenty minutes. On our recommendation [to Harry Stone], Pee Wee brought the group down. They were neat, well-dressed, enthusiastic. They displayed good showmanship and good entertainment. They just said, "We like it in Louisville, but we would very much like to come to Nashville."

left: 1938 *WSM program release*
featuring Pee Wee King and
His Golden West Cowboys.

right: J. L. Frank *(top left) and*
two of his acts, Gene Autry
(back row, fourth from left) and
Pee Wee King and His Golden
West Cowboys, *visit the WSM*
studio. Posing with them are
comedians Sarie and Sallie *and*
Asher Sizemore *with his sons,*
Buddy Boy *and* Little Jimmie.

ALTON DELMORE:

Joe Frank goes, I think, as one of the most neglected persons in the entire field of
country music. Joe was an outstanding person who could prod out real talent
when he found it. He was a down-to-earth businessman who knew what would
go in the game. He talked and acted like a plowboy but had a tremendous
knowledge of the entertainment world. He always had his heart in his work and
always had a good word for down-and-out musicians and a handout if they
asked for it . . . and a lot of times when they didn't ask for it. I give Joe Frank
credit for putting the Grand Ole Opry in the big-time class and big-time money.

Pee Wee was the first Opry act to join the Musicians Union, and, in
1938, became the first to appear in a movie when he made a cameo appearance in Gene Autry's *Gold Mine in the Sky.*

PEE WEE KING

I think they asked us to join the Opry because we were microphone minded.
There was no hesitation. No drawn-out pauses between our tunes. We knew what
we were doing because we were organized. This was the way we made a living.

Most of them who were on the Grand Ole Opry were farmers and had jobs and did this on Saturday night only. We made our living in the music business.

One of those who appreciated Pee Wee's style and sophistication was a struggling young singer, Eddy Arnold. Originally from rural Tennessee, Eddy was living in St. Louis in 1939 when he heard that Pee Wee's singer, Jack Skaggs, was leaving. He wrote a letter that ended up in the hands of J. L. Frank and followed it with an audition disc. Hired as of January 1940, Eddy later joked that he spent as much time selling Pee Wee's songbooks and sweeping out the auditorium as he did onstage, but he came to share Pee Wee's goal of broadening country music's appeal.

Many Opry listeners only knew Pee Wee's name. He didn't sing, and was so self-conscious about his starkly northern accent that he usually left emceeing duties to his band-members. Because he'd never been *country*, Pee Wee wasn't betraying or forsaking country music in edging closer to pop. More contentiously, he probably introduced the electric guitar and drums to the Opry stage. Always out of place on the Opry, Pee Wee returned to Louisville in 1947 to work in what was then the new medium of television. He went on to cowrite three songs that became pop and country standards, "Tennessee Waltz," "Slow Poke," and "You Belong to Me."

Eddy Arnold singing with Pee Wee King's Golden West Cowboys.

Roy Acuff: "I was hired at the Opry as a fiddle player. Country music in the late 1930s was mostly instrumental. I never would have lasted as a fiddle player. I've stuck around all of these years because of my singing."

Roy Acuff: February 1938

GRANT TURNER:

Roy Acuff gave the Grand Ole Opry its voice.

Roy Claxton Acuff was born in Maynardville, near Knoxville, Tennessee, on September 15, 1903. He grew up on a tenant farm in the foothills of the Smoky Mountains, and played semipro baseball until sidelined by a debilitating bout of sunstroke. During the layoff, he honed his skill on the fiddle, and, after his recovery, he formed the Crazy Ten-E-Seeans. Based in Knoxville, Roy Acuff first appeared on the Grand Ole Opry in October 1937, but didn't do well.

DAVID COBB, WSM *announcer:*

I sincerely did not want to say anything to hurt Roy's reputation, but I said the sooner he found another way to make a living, the better it would be for him.

PEE WEE KING:

My manager, Joe Frank, was the one who gave Roy his first big boost. He contacted Roy and said, "Man, you're missing the big boat. You don't have to be stuck in a little town like Knoxville. Come on down to Nashville. You can go national." Roy was skittish about leaving Knoxville, especially since he'd been turned down by the Opry once.

Roy was offered another on-air audition on February 5, 1938.

DAVID STONE:

There was a gap in the program. Someone stopped too early or didn't show up. I crooked my finger at Roy. He came out and I introduced him, and Roy said he was going to sing "The Great Speckled Bird." Come Monday morning, the powers that be wanted to know who was the guy singing about the bird. But as the morning went on, the lanky guy who was head of our mail department called up and said, "What are we going to do about all these letters coming about something to do with a bird?" We went down to the mail room and there were several stacks of mail just for Roy.

ROY ACUFF:

You didn't get on the Opry for singing a song or having a hit number. They didn't ask you if you ever recorded. They didn't care. You had to be a showman. The only way you could get on was to have something to show and prove it. When I came back, I was supposed to fiddle, and I did. But I sang "The Great Speckled Bird" that night. The audience reaction was overwhelmingly positive. The next day, we had to be in Dawson Springs, Kentucky, then I went back to Knoxville, and in two weeks they sent my mail. It came in bushel baskets.

The Delmore Brothers were the Opry's biggest attraction, and they took up for the performer who would soon supplant them.

ALTON DELMORE:

On Monday morning I went to see David Stone about the band we wanted to play with us. He wanted to get us back on the road. He asked me, "Have you decided who you want to play your dates with you?" "Yes, we want Roy Acuff." "And, if I may ask, who the hell is he?" "He's the leader of the last band that played last Saturday." "I'll be goddamned if I think I'll ever be able to

The group Roy Acuff brought to the Opry in 1938. From left: Clell Summey, Jess Easterday, Imogene "Tiny" Sarrett, Acuff, and Red Jones.

understand you crazy hillbillies. Here you are picking the worst band that played."

At the Delmores' request, David Stone wrote to Roy Acuff offering him a job:

> *Dear Roy,*
>
> *I am in receipt of your telegram advising that you will be here for programs starting the 19th. I will book you for a spot on the Grand Ole Opry, and also a series of 7:00 a.m. programs starting Monday February 21st.*
>
> *I am teaming you up with the Delmore Brothers for several personal appearances. These boys have tremendous popularity*

*in this territory, but they cannot manage or build their own unit
so I think it would be a great combination for the two acts. I
think I can get some good dates right away and start you out as
soon as you get here. This will save a great deal of time in
getting your build up with the WSM audience.*

*Yours very truly,
David P. Stone.
February 10, 1938*

ROY ACUFF:

*That song, "The Great Speckled Bird," was what done it. I'd heard the song over
around Knoxville and paid a guy to copy it down for me. It was written by a
preacher in Springfield, Missouri. I met him once. I never knew who the writer
was all those years. The song was stolen from him.*

*When I came to the Opry, I called my band the Crazy Ten-E-Seeans. David
Stone wanted a name change. I came up with Smoky Mountain Boys to get in a
plug for my homeland of east Tennessee. You know, if it hadn't been for the
Opry, I think I might have fallen by the wayside. It was like a network show.
With the fifty-thousand-watt clear channel, we were covering everything from the
Rocky Mountains to Maine, and from Canada into the islands off the Florida
coast. I didn't realize how different my singing was until the mail started coming
in. The letters would mention how clear I was coming through, and how distinct
my voice was, and how they could understand the words. When I got started, my
goal wasn't wealth. I only wanted to do something I enjoy. No city of any size
would accept hillbilly performers, so we played schoolhouses out in the woods
and small theaters in small towns. Twenty-five dollars was a big gate. I didn't get
my first one-hundred-dollar gate until along about 1940. That was at the
McFadden School in Murfreesboro.*

ALTON DELMORE:

*Roy was a hungry person. Not for food or security, but to make a little niche. I
believe Roy's carelessness for security really benefitted him more than anything
because he didn't seem to worry if we had a good date or a bad one as far as*

money was concerned. He just wanted to make good as an entertainer. And he was a natural salesman. He could sell himself on the stage anytime.

The Delmore Brothers left the Opry seven months after Acuff arrived. By then, Judge Hay was back, encouraging Acuff to sing the "heart" songs. Acuff complied, and his influence became inestimable.

HANK WILLIAMS:

Roy Acuff is the best example of sincerity in singing. He's the biggest singer this music ever knew. You booked him and you didn't worry about crowds. For drawing power in the South, it was Roy Acuff then God. He'd stand up there singing, tears running down his cheeks.

ROY ACUFF:

I like to get into the mood of a song. If you don't feel it, you can't sing it. You can't fool a person out there. I've cried onstage, not just for that audience, but I've cried because I wanted to cry. Because it was hurting.

Roy Acuff gives it all he's got with guitar player Lon Wilson and right-hand man Pete "Bashful Brother Oswald" Kirby adding the harmony.

Roy Acuff saw it all, from rural string bands to the dawn of New Country. To him, country music was just that: music for, by, and of country people. No compromise, no artifice, no concessions. Those who live and die by chart statistics might wonder why the man dubbed "The King of Country Music" just barely figures in the chart books, but Acuff made his mark before the country charts started; in fact, his success was one of the reasons that the music industry took country music seriously enough to start a country chart.

Bill Monroe: October 1939

Bill Monroe.

Bill Monroe was better known than Pee Wee King or Roy Acuff when he came to the Opry. As one of the Monroe Brothers, he'd sold hundreds of thousands of records in the late years of the Depression, and the brothers had been a big draw in the Carolinas. When Bill Monroe auditioned at the Opry, he was leading his Blue Grass Boys, but had yet to develop the style of music that would later be known as bluegrass.

Despite their success as a team, the split between Bill and his brother Charlie was far from amicable.

MINNIE PEARL:

They say that if Bill had to travel east to get a booking, he would go out of his way to go by his brother's house in Kentucky and get him out of bed in the middle of the night just so they could have a fight.

CHARLIE MONROE:

He won't last on the Opry. Wait 'til people find out how difficult he is to get along with.

The Monroe Brothers had been a partnership in which Bill was the junior partner, but he never again took a backseat. His opinions on how his Blue Grass Boys should look and play were unbending. He dressed soberly and required that his band members did likewise. Unlike other country acts at that time, they did little or no comedy and barely moved onstage.

BILL MONROE:

After Charlie and me broke up, I was searching for a name for my group, and I wanted a name from the state of Kentucky. Before I come to WSM, I'd already decided on using the name "bluegrass," because that's what they'd call Kentucky, the Bluegrass State, so I just used Bill Monroe and His Blue Grass Boys. I showed up at WSM on a Monday morning, and I met the Solemn Ol' Judge. David Stone and Harry Stone was there. They was all goin' out to get some coffee and something to eat. They told me that Wednesday was the audition day. So they come back and I sang "Mule Skinner Blues," "Bile Them Cabbage Down," numbers like that, and a gospel song.

CLEO DAVIS, *Bill Monroe's guitarist:*

They put us in one of the studios, and we really put on the dog. We started out with "Foggy Mountain Top," then Bill and I did a duet with duet yodel, fast as white lightning. We came back with "Fire on the Mountain" and "Mule Skinner Blues." That sewed it up.

BILL MONROE:

They said I could go to work for 'em that Saturday, or I could go on lookin' for another job. Maybe I could make more money. I told 'em I wanted to be at the

One of the earliest incarnations of the Blue Grass Boys, around late 1939 or early 1940. From left: Art Wooten, Bill Monroe, Cleo Davis, and Amos Garren.

Grand Ole Opry. They said, "Well, you're here, and if you ever leave, you'll have to fire yourself."

Bill Monroe was the only Opry performer not to admit to nerves on the first night.

BILL MONROE:

I wasn't a bit nervous that first night because I knew I could do what I was up there to do. I sung "Mule Skinner Blues," and it got three encores. The management just stood and looked at us. They knew the music was altogether different. They didn't know me, but they knew I had a music that would fit in at the Grand Ole Opry. It would be fine for the farm people, the country people. It had a hard drive to it. Back then, they just drug the music out. Our music was pitched up at least two or three changes higher than anyone had ever sung it at the Opry.

CLEO DAVIS:

Performers such as Roy Acuff, Pee Wee King, and Uncle Dave Macon who were standing in the wings could not believe when we took off so fast and furious. Those people couldn't even think as fast as we played. There was nobody living who had ever played with the speed we had.

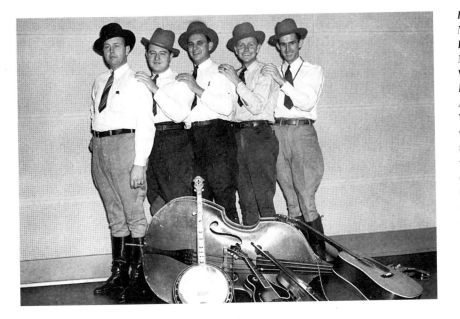

From left: Bill Monroe, Howdy Forrester, Clyde Moody, Cousin Wilbur (Wesbrooks), David "Stringbean" Akeman. Cousin Wilbur: "Sometimes we'd go to bed one night a week, and it was a good thing we didn't go to bed more often, because if we had, we wouldn't have had no money to pay the bill."

One of the very few surviving photos of the classic lineup of the Blue Grass Boys. Onstage at the Opry for Purina, from left: Lonzo Sullivan of Lonzo and Oscar clowning to the side; Chubby Wise, Bill Monroe, Lester Flatt, and Earl Scruggs.

Bill Monroe: "The Opry goes out over WSM, and those are my initials, William Smith Monroe."

Ricky Skaggs: "I think, on some level, Bill really believed that the station needed a powerful good name, and they named it after him."

BILL MONROE:

I dress the way a lot of Kentuckians used to dress years ago. I think it was a help to the music to dress as we did. I never would have dressed up like the other bands. I wanted to let people know that my music was up where I wanted it. It wasn't no low, down-to-earth music. I want people to listen to it. I want people to know I'm playing it for them, right from my heart to theirs.

In 1945, Bill Monroe hired Lester Flatt and Earl Scruggs, and bluegrass music began to take shape on the Opry stage.

BILL MONROE:

Back in the early days, Stringbean was the first banjo picker with me. I'd heard the banjo back in Kentucky, and I wanted it in with the fiddle and the rest of the instruments. Stringbean give us a touch of the banjo, but he quit. He went into the service. When I heard Earl, I knew the banjo picking would fit my music. He could take lead breaks like the fiddle. Without bluegrass, the banjo never would have amounted to anything. It was on its way out. Fiddlers would have been mighty scarce without bluegrass, too.

RICKY SKAGGS, *Opry star:*

He was looking for a sound he could call his own, and with the addition of Flatt and Scruggs, his music had the drive that he'd been looking for. It had taken a while, but he'd found his sound. It was old-time music on steroids. It was old, but it was cutting edge. It would please the old-timers, but it appealed to a younger generation, too. The gospel quartet numbers really solidified their following. They may not have lived the life they were singing about, but, man, could they sing about it.

JAKE LAMBERT, *bluegrass musician:*

Monroe's band became one of the hottest groups working the Opry. Bill purchased a stretch automobile and they were on the road almost seven days a week. When they finished a Friday night show they would head for Nashville and the Opry. Most of the time they would leave as soon as the Opry was over and travel the rest of the night to do a Sunday matinee—maybe four hundred miles away. Flatt said that there were many times [his wife] Gladys would bring his clothes to the Opry and he would never go home. For both Lester and Earl, the road seemed to be endless. The personnel of the Blue Grass Boys in 1946 and '47 was Monroe, Flatt, Scruggs, Chubby Wise, and Howard Watts. This band would go down in bluegrass history as being probably the best ever assembled.

After just two years, Flatt and Scruggs became disenchanted.

JAKE LAMBERT:

Flatt and Scruggs, as well as the rest of the boys, were making about sixty dollars a week, and that wasn't bad money, except for the long hours. Earl was the only one in the group with a high school education, and he took care of the money. He told me that on many Saturdays, when the Blue Grass Boys rolled into Nashville for the Grand Ole Opry, he would be carrying between five to seven thousand dollars. So both Flatt and Scruggs could see where the money was. They knew it would never be as sidemen.

In 1948, Flatt and Scruggs left to form their own band, but Bill Monroe recruited literally hundreds more Blue Grass Boys. Many, like Flatt and Scruggs, would eventually lead their own bands, and some would attempt to take bluegrass in new directions, but Bill Monroe's vision of his music was unbending, and he would always remain caustic and dismissive of those who deviated from it.

BILL ANDERSON, *Opry star*:

The thing about Bill Monroe and his music is that he was very creative and flexible to a point, and then he became very rigid. I watched him one time in the dressing room. He was working on a new song, an instrumental. The Blue Grass Boys were feeling their way through it, improvising and changing it, but once they got it to where he liked it, he didn't want it changed at all. He let his guys be flexible until they got it to where he wanted it, then he set it in concrete.

Minnie Pearl: November 1940

Opry stars had told jokes . . . plenty of them, but there had been few comedians on the show until Sarah Ophelia Colley brought her alter ego, Minnie Pearl, to the Opry stage. Born into a prosperous middle-class family, Sarah Colley aspired to be a professional actor until she developed her Minnie Pearl character on the rural theater circuit. In the fall of 1940, she appeared as Minnie Pearl at a bankers' convention in her hometown, Centerville, Tennessee.

MINNIE PEARL:

I got a call from Harry Stone. He said that Bob Turner, a Nashville banker who was a friend of my father's, had seen me do a country girl character at a convention. "He says, you ought to be on the Opry. Would you like to audition for us?" I won't pretend that I always wanted to be on the Opry. I'd never thought about it one way or another, except I didn't particularly like the music. I auditioned in my street clothes. I still wanted to be Ophelia Colley, dramatic actress, doing a comedy part. I wasn't yet ready to be Minnie Pearl. The first night I was so scared. Judge Hay gave me the very best advice any performer can get. "Just love them, honey, and they'll love you right back."

Minnie Pearl became the small-town gossip and chatterbox that most of her listeners knew only too well. Her routine included regular updates on

her brother, her Uncle Nabob, and her boyfriend Hezzy. Minnie's imaginary family became extended family for many listeners.

left: **Sarah Ophelia Colley** *aspired to be* **Ophelia Colley** *on Broadway, not* **Minnie Pearl** *on the Grand Ole Opry.*

right: *"How-dee!"*

MINNIE PEARL:

Minnie started out as a gentle, very authentic girl from the mountains, but she's more brassy than when she started. I created the character in 1938. I had a job producing amateur plays around the Southeast, and I began to collect country stories and I created this character. I thought "Minnie" and "Pearl" were the two nicest country names I could think of. I'm from Centerville, Tennessee, and my father had a lumber business. There was a railroad that had a loading switch

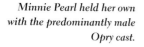

Minnie Pearl held her own with the predominantly male Opry cast.

three miles from Centerville. It was called Grinder's Switch because the largest family that lived there were the Grinders. When WSM let me come on the Opry, they said, "We think you ought to have a locale," so I picked Grinder's Switch because I didn't think anybody would be offended because so few people lived there. I've peopled it with my own people. I'm the only person who can see and hear the sound of the people who live there whom I've created. Minnie's a mountain girl and she has never worried about her education, and she has never been intimidated by educated people. I just love to put on her white cotton stockings and one-strap Mary Jane shoes.

When I first brought Minnie Pearl to the public on the radio, I used a very different type of salutation. It was "How-dee, I'm just so proud to be here," but the decibels were different.

PEE WEE KING:

Early on, she was working for Roy Acuff [on the road], and she hadn't perfected her introduction. She said, "How-dee. I'm just so proud I could come." And Acuff told her she'd have to change the last bit.

MINNIE PEARL:

Now I scream it out loud. When I went on the Prince Albert network portion of the Opry in 1942, the agency in New York suggested that I scream it as a promotional stunt. The announcer said, "When Minnie Pearl says 'How-dee,' say 'How-dee' right back." Over the years, I got louder and louder, and the audience got louder and louder.

From 1948 until 1958, Minnie Pearl had a successful comedy partnership on the Opry with Rod Brasfield. They referred to their style of comedy as "double comedy" because there was no straight man.

MINNIE PEARL *and* **ROD BRASFIELD** *routine:*

MINNIE: How-dee! I'm jes so proud t'be here!
Hezzy was over to see me on Wednesday and he brought a s'prize! (When Hezzy brings anything, it's a s'prize!) He brought over a box of candy and a box of nuts. He says to me, "I know you don't care about sweets, so I brung the candy over to your mammy, and nuts to you!"
Then me and Hezzy went in the front room and set down on the double settee. Oh, it was so romantic! He was a-settin' there and I looked into his eyes . . . and he looked into my eyes . . . and then he says . . .

ROD: Hi-dy, Minnie!

MINNIE: Well, Rod Brasfield! You come right in between me and Hezzy!

ROD: I did, Minnie? You mean I was caught in the big squeeze?

MINNIE: Yes, I was jes' about to tell about Hezzy kissin' me . . .

ROD: Why, Minnie Pearl! You mean to say you're one of them gals that kiss and tell?

MINNIE: Why sure, Rod, what's wrong with that?

ROD: I thought it was only the fellers that kiss and tell.

MINNIE: Uh-uh, Rod . . . it's the fellers that kiss and exaggerate! But ain't it funny, Rod. . . . I 'member the time when if my pappy caught a feller kissin' me he'd almost shake the feller's teeth out.

ROD: And what does he do now, Minnie?

MINNIE: Almost shakes his hand off!

ROD: I know just what you mean, Minnie. When I started to call on my gal, Suzie, Her poppy used to stand a shotgun in the corner with a lily in both barrels.

MINNIE: And he don't do that no more, Rod?

ROD: Nope . . . He puts a travelin' bag in the corner with two tickets to Niagara Falls!

(From the Prince Albert Grand Ole Opry, February 13, 1954)

Ernest Tubb: January 1943

Ernest Tubb, like Bill Monroe and Roy Acuff, pioneered a new style of music. Tubb's gritty honky-tonk music had its origins in Texas and Oklahoma barrooms in the years after the repeal of Prohibition. He was the first to bring beer-joint music to the Opry stage, and his addition to the cast proved that the show was looking beyond its traditional base in the Southeast. Tubb had already recorded his signature tune, "Walkin' the Floor Over You," and was on the point of taking his career to the next level when he appeared on a 1943 New Year's Day show in Gadsden, Alabama, with Pee Wee King. J. L. Frank proposed to Ernest that he come to Nashville to join the Opry, and Tubb readily agreed.

ED LINN, *journalist, in* Saga *magazine:*

Ernest Tubb began singing in the oil-field honky-tonks of Texas in the late 1930s. It was a poor Saturday night that didn't produce a couple of interesting brawls. Tubb had to meet the competition as best he could. "The harder they fought," he says, "the louder we played." One night, a friend took a five-minute break and came back to find a bullet-ridden body sprawled across the wreckage of his guitar. It was disconcerting. Good guitars were hard to come by in those days.

Ernest Tubb.

ERNEST TUBB:

I don't read music and I'd fight the man who tried to teach me. I don't care whether I hit the right note or not. I'm not looking for perfection. Thousands of singers have tried that. I'm looking for individuality. I sing the way I feel like singing at the moment. I never sang for the dollar. I sing because I want to sing.

PEE WEE KING:

Ernest knew he was taking a big chance when he quit his job at the radio station in San Antonio and gave up the good-paying gigs he played at the honky-tonks around there. But he hedged a bet. He left his wife and children behind and told them he would try out Nashville first. It didn't take long for Ernest to become popular. Within a few weeks he was getting bushels of mail. He had a certain spark that set the Opry on fire every time he played.

Wartime crowds gather on Nashville's Broadway to hear Ernest Tubb and Whitey Ford—the "Duke of Paducah" (with his arm in the air). Eddy Arnold awaits his turn, sitting to the right.

JUSTIN TUBB, *Opry star and Ernest's son:*

To me, that's when he became a star, to be that far away, and pick him up on the radio. Being made a member of the Grand Ole Opry was the most important thing in my dad's life. It was his badge of having made it. This was the tops in radio when people would listen to radio like they watch TV now. It was very important to him to be back here every Saturday night for the Opry. He traveled more than anyone on the show, except maybe Little Jimmy Dickens, but he bent over backwards to be in for the show.

WILLIE NELSON:

The first songs I ever learned were out of Ernest Tubb songbooks. I was as big an Ernest Tubb fan as people ever were Elvis fans or Beatles fans. I grew up with him back in the 1940s.

HAL SMITH, *Texas Troubadour:*

I remember women keeling over in Louisville when he sang there. They had to take them away on stretchers. He was as big as Sinatra, only with a different, country audience.

The Ernest Tubb Midnite Jamboree, 1940s.

Distressed when fans told him they couldn't find his records, Tubb opened the Ernest Tubb Record Shop on Commerce Street, Nashville, in May 1947. Although it was within walking distance of the Opry, more than seventy percent of the store's business was mail order. Tubb bought airtime on WSM after the Opry finished, and his Midnite Jamboree soon became a showcase for younger talent.

From the earliest days, Opry shows were made up of regular performers along with guest artists, some of whom just happened to be in Nashville on a Saturday night. Over the years, the concept of membership evolved, and by the 1940s it was fairly formalized. In exchange for a commitment to perform regularly on Saturday nights at the Opry, members could use the Opry name to advertise their road shows during the week. Though many of the earliest country stars—the original Carter Family, Jimmie Rodgers, Charlie Poole, Jimmie Davis, Gene Autry—did not appear on the Grand Ole Opry, the addition of Pee Wee King, Roy Acuff, Bill Monroe, Minnie Pearl, and Ernest Tubb made Opry membership the topmost rung of the country music business.

Program for Grand Ole Opry — Saturday December 18 — 8:00 to 12:00 p.m.

Purina—6:30 to 7:00

* * *

Studio—7:00 to 8:00

* * *

Purina—8:00 to 8:30

Bill Monroe—Doghouse Blues
Zeke Clements—Smoke on the Water
Bill Monroe and Clyde Moody—I Wonder Where You Are Tonight
Uncle Dave Macon and Dorris—Keep My Skillet Good and Greasy
Daniel Quartette—Every Time I Feel the Spirit
Jam-Up and Honey—Jokes
Golden West Cowboys—Riding Up to Glory
Sam and Kirk McGee—Who Broke the Lock
Chubby Wise—Cacklin' Hen
Bill Monroe—Lil Liza Jane
Uncle Dave Macon and Dorris—Lonesome Road Blues

* * *

Crazy Water Crystals—8:30 to 9:00

Paul Howard—Be Honest with Me
Marie and Clyde Dillaha—Cowards Over Pearl Harbor
Eddy Arnold—Mommy Please Stay Home with Me
Crook Brothers—Shortnin' Bread
Robert Lunn—I'm in the Army Now
Lonnie and Tommy Thompson—Raise the Window Mother Darling
Possum Hunters—Billy in the Low Ground
Smith Sisters—No Letter Today
Uncle Rufus—Great Grand Dad
Gully Jumpers—Arrington Breakdown
Paul Howard—Dear Old Sunny South by the Sea

* * *

Royal Crown—9:00 to 9:30

Golden West Cowboys—Goodbye Liza Jane
Fruit Jar Drinkers—Eighth of January
Ernest Tubb—Answer to Walking the Floor Over You
Curly Williams—I'll Be Around Somewhere
Bill Monroe—California Blues
Spike and Spud—Midnight Flyer
Fruit Jar Drinkers—Big Joe
Ernest Tubb—I Dreamed of an Old Love Affair
Curly Williams—There'll Be Some Changes Made
Becky Barfield—I Want Someone
Hal Smith—Cotten Eyed Joe

* * *

Prince Albert—9:30 to 10:00

Roy Acuff—Whoa Mule Whoa
Roy Acuff—Put My Rubber Doll Away
Minnie Pearl—Columbus Stockade
Mack McGarr—Rock and Rye Polka
Ford Rush—Put on Your Old Gray Bonnet
Old Hickory Quartette—Molly Darling
Whitey Ford, the Duke of Paducah—Jokes
Jimmy Riddle—12th Street Rag
Roy Acuff—When the Saints Go Marching in
Hoe Down—Fishers Hornpipe

Wall Rite—10:00 to 10:15

Bill and Clyde—I'm Going Back to Old Kentucky
Clyde Moody—If I Had My Life to Live Over
Blue Grass Quartette—Old Country Church
Sally Ann—Put Me in Your Pocket
Chubby Wise—Wagoner

* * *

Weatherman—10:15 to 10:30

Daniel Quartette—Heaven's Radio Station Is on the Air
Uncle Dave Macon and Dorris—You Are Getting More Like Your Dad Every D
Eddy Arnold—I Walk Alone
Marie and Clyde Dillaha—I'm Sending You Red Roses
Possum Hunters—Billy Wilson
Uncle Dave Macon and Dorris—From Jerusalem to Jericho
Daniel Quartette—Jesus Hold My Hand
Possum Hunters—Possum Hunter's Dream

* * *

Cherokee Mills—10:30 to 10:45

Roy Acuff—The Heart That Was Broken for Me
Roy Acuff—Radio Station S-A-V-E-D
Rachel and Oswald—Jessie James
Jimmy Riddle—Put Your Arms Around Me
Jug Band—Blackeyed Susan

* * *

Lazyu—10:45 to 11:00

Crook Brothers—Golden Slippers
Uncle Rufus—My Mother's Prayer
Sam, Kirk, Floyd and Goldie—Chittlin' Cooking Time in Georgia
Robert Lunn—Tooth Picking Time in False Teeth Valley
Lonny and Tommy Thompson—Open Range Ahead
Gully Jumpers—Breakdown in T

* * *

Roy Acuff Song Book—11:00 to 11:15

Roy Acuff—Write Me Sweetheart
Roy Acuff—What Good Will It Do
Rachel and Oswald—Weary Lonesome Blues
Roy Acuff—Tear-Stained Letter
Jimmy Riddle—12th Street Rag

* * *

Ernest Tubb Song Book—11:15 to 11:30

Ernest Tubb—I'll Get Along Somehow
Ernest Tubb—When the World Has Turned You Down
Ernest Tubb—Drop Your Net
Ernest Tubb—I'm Wondering How

* * *

Saf-Kill—11:30 to 11:45

Golden West Cowboys—Pretty Little Widow
Little Becky Barfield—Keep a Light in Your Window Tonight
Trio—There's a Blue Sky Way Out Yonder
Pete Pyle—I Dreamed of an Old Love Affair
Spike and Spud—Song of the Blind
Golden West Cowboys—Little Girl Go Ask Your Mama

* * *

11:45 to 12:00

Paul Howard—With Tears in My Eyes
Smith Sisters—We'll Keep 'Em Flying
Curly Williams—When My Blue Moon Turns to Gold
Zeke Clements—I Dreamed I Spent Christmas in Heaven
Fruit Jar Drinkers—Jackie Boy
Paul Howard—Home in San Antone
Curly Williams—Where We Never Grow Old
Fruit Jar Drinkers—Dixie—Home Sweet Home

Grand Ole Opry program, December 18, 1943.

GRAND OLE OPRY®

NEW MEMBERS: 1940s

David "Stringbean" Akeman

Eddy Arnold

The Bailes Brothers

Rod Brasfield

Lew Childre

Cowboy Copas

The Cackle Sisters

John Daniel Quartet

Little Jimmy Dickens

Annie Lou and Danny Dill

Milton Estes and
His Musical Millers

Red Foley

The Duke of Paducah
(Whitey Ford)

Wally Fowler and
the Oak Ridge Quartet

Paul Howard and the
Arkansas Cotton Pickers

Johnnie and Jack

Grandpa Jones

The Jordanaires

Bradley Kincaid

Lonzo and Oscar

Clyde Moody

George Morgan

Minnie Pearl

The Poe Sisters

Old Hickory Singers

Ernest Tubb

Curley Williams and
His Georgia Peach Pickers

Hank Williams

The Willis Brothers

MINNIE: HOW-DEE! I'M JES' SO PROUD T'BE HERE!

A YOUNG GAL SURE HAS TO BE MIGHTY CAREFUL THESE DAYS WHEN IT COMES
TO FELLERS... ~~THREE-FOUR WEEKS AGO I LET A FELLER KISS ME...AND~~
~~EVER SINCE THEN HE'S BEEN TRYIN' TO BE INTRODUCED TO ME!~~
just now a feller backstage tried to kiss me —
THIS FELLER WAS KINDA CUTE, THOUGH...HE SAYS, "YOU REMIND ME OF
THE OLD SAYIN' 'SWEET SIXTEEN, AND NEVER BEEN KISSED'!"...AND I
SAYS, "OH, DO I LOOK LIKE SWEET SIXTEEN?" AND HE SAYS, "NO, BUT
YOU LOOK LIKE YOU NEVER BEEN KISSED!"...

FOLEY: MINNIE, WITH ALL YOUR TALK, I HAPPEN TO KNOW THAT YOU AIN'T THE
TYPE OF GAL WHO BELIEVES IN LOVE AT FIRST SIGHT...

MINNIE: OH, YES I AM, RED...LOTS AND LOTS OF FELLERS HAS FELL IN LOVE WITH
ME AT FIRST SIGHT...

FOLEY: THEY HAVE??

MINNIE: THEY SURE HAVE. I WISH THERE WAS SOME WAY I COULD KEEP 'EM FROM
TAKIN' A SECOND LOOK!

FOLEY: BUT MINNIE - YOU ALWAYS SAID YOU WERE SAVIN' YOUR LIPS FOR THE
MAN YOU LOVE!

MINNIE: THAT'S RIGHT RED..I'M SAVIN' MY LIPS..BUT IT'S LIKE SAVIN' DOLLARS
I WANNA PUT 'EM WHERE THEY'LL GATHER THE MOST INTEREST! BUT RED,
DO YOU KNOW ~~THAT~~ *That there's* ONE ~~THING~~ *word* ~~IS~~ *makes* THAT ~~KEEPS~~ A GAL ~~FROM BEIN'~~ *either* POPULAR! *or unpopular*

FOLEY: NO!

MINNIE: THAT'S IT!
WELL, NOW FOR SOME NEWS FROM GRINDERS SWITCH!

(MINNIE CONT'D OVER)

5

COAST TO COAST

From the time WSM station manager Harry Stone sold thirty minutes of the Grand Ole Opry to Crazy Water Crystals, there was no shortage of sponsors. Manufacturers with products aimed at rural consumers, like Allis-Chalmers, International Harvester, Penn Tobacco, and Carter's Chickery, stood in line. But Harry Stone wanted to get at least a portion of the Opry on a national radio network. WSM's fifty-thousand-watt signal was strong, but reception outside the South depended upon location and atmospheric conditions. If the Opry was on a network, it would be carried on local stations and come in clearly from coast to coast.

Harry Stone was especially keen to get a network slot because, in 1933, Alka-Seltzer began sponsoring a segment of the Opry's rival, Chicago's WLS Barn Dance, on NBC's Blue Network. WSM was already an NBC affiliate, broadcasting NBC network shows such as *Amos 'n' Andy*, *Vic and Sade*, and the *Lucky Strike Dance Hour* locally, but the Grand Ole Opry needed a sponsor to become a network show itself.

Another five years passed before one of the Opry's newer sponsors, tobacco manufacturer R. J. Reynolds, approached NBC with the idea of bringing thirty minutes of the show to the network. It was a good moment to take the Opry nationwide. The new stars—Roy Acuff, Pee Wee King, and soon Bill Monroe and Minnie Pearl—were coming into their own. The country record business was recovering from the

Page from a Prince Albert show script.

Roy Acuff and his Smoky Mountain Boys (and Girl) celebrate the Opry going coast-to-coast.

Depression, and pop singers like Bing Crosby were beginning to "cover" country songs. Country music was becoming a commercial force, and the Opry's stars had just the right mix of modernity and tradition.

R. J. Reynolds's Prince Albert brand sponsored the networked segment on what would become known as the Prince Albert Opry. Although Roy Acuff had only been on the Opry little more than eighteen months, he was chosen as the host.

JUDGE HAY:

Various portions of the show had been sponsored for many years, so we who work behind the mics attached no particular significance to the Prince Albert sponsorship at first. The arrangements were made by the William Esty Company, the New York advertising concern, which handled the [Reynolds] account. Mr. Marvin there had the idea in the back of his head to put the Opry on the NBC network. He came in for much ribbing [from] many members of his profession, but he stuck to his guns and found that there was considerable interest in our efforts to entertain with homespun music and comedy. Heretofore, we had not made any effort to produce the show in the accepted sense of the word, so we had to be snatched off the air at the end of our thirty minutes. With that exception, the half-hour went over pretty well. Before the next week rolled around, we had timed our opening and closing. The stations included in the Prince Albert deal were located all the way from the southeastern zone to the West Coast.

JUDGE HAY *introducing the first Prince Albert portion of the Grand Ole Opry, October 14, 1939:*

Friends, these are the same people you've been listening to for fourteen years; the only difference tonight is that they're coming to you from the Mexican border to the mountains of Virginia. Our show is ready to ride right down the middle of the road to our friends and neighbors throughout America.

JACK DeWITT:

The Prince Albert deal surprised me because I'll never forget writing to the president of NBC, Bobby Sarnoff, son of the general [NBC founder David Sarnoff]. I told him we had an awful lot of talent here and we'd like to put our programs on NBC. He wrote back and said, "We're not interested in country music. Perhaps you had better try CBS." But you had the same attitude here in Nashville. We started the first FM station [in October 1940] because Edwin Craig was embarrassed in front of the [upper class] Belle Meade crowd because of the Grand Ole Opry. He thought that broadcasting classical music on FM would help.

With the Prince Albert sponsorship, nationwide Opry tours, and country songs taking over the airwaves, national magazines began taking an interest in the Grand Ole Opry for the first time. Most of the pieces were patronizing, but the writers couldn't fail to be impressed with the Opry's hold upon its audience or with the size of that audience.

DON EDDY, *journalist, in* American Magazine:

One 30-minute segment is piped over the full coast-to-coast NBC network, during which pollsters say it has 9,500,000 faithful listeners. The cast varies from 120 to 137 performers, depending on how many show up. Pay is small (one featured singer gets $19.50 a week) but advertising value to the individual is

Stills and a lobby card from Republic Pictures' Grand Ole Opry movie, directed by former railroad worker Frank McDonald. Critic Evelyn Keyes said, "I've never seen anyone as terrified of directing as Frank McDonald." Regardless, he directed over a hundred movies, mostly low-budget westerns.

enormous. There are surprisingly few women on the show because (a) women don't like to be laughed at, and (b) backwoodsmen in the audience with their wives would get their ears slapped down if they stared at a strange female, much less applauded her. That is why Cousin Minnie Pearl deliberately tries to make herself homely.

The Opry also attracted the attention of Republic Pictures, and in 1940 several Opry members were in a Republic feature, *Grand Ole Opry*. To secure Republic's commitment, Judge Hay brought the producer to Uncle Dave Macon's house near Murfreesboro, Tennessee.

JUDGE HAY:

After dinner, Uncle Dave invited us to be seated under a large tree in his front yard, where we discussed the possibility of a Grand Ole Opry picture. As the producer and [I] drove back to Nashville, that experienced executive said, "I have never met a more natural man in my life. He prays at the right time. He cusses at the right time, and his jokes are as cute as the dickens."

Knoxville News Sentinel, 1940:

The other night, Acuff and the other Opry players were a bit spryer with their songs and wits than usual. The Hollywood scouts were in the audience. Republic Pictures had a producer, director, and writer there listening. "Roy and the others will start packing soon for California," said Jack Harris, WSM publicity director.

"Cameras are to start grinding on May 1." The WSM man said that the picture was originally scheduled with Gene Autry, but that didn't go through.

The movie was short (just over one hour), and the plot was flimsy and didn't have much to do with the Opry, but it was significant that the movie colony in Hollywood thought that *Grand Ole Opry* was a salesworthy title for a nationally released picture.

JUDGE HAY:

We got the contract to do a Republic picture. Uncle Dave Macon was in it, and he always said that he couldn't get along without his country ham. Uncle Dave and I went out to Hollywood on the train. Roy Acuff had a station wagon and drove all the way along the southern route with very few stops. Uncle Dave told Roy, "I'm not sure we're gonna get enough to eat out there. I've got three country hams. I want you to put them on top of your bus so we'll be sure to have something to eat." Uncle Dave would go into restaurants out there and tell the cooks that he wanted a large order of eggs to go with his country ham so he wouldn't get too lonesome. Then he insisted that Roy carry the crates back to Tennessee so that he could use them for chicken coops. When Uncle Dave visited the shore of the Pacific Ocean, he took out a tobacco sack and filled it with wet sand. That was a token of his visit to the West Coast. We worked, I guess, two or three days on the picture. It had two hundred scenes and each scene was a minute or less. Finally the director told us we could come over to a little shed and watch the rushes. After a couple of minutes, Uncle Dave came on. His son Dorris was standing beside him in the movie plunking a guitar, looking like a wooden Indian. Uncle Dave looked up there at the screen, stood straight up, and said, "Wheeeeeeee, that's me!" Hollywood has seen many unusual people, none more so than Uncle Dave.

ROY ACUFF:

Hollywood, I came to find out it was phony. I'd say seventy-five percent of Hollywood is phony and maybe twenty-five is pure, whereas I'd say that our business with the Grand Ole Opry is maybe ninety percent pure.

Movies weren't the only other industry to benefit from the rapidly growing Opry business. When World War II ended in 1945, there were still no recording studios or record companies in Nashville, but there was one pioneering music publisher.

VITO PELLETTIERI:

The two men who are responsible for Nashville being Music City are Roy Acuff and Fred Rose. Fred was on WSM and he'd written songs for Gene Autry. I says, "Fred, I'm having trouble clearing tunes. I just wish we had a publisher here that can do it. Nobody will take the hillbilly tunes. Nobody wants them, and I've got to have them." He said, "Well, I can help you out if you get Roy Acuff interested in this thing." So I went to Roy and I told him what Fred had said. Roy said, "Yes, I'll be interested." He asked me what kind of fellow Freddie was, and I told him the finest there was. And that was the beginning of Acuff-Rose, the publishing company.

left: **Fred Rose and Roy Acuff. Hank Williams: "Fred Rose came to Nashville to laugh, and he heard Roy Acuff and said, 'By God, he means it.'"**

right: **One of Roy Acuff's first songbooks.**

Roy Acuff's

FOLIO OF

Original Songs

FEATURED OVER WSM GRAND OLE OPRY

DAVID STONE:

Roy was selling songbooks. He had a little trailer home out on the east side, and he had girls come in daily and stuff them in the mail. So he and Freddie got into the publishing business, and it blossomed from the first day. Roy advanced some money to Fred. The money was put in five different banks, so Roy said nothing could happen to all five accounts at once.

ROY ACUFF:

We were like blind pigs searching for an acorn. I was selling a lot of songbooks and I had accumulated a little extra money. I wanted to make some kind of investment, and I knew there wasn't anyone publishing country music, at least not in a big way. I talked to Harry Stone and Vito Pellettieri, who knew Fred real well and knew a lot about music. Finally, I went to Fred, and he thought I was kidding. But it kind of got to him. I told him I had saved twenty-five thousand dollars and I took it to the bank to put in his name. That's how much I trusted him. That money didn't come from personal appearances and it didn't come from playing the Grand Ole Opry. It came from selling songbooks because I knew my songs were hotter'n a pistol. I paid eighty-five dollars for a spot on the Opry broadcast advertising a book of my songs with pictures, and by Wednesday there were twenty-five thousand letters in the post office. People paid twenty-five cents apiece for them.

WESLEY ROSE, *Fred Rose's son:*

Nashville wasn't a music town. But there was the Grand Ole Opry, and that was the reason we stayed. The fact that the Opry was here made us decide to settle in Nashville permanently. The artists were available every weekend and we could take our songs to them. Nowhere else in the world did artists congregate like that every weekend.

Despite the Opry's ever-increasing crowds at home and on the road, it had yet to find a semipermanent base. The primitive Dixie Tabernacle was already deemed unsuitable when the owner precipitated another move.

"THIS WILL RUIN EVERYTHING"— THE OPRY PLUGS IN

Electric steel guitars were introduced in the early 1930s and became popular in western swing bands and big bands where acoustic instruments had to do battle with larger ensembles. One electrified instrument would have created an imbalance in the early Opry groups, but that wasn't the reason they weren't on the show. Judge Hay was dead set against them, and his opinions were shared by many within the Opry cast. If Hay was a pioneer, he was also a purist, and saw no contradiction there.

PEE WEE KING:

We proved that country music doesn't have to sound old-timey. The first time Judge Hay heard me play my accordion, he said, "What is that thing?" I said, "It's an accordion." He said, "That's not a country instrument." Every time we'd introduce a new instrument on the Opry, Judge Hay would get upset. His glasses would come down on his nose. He would call me over, and I knew I was in for a lecture. That's what he did when we did a show with a drum for the first time. He said, "Pee Wee, there's no room on the Opry for that."

Pee Wee King with the offending accordion.

SAM McGEE:

Fellow by the name of McLemore had this electric steel guitar. I heard him play the thing and I thought it was pretty. Never heard one before, so I bought it offa him. I got by with it for two Saturday nights on the Opry, and on the third I was ready to play on our half hour, and Judge Hay came out and tapped me on the shoulder.

BASHFUL BROTHER OSWALD:

Judge looked at it, and he said, "We're not ready for that thing yet, sonny boy. Take it back home."

ROY ACUFF:

This will ruin everything.

KIRK McGEE:

It wasn't too long after, Judge Hay was gone. Then they had electrified instruments in every band.

Ernest Tubb's electric guitarist, Jimmie Short, didn't make the journey to Nashville, and Harold Bradley subbed for him in this 1943 shot. Toby Reese is on bass.

JUSTIN TUBB:

My dad started using the electric guitar so people could hear him in the honky-tonks where he worked. He delivered beer for a company out in west Texas, then he'd get up and play for tips, and you couldn't hardly hear him over the drunks. Some of those west Texas honky-tonks can be kinda noisy.

GRANT TURNER:

It was 1943 when promoter Joe Frank insisted that his new star, Ernest Tubb, be allowed to use electrified instruments. He would not have sounded like his records otherwise.

✦　　✦　　✦

DAVID STONE:

The owner of the tabernacle on Fatherland got fussy and wanted a big cut, so we had to move on.

HARRY STONE:

I don't remember who was governor of Tennessee at the time, but I went to see him and asked permission to use the War Memorial Auditorium just across the street from WSM's offices. Despite the ruling against commercial use of the facilities, I convinced him this was art and culture and [in July 1939] he let us have it.

PEE WEE KING:

When we arrived at the Opry in 1937, admission was still free. People would arrive early and eat dinners they'd brought from home on the ground. [My manager] Mr. Frank was looking out at the throng of people waiting for the show to start, and he said to David Stone, "You're missing the boat. You should charge a small admission. Maybe a dime or a quarter." Mr. Stone said, "Why should we charge? We're getting a lot of valuable advertising out of these free shows." Mr. Frank said, "When you give something away, people don't value it as much as they should, but if you charge even a small amount, they know it's something special."

JUDGE HAY:

If, as Hay said, the Opry's first admission charge was a quarter, by 1941, it had increased to fifty cents.

We put a small price of twenty-five cents on the seats in an effort to handle the crowds, but the auditorium was soon filled to overflowing. Imagine a theater turning crowds away year after year.

HARRY STONE:

The upholstery at the War Memorial was a gum-chewers' heaven. Going there set us back ten years. I listened to this committee spell out all the reasons why we should not only be put out, but put in jail. But it sure was a nice place.

The War Memorial was close to the State Capitol, and the litter left by the Opry crowd was the last straw. Once again in search of a home, WSM approached the trustees of the Ryman Auditorium. The Ryman was built in 1892 by Captain Tom Ryman, president of the Nashville, Paducah, and Cairo Packet Company. It was, Ryman wrote, "purely an outpost to catch sinners." A reformed sinner himself, Ryman built the hall so that the evangelist who had turned his life around, the Reverend Sam Jones, might have a place to preach.

A spectacular venue, Nashville's War Memorial Auditorium was home to the Opry for almost four years between 1939 and 1943. Onstage in 1939, Roy Acuff is backed by Bashful Brother Oswald on Dobro.

Judge Hay with Sam McGee (holding the sheep) and Lonnie Wilson of Roy Acuff's Smoky Mountain Boys.

JACK DeWITT:

The Ryman was run by a group of prominent Nashvillians who got no money out of it. They brought in all sorts of plays and so on. The businessmen who helped run it included Horace Hill [chairman of the local grocery chain, H. G. Hill], Mr. Clements of National Life, and Dan May, the Jewish manufacturer. We rented it from them. I had to deal with Horace Hill. The first thing I had to do was find Horace. He never got to his office until five o'clock in the afternoon, and after that we had to go down and see him and hope that he was there. So he set the amount that we would pay them.

On June 5, 1943, the Opry began at the Ryman on a regular basis. Even with paid admission, every show was sold out with hundreds turned away every week.

PEE WEE KING:

The reason the Ryman was ideal for the Opry was its acoustics. I don't know the technical reason why the sound was so incredible, but I believe the wood in the auditorium absorbed the sound of the music, and it just stayed there. It was like being inside an old violin, surrounded by good seasoned wood. Not even the backstage noise could destroy the sound. And talk about noise! It was a free-for-all back there; a lot of the tune-ups and rehearsing took place in full view of the audience. Sometimes, the only way to tell who was performing was to see who was at the microphone. There were almost no dressing room facilities. Just one area for men and one for women. There were two washrooms to accommodate as many as two hundred performers.

MINNIE PEARL:

At first, I was horrified by the seeming disorganization. I had come from directing plays. On the Opry, it wasn't unusual for an announcer to say, "And now we're proud to present so-and-so," and someone would whisper, "He ain't here, he's gone to get a sandwich," which didn't fluster the emcee, who'd say, "Oh well, he'll be back in a minute. Meanwhile, let's hear from the Fruit Jar Drinkers."

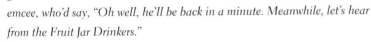

Crowds started lining up Saturday afternoon for the 8:00 p.m. show at the Ryman.

Many dreamed of visiting the Opry; some dreamed of playing there.

BUCK WHITE *of the Whites, Opry stars:*

First time I came to the Ryman, it was like the first time I'd gone to the Alamo. I thought I was stepping into a holy place. It was full of spirits. Good spirits.

BILL ANDERSON:

I listened to the Opry as a young boy down in Georgia, and they used to call WSM the "Air Castle of the South," so I always thought the Opry was held in a castle. The first time I came I was about fourteen, and I was so disappointed because I had visions of this big castle sitting out on a big piece of land. And here was this little auditorium on Fifth Avenue. It was falling apart and there were holes in the curtains, and I thought, This isn't the castle of my dreams at all. We had seats downstairs under the balcony. My mother had bought a new dress to go to the Opry, and someone spilled a soft drink upstairs and it leaked down on her new dress. Once the curtain opened and the music started, I didn't care. It wasn't broken down into two different shows then, but by 10:30 my mom and dad and sister had had enough and they went back to the hotel. I said, "Not

me." I sat there until midnight, then walked around the corner to the Ernest Tubb Record Shop for the Midnite Jamboree. I was just like a sponge soaking it all up, but getting into that business was a dream I didn't dare dream.

WILLIAM R. McDANIEL *and* HAROLD SELIGMAN, *journalists:*

Although the show lasts from 7:30 p.m. until twelve midnight, many of the fans sit through the entire program. Others leave about ten, after they have seen most of the performers. As a rule, the entertainers appear at least once before ten, and once again after ten. This makes room for many of the throng who wait outside the auditorium in the hope of getting a seat in the last portion of the show. The turnover in audience permits the show to play to an average audience of five thousand. Demand for tickets is greater in the summer months, and the show is sold out many weeks in advance. Fans holding general admission tickets begin lining up in front of the auditorium by the middle of Saturday afternoon to assure themselves choice seats when the doors are opened at six. By that time, crowds are usually lined up eight abreast for two blocks. Audience turnover is higher in the summer, mainly because it gets steaming hot in the auditorium, despite exhaust fans, personal cardboard fans, and shirtsleeves.

Jim Denny, who'd been the Opry's bouncer at the Dixie Tabernacle, realized that there was some money to be made from the crowds before they got to see the show. "Denny," wrote journalist George Barker, "had the genius of being able to do a little something for himself all the time he was doing a first-rate job for his boss."

VINCE HIMES, *Jim Denny's employee:*

Jim Denny ran the concessions. That included soft drinks and hot dogs, which were sold to people waiting in line outside the Opry for tickets. People started lining up around two or three p.m., and they'd get pretty hungry. The War Memorial and the Ryman weren't air-conditioned, so it got very hot in those buildings during the summer. We sold a lot of fans.

Several years would pass before Denny took over the Opry's Artists Service Bureau. During the war years, he ran the concessions and opened one of Nashville's first recording studios so that soldiers stationed in nearby Fort Campbell could record messages to send home.

During the war, the Grand Ole Opry became more popular than ever. Servicemen from the South were sent across the country and then around the world, and they took their music with them. The Opry's homespun music and humor seemed inextricably tied to the vision of hearth and home that inspired the troops. Ernest Tubb and Roy Acuff became household names during the war years. Acuff's searing emotionalism went hand in hand with his music's spiritual high ground, while Ernest Tubb sang simply and movingly of loss and separation in songs like "The Soldier's Last Letter" and "It's Been So Long, Darling."

In 1941, several Opry performers were recruited for a Camel road show. The Esty Agency, which handled the Opry sponsor Prince Albert, organized the Camel Caravan on behalf of R. J. Reynolds's Camel brand. Until the Opry performers joined the cast, all of the artists had been pop or jazz since the Camel Caravan's inception as a radio show in 1932.

MINNIE PEARL:

Someone had the idea of putting the Camel Caravan on the road with three units of the show traveling around the country entertaining servicemen. They organized a troupe from Hollywood, one from New York, and one from

*The Camel Caravan
Opry troupe in Florida.*

Nashville. Mr. Frank sold the Esty Agency on using Pee Wee's show for the Opry *Camel Caravan.* The young men on the bases came from all over the country, many from places too far from Nashville for us to perform at because we always had to be back home for the Saturday broadcast. We started in August 1941. Europe was at war, but the United States wasn't, and most Americans didn't think we ever would be. For nineteen months, we worked three shows a day. In addition to my regular fifty dollars a week from Pee Wee, the Esty Agency offered me additional fifty dollars if I would act as chaperone to the cigarette girls, who'd walk through the audience passing out sample packets of Camels.

In May 1942, almost six months after the United States entered the Second World War, the government introduced gasoline rationing, and the draft had already depleted the ranks of sidemen, but Opry stars continued to tour far and wide.

In her newspaper, the *Grinder's Switch Gazette,* Minnie Pearl described a typical "all-night jump."

*The Camel Caravan
touring truck.*

Work the Opry 'til midnight — take time out to load up, killing an hour in the process — start out of Nashville saying to ourselves that we positively will not stop to eat 'til we've gone at least seventy-five or one-

hundred miles. Lots of chatter the first fifty miles or so, everybody discussing the latest Opry news. Things begin to quiet down. The motor hums, miles slip by, the driver is wide awake. Into towns and out. Sleepy little towns where sensible folks are asleep like we ought to be. Lights of an all-night café show up ahead.

Pull over to one side. "Let's eat." Sleepy musicians pile out and into the café. "Coffee." See what's on the jukebox. "Got Eddy's new record. There's one of Tubb's. Here's Roy's 'Silver Trumpets.' Play that one. Better move on, we got miles to go fellas. Into the car again. Let me sit in the front with the heater. My feet are ice." Settling down for another forty or fifty miles. "Hey, wake up, somebody. I can't take it any longer. I'm dead. My eyes are plumb shut." "I'll take it. Wait'll I get out and stretch." "What time is it anyway?" "About 5:30. Almost time for breakfast." "Not yet, let's try to make it to Plainville. It's only fifty miles from here." Quiet again. All of a sudden, there's a bumping sound, not so bad at first. Gets worse. "What's that?" "Tire." "Get out, won't take long." "That spare okay?" "Fella said he wouldn't guarantee it." "Put it on. May be a filling station down the road." "Why can't we have those flats closer to town?" Stop for breakfast. "We ought to make it in time to clean up a little before the show." Back in the car again. Lively chatter now. Coffee and breakfast have waked us all up. "Try that new number. You start it." Singing for twenty or thirty miles. Best rehearsing in the world, right there on the road. "Are we on the right road? Haven't seen a highway sign for miles." "What's the time?" "Okay, we'll make it if we don't have any more hard luck. Where do we show tomorrow? We've showed there. Good town. Rotten hotel. You remember, we showed there with the tent show summer before last?" "Let's get a Coke or something. I'm hungry again." "Let's wait and eat 'til we get there. There's the town now. There's one of our showbills. I hope we pack 'em in. Say, where's the auditorium?"

MINNIE PEARL:

Eddy Arnold opened with "I'll Be Back in a Year, Little Darlin'," and the boys loved it because they thought they'd be home in a year. Then, after Pearl Harbor, he opened with that song one night and got booed all the way through. The

The Camel Caravan's cigarette girls passed out free smokes and raised morale among the servicemen.

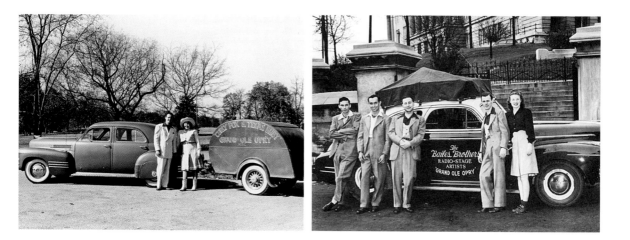

Curly Fox and Texas Ruby (left) and the Bailes Brothers (right) were among the acts that turned their touring transportation into advertising.

Caravan ended in 1942. It was too expensive to get us all the way back to Nashville on Saturday night, and travel was becoming more and more difficult with gasoline rationing and all the rubber for tires going to the war effort.

PEE WEE KING:

One time when Minnie was with us, we were traveling back to Nashville. During the war, we were always having flats because the tires were made of synthetic

Pee Wee King and his fiddle player, Speedy McNatt, ensure that their latest record is on the jukebox.

rubber. We'd already had twelve flats on that trip, and we were hot and tired and frustrated and late. I was mad as hell. I said "All right, everyone, get out. I'm gonna throw this tire through the windshield." Minnie said, "Gus, I do believe Pee Wee is upset." Gus was my brother-in-law and road manager. He said, "Minnie, I've never seen Pee Wee mad at anything before, but I think you're right. He's cussing in Polish." Minnie said, "I thought he was using cuss words I'd never heard before."

There have been very few Saturday nights when the Opry wasn't broadcast over WSM, but one came toward the end of the war.

Report in MINNIE PEARL'S Grinder's Switch Gazette:

On Saturday April 14 [1945], the WSM Grand Ole Opry was not on the air. All of the radio stations and all of the networks observed a three-day period of mourning for our late President, Franklin Delano Roosevelt. For those three days, the usual programs were cancelled, including the OPRY. Announcements were made over WSM to the effect that the OPRY would not be held that Saturday night. For the benefit of those who had not heard the announcement

"THE NEWS, THE GRAND OLE OPRY . . . AND THAT WAS IT!"

LORETTA LYNN *in Butcher Holler, Kentucky:*

I loved Ernest Tubb even when I was a little girl. I'd lay by the radio on Saturday night with my head right up next to it. I'd have a coat or something around me. I'd go to sleep crying when he'd sing, "It's been so long darlin' since I had a kiss from you." It was wartime, you know. During the war, Daddy would say, "We're gonna save the batteries on the radio." It was an old Philco radio. We listened to the news and the Grand Ole Opry, and that was it!

JEAN SHEPARD *in Pauls Valley, Oklahoma:*

We listened to the Opry on a sharecropper's farm in Oklahoma. We saved up and scrimped every year to buy a $2.98 battery for that radio. My daddy run a

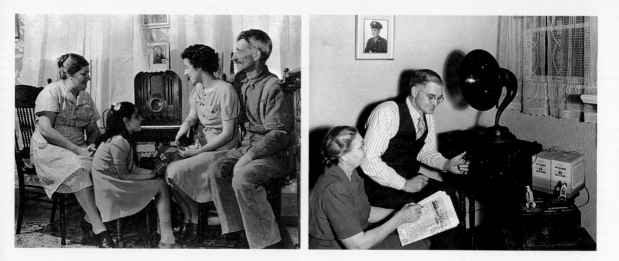

*left: **Listening to the Opry has always been a family affair, with something for every generation.***

*right: **Many people saved their battery power to listen to the Grand Ole Opry on Saturday nights. Some people even took the battery out of their trucks to hook up to the radio.***

ground wire down to this lead pipe in the ground. I'd go out to the cistern and get some water and pour water around it so we could knock the static out. The Opry would come in loud and clear and it'd be wonderful. Grant Turner would say, we have cars here from Michigan and Texas and Oklahoma and Ohio, and I'd think, "How in the world did those people get there?"

JIM McREYNOLDS *of Jim and Jesse in Carfax, Virginia:*

We grew up in the mountains in Virginia, and the only entertainment we had was an old battery radio. On Saturday nights, the whole family would gather in and listen to the Grand Ole Opry. Back then, if you were a member of the Opry, you were there every Saturday night. You could always count on Monroe and Acuff and so on. We grew up in a family that played old-time music, and you'd listen to the Opry on Saturday night, and you'd spend all next week trying to copy what you heard.

JEANNIE SEELY *in Titusville, Pennsylvania:*

I was born in 1940, and I remember the times when Edward R. Murrow or President Roosevelt was on with announcements about World War II, which I didn't understand. All I knew was you had to be quiet. Then we'd turn on the Grand Ole Opry, and everyone sang along and clapped. I couldn't understand why it wasn't always there. You should be able to always turn that button and hear the Opry and Ernest Tubb. If we couldn't pick up the Opry, we'd pile into the car and go find someone who could pick it up.

★ ★ ★

and had come from a distance to see the OPRY there was a short musical
program at the Opry House for which tickets were not required.

PEE WEE KING:

I was substituting for Roy Acuff when President Roosevelt died. The Judge came
to me and says to me, "Would you do your stage show while the network takes
over? Just entertain our audiences here at the Ryman?" I said, "Well, sure." I told
Buddy Harroll, our trumpet player. "Buddy, run out in the bus and bring your
ax in." Buddy says, "King, you kiddin'? A trumpet on the Opry stage?" I says,
"Yeah." I told the audience, "The network has taken over our radio time
eulogizing our late president, so if you don't mind, we'd like to show you what we
do in our stage shows. First, everyone, please bow your head in respect." I played
"My Buddy" on the accordion. We had everybody in the audience in tears. Then
Buddy went straight into "Bugle Call Rag," and Judge Hay almost jumped off
the stage.

By war's end, the Grand Ole Opry had become the most popular country music radio show, and every up-and-coming country star wanted to
work on it. The Opry offered something for everyone: old-time rural
music from Uncle Dave Macon and Sam and Kirk McGee; Bill Monroe's
bluegrass; Ernest Tubb's honky-tonk music; Roy Acuff's heartfelt Ap-
palachian music; Minnie Pearl's comedy; Eddy Arnold's crooning; and
Pee Wee King's sharp-tip western swing. The show was breathlessly fast-
paced, designed in such a way that if there was someone you didn't like,
you'd barely have time to reach the dial before he or she was off. The
rapidly evolving lineup and innovative managers behind the scenes would
take the show to even greater heights in the years ahead.

6

STAR TIME

By the end of the Second World War, no one seriously questioned the Grand Ole Opry's preeminence. There were hundreds of radio barn dances on stations great and small, but the Opry was the dream of every performer on every small-town radio barn dance, and the Opry's management team was determined to keep it that way. But there were clouds on the horizon. For one thing, no one foresaw the impact that television would soon have on "live" radio. When Pee Wee King left the Opry in 1947 to work on a television station in Louisville, Kentucky, the feeling was that he'd be back in six months. Even so, as the Opry's new management team took shape in the years immediately after the war, the future looked rosy and assured.

Judge Hay was still at the Opry, but only as an announcer. In 1945, he wrote the first history of the show, *A Story of the Grand Ole Opry*. It was a slender booklet sold only at the Opry's concession stands, but it showed that the Solemn Old Judge already appreciated the significance of what he'd created twenty years earlier. Vito Pellettieri still stage-managed the show, and Harry Stone was still WSM station manager, but his brother, David, had left. The Opry's former bouncer, Jim Denny, had taken over David's role at the Opry's Artists Service Bureau. Shortly before the war, Jack

Ott Devine, who would become manager of the Opry in 1959,
George Reynolds, Jack Stapp, Harry Stone, and Judge Hay.

Stapp had come to WSM as program director, and returned after serving overseas. A quiet, diffident man, Stapp had worked at CBS radio in New York and helped professionalize the Opry. Edwin Craig still oversaw the Opry from his position on the board of National Life, and brought back his old friend Jack DeWitt to the newly created post of president of WSM. DeWitt was born on Fatherland Street in East Nashville, near where the Opry was held between 1936 and 1939, but his interest in radio was almost entirely technical. As a part-time engineer, he'd helped install WSM in the National Life building, and was chief engineer between 1932 and 1942. DeWitt's appointment as president placed him over Harry Stone, and this was probably Craig's way of trying to limit Stone's authority.

JACK DeWITT, WSM *president*:

I came back to WSM in 1947. I used to go to the Opry every three or four months. I would go down and sit in the front seat at the Ryman. Then I'd go backstage and see the guys. I wanted to show them that I had a great interest in the Opry, which I didn't at all. I like what's called good music, but I didn't let them know that if I could help it.

Jack DeWitt happily left the Opry to Harry Stone, Jack Stapp, and Jim Denny. They couldn't risk a new star spearheading a rival barn dance, so one of their top priorities was to recruit up-and-coming artists from other radio barn dances. The Opry was still paying "scale" (the minimum mandated by the musicians' union for broadcasts), but could entice young stars with its prestige, huge listenership, and lucrative tours.

JACK STAPP:

The one thing I wanted to do was to get the best country talent at the Grand Ole Opry. Every time one of our artists would say, "Hey, I just heard a great singer down in Shreveport, you ought to get him," I'd get on the phone and I'd call him. I'd ask him if he wanted to come to Nashville.

The answer was almost invariably "Yes."

MARIE CLAIRE, *Jim Denny's assistant:*

Jim Denny greatly improved the quality of country bookings through the bureau. Where Opry acts once played schoolhouses and tiny halls, Denny had them in auditoriums, arenas, and fairs. He had a deep, gruff voice. He liked to wear brown pinstriped suits, and he walked down the hall like a bear. He scared some people to death.

The first problem facing the new management in the postwar years was how to handle an Opry star who sometimes gave the impression that he was bigger than the show itself: Roy Acuff. The host of the Opry's networked Prince Albert show, Acuff was not only the biggest star in country music, but one of the biggest stars in all popular music. War reporter Ernie Pyle reported that the Japanese troops at the Battle of Okinawa screamed, "To hell with Roosevelt! To hell with Babe Ruth! To hell with Roy Acuff!" When National Life salesmen went on the road, they were trained to say, "Good morning, I work for the company that owns the Grand Ole Opry, and Roy Acuff asked me to come by and give you a personal hello. May I come in?"

The war in Europe was over, but hundreds of thousands of GIs remained there, and, with the fighting ended, they could focus a little more upon entertainment. Their choice: Roy Acuff and the Smoky Mountain Boys.

Jim Denny had come to Nashville on his own at age eleven in 1922. Jim Denny: "I got off the train and all my money was in a little tobacco sack. I had about forty cents. I got a job selling the Tennessean up and down Church Street. Between editions, I delivered telegrams, and I was adopted, sort of, by the women in the bordellos north of the Capitol. Most of their business was arranged by telegram. Very often, answers were required, so I got to carry the messages both ways. They were always good for a fifty-cent tip, a good meal, and conversation."

THE FIRST CARNEGIE HALL SHOWS

No event better underscored the fact that country music had a nationwide following than the first Carnegie Hall concerts in September 1947.

Billboard *magazine, November 1947:*

Staid Carnegie Hall has been re-bopped by Lionel Hampton and jived by Woody Herman, but Thursday and Friday September 18 and 19, it was con-quered by hillbilly music and the place will never be the same again. A cornbilly troupe called the Grand Ole Opry featuring many performers appearing regularly on the air show of that name took over the house and proved to the tune of $12,000 gross that the big city wants country music. The promoters, Sol Gold, Abe Lackman and Oscar Davis, got more than a kick out of it because they garnered about $9,500 with a talent nut of about $5,000. If nothing else, the hillbilly concerts demonstrated several important things. First, New York is sold on hillbilly music. These weren't just curious onlookers out for a night of novelty. These were serious devoted fans, almost rabid in their wild enthusiasm. Such screaming and wild applause after each number hasn't been heard in town since Frank Sinatra brought out the bobbysoxers at the Paramount. Instead of juveniles, these were people beyond their teens who knew all the numbers and entertainers, which is proof positive that they listen to all the shows featuring these performers.

From the Grinder's Switch Gazette, *September 1945:*

Word has just now reached us that last winter for almost six months the Roy Acuff recording of "Great Speckled Bird" was among the top ten numbers on the Mediterranean Hit Parade chosen from requests sent in by G.I.s in that section of the world.

From Radio Daily, *October 1945:*

A tally of 3,700 votes cast by G.I. listeners in the European areas during a two-week popularity contest over AFN's Munich Morning Report *between Frank*

MINNIE PEARL:

That was the first time I realized how far-flung country music had become. The boys had come home from the service and many who'd never been exposed to country music before they left were now fans. It's hard for some of the new country artists to realize how limited we were in the early days. Through the mid-1940s, country music performers didn't play the big halls or the class houses. We showed in high school auditoriums, one-room schoolhouses, beer joints, and fairs.

ERNEST TUBB:

People couldn't believe country music was being played at Carnegie Hall. The radio and newspaper people ignored us the first night we were there, but we turned away six thousand people and the next night every reporter was there. We played two nights and even then didn't play to everyone.

★   ★   ★

Sinatra and Roy Acuff showed a 600 vote lead for Acuff. As a result, a new show called Hillbilly Jamboree *will be launched by AFN Munich soon.*

From the Grinder's Switch Gazette, *November 1945:*

While Roy Acuff is in Hollywood, Saturday night Opry fans will still be able to hear him and the Smoky Mountain Boys on the Prince Albert program. Arrangements have been made to "pipe" his part of the program from Hollywood through to WSM, where it will go out as part of the network show.

Despite characterizing Hollywood as seventy-five percent phony, Acuff made five movies between 1942 and 1946, and toured nationwide, making it hard to meet his Opry commitment.

Before satellites, radio shows were transmitted across the network by phone lines, and Roy Acuff used the same technology to appear on the Opry in voice if not in person.

From the Grinder's Switch Gazette, *January 1946:*

A lady arrived at the Opry House back in November and was walking down the aisle to her seat just as Roy Acuff by wire from Hollywood was introducing Gene Autry, also in Hollywood. Autry sang a song. The lady, being familiar with the voices of both Roy and Gene was somewhat confused hearing them and not being able to see them. She walked up to the doorman and said, "How much extra does it cost to see 'em?"

Roy Acuff was beginning to test his popularity in ways that sometimes dismayed his costars. In 1943, Acuff's Prince Albert Opry show had gone from partial networking to the full NBC network. There was a celebration at the Ryman, but Tennessee governor Prentice Cooper wouldn't attend. Saying he'd be no party to a circus, he added that Acuff was bringing disgrace to Tennessee by making Nashville the hillbilly capital of the United States. He would be the last Tennessee governor to take that stand, but Acuff was determined to make him pay for it. With a governor's race looming in 1944, Acuff secured the Republican nomination.

PEE WEE KING:

Roy called me before he announced his candidacy. He said, "Pee Wee, you're a Republican, and I want you to help me. I'll throw in fifty thousand dollars of my own money, and we'll draw crowds like you've never seen. We'll play all the little foothill towns and courthouse squares all over Tennessee, and I'm confident we'll

win." He was right about drawing the big crowds. Everybody came to hear ol' Roy sing, but they didn't vote for him. He got whipped by the Democrats.

Undeterred, Acuff decided to try for the Republican nomination again in 1948, but was defeated yet again.

In 1946, between runs for governor, Roy Acuff left the Opry in a dispute over salary. Rather than give in to his demands, the Opry hired Red Foley away from WLS's National Barn Dance to replace him on the Prince Albert segment.

Roy was the first Opry star to sign a deal for product endorsement. Cherokee Mills reached an agreement with him to use his name on their flour. Later in the 1940s, J.C. Penney would license his name for a line of clothing.

RED FOLEY:

I guess I never was more scared than I was the night I replaced Roy Acuff on the network part of the Opry. The people adored Roy and a lot of them didn't believe

Roy Acuff: "It isn't easy for a country boy like me to stand up here and try to make a political speech. I intend on staying up here, being one of you, and I promise not to bring politics again to the Grand Ole Opry."

he'd quit. They thought I was a Chicago slicker who had come down to pass himself off as a country boy and bump Roy out of his job. It took me about a year to get adjusted. But, boy, that first night on the Opry stage was a nervous time. While I was wishing Roy luck and saying goodbye, there were old women crying in the front row. I'd been warned people might throw tomatoes at me—without taking them out of the can.

HILLOUS BUTRUM, *Opry bass player:*

Foley wasn't a real showman, but I've never seen anybody else able to hold an audience the way Red did, except maybe Hank Williams. We were playing the Showboat in Las Vegas once, and everybody was drinking and gambling and living it up. Red came out and did "Peace in the Valley," and it was like someone had turned off a switch. We asked him how he had the nerve to sing a hymn in a place like that and how he could make it go over so strongly, and he said, "I pick out two people and just sing to them. I begin to reach them, and then it spreads."

Early in 1947, Roy Acuff returned from an extensive West Coast trip, and was hospitalized. Two of his first visitors were Harry Stone and Ernest Tubb. According to Acuff, the conversation went like this:

Roy Acuff in a promotional shot for RC Cola.

Harry said, "Roy, the Opry is losing many of its people, and it looks like maybe we're going under if you don't come back and be with us. Come and help us out. We wish you would change your mind, and come back." [I replied], "Harry, if I mean that much to WSM and the Grand Ole Opry, I will come back and do everything I can to help the Opry at all times."

Roy Acuff returned April 26, 1947, as host of the Opry's Royal Crown segment, but Red Foley remained at the helm of the Prince Albert show. Always an astute businessman, Acuff might have sensed that his career had peaked. He returned just as another Opry star, Eddy Arnold, was wondering if he really needed the Opry. Arnold's answer would be different than Acuff's. A pioneer country crooner, Eddy Arnold's star had risen meteorically in very few years. It had been just five years since he'd left Pee Wee King and gone to see Harry Stone.

Roy Acuff was a showman extraordinaire. In addition to singing and playing the fiddle, he was a champion with a yo-yo and could balance a fiddle on its bow on his chin.

EDDY ARNOLD:

I said, "Mister Stone, I love Pee Wee, but I'm going to leave him. I'm not making any money and I'm not getting anywhere. I have a wife and mother to support, and I'm quitting whether you hire me on my own or not. What I'd like to do is work for you on this station." How I ever got up the nerve to ask Harry Stone to give me my own program, I'll never know. Mister Stone looked at me a second or two, blinked, and said, "Eddy, you have a job." I didn't earn a lot on WSM, but Harry Stone saw to it that I got enough to get by. I'll never be able to repay Harry Stone for having faith in me. Gradually, he arranged for me to appear on other WSM programs, and finally the Grand Ole Opry.

In 1944, Harry Stone arranged for Eddy Arnold to get a recording contract with RCA, and in the years immediately after the war, Eddy sold millions of records and became the first country artist to consistently cross over into the pop charts. He dominated the country charts to such an extent that just one other artist scored a number-one hit in 1948.

Eddy's Arnold's manager, Colonel Tom Parker, later managed Elvis Presley, and saw the Opry tying up his star on Saturday night at minimum wage. Repeatedly, the Colonel told Eddy that the Opry needed him more than he needed the Opry, and, in 1948, Eddy came to share that opinion.

EDDY ARNOLD:

Someone said to me, "The Opry made you." I said, "If it made me, then why hasn't it made the Fruit Jar Drinkers?"

Even off the Opry, Eddy Arnold was so influential that the Opry had to accommodate him. Colonel Parker arranged for Eddy to host a radio show

After Eddy left Pee Wee King, Judge Hay dubbed him "The Tennessee Plowboy." Success came quickly. Little Roy Wiggins, Eddy's steel guitarist: "We'd leave Nashville on Sunday night. We'd get home during the day on Saturday, play the Opry Saturday night, and leave again Sunday night."

sponsored by Purina. It was offered to WSM for transmission on Saturday night, but WSM turned it down because it would interrupt the Opry. Purina then offered it to WSM's rival, WLAC, for Friday night.

IRVING WAUGH:

I told Purina that if they ever put the Eddy Arnold show in this market, it had to go on WSM because we were the country station. I told him that if he went to another station on Friday night we would put a live country music show against him, in front of him, and behind him. I said, "I hate to say this because it sounds as though I'm threatening you, but this means so much to our company." He finally said, "You can have it, but you'll have to do what you said you'd do if the show went on the other station. You'll have to build a live show in front of it and behind it."

And so, in 1948, the *Friday Night Frolics* was created as a sister show to the Saturday night Opry. With a live audience in the WSM studio, it fulfilled the commitment to Purina, and allowed the station to offer sponsorship opportunities to advertisers waiting for a spot on the Opry itself. The frolics would later become the *Friday Night Opry*, moving from WSM Studio C to the Ryman on September 11, 1964.

Even with Eddy Arnold gone, the Opry was still drawing top up-and-coming stars: George Morgan, Little Jimmy Dickens, Hank Williams, and Hank Snow.

George Morgan: September 1948

GEORGE MORGAN:

One Saturday night, I was back in Barberton, Ohio. I heard Eddy Arnold say goodbye to the Opry audience. I wondered who would be replacing Eddy, and on Monday morning I got a call from WSM asking me to audition.

George Morgan and band perform at the Friday Night Frolics, broadcast from WSM Studio C. Many Opry members performed not only on the regular Saturday night show, but on daily programs and the Frolics as well.

Unusually, George Morgan was brought to the Opry before he'd made his first record. He was appearing regularly on the WWVA Jamboree, and the Opry had heard enough good reports to entice him to Nashville. Columbia Records signed him as soon as he arrived, and his first record, "Candy Kisses," became his signature hit. In 1972, he introduced his daughter, Lorrie, a future member, from the Opry stage.

Little Jimmy Dickens: February 1948

Compensating for his small stature (four feet, eleven inches in cowboy boots) with a brassy personality, Little Jimmy Dickens has been an entertainer more than a singer, but for many years he recruited some of the most innovative musicians in Nashville and could perform ballads as adeptly as the novelty songs for which he's best known.

GRANT TURNER:

Roy Acuff did a radio show from his den on Sunday afternoons. It was the first time anyone had done this on WSM. His wife, Mildred, built a fire during the winter. Roy had met Jimmy in Saginaw, and he told Jimmy that if he came to

Little Jimmy Dickens in hot pursuit of June Carter on the Jefferson Island Salt portion of the Opry.

Nashville, he'd get him on the Grand Ole Opry, but the first time Jimmy was on WSM was on Roy's program from his den.

LITTLE JIMMY DICKENS:

When Roy Acuff came to Saginaw [Michigan], it was very cold. He asked me, "What are you doing in this cold country?" I said, "Well, it's a living, you know. I'm working." He said, "We've got to see about getting you out of here. Would you be interested in coming to the Opry?" I said, "If you told me I was going to the Opry, I don't know if I'd live long enough to make it." I didn't sleep for two days and nights. [After the first show], I went back to Saginaw and forgot about it. Then I got a call to do another guest spot. Mr. Acuff said, "You'd better bring enough things with you. I think you're going to stay." Sure enough, he said, "I want you to stay around here, do my program, and stay at the house until we can get you straightened out."

I just went from doing Mister Acuff's programs to my own. I did early-morning programs on WSM for a pretty long period of months, so I figured by doing that they were going to put me on the Opry as a regular member. I more or less just slid into it.

Little Jimmy Dickens songbook, published 1956.

Little Jimmy was also signed to the Opry without any hits or even a recording contract, but he, too, was acquired by Columbia Records and used the exposure afforded by the Opry to make his first records, "Take an Old Cold Tater (and Wait)" and "Country Boy," into big hits.

There were years between 1957 and 1975 when Little Jimmy Dickens only guested on the Opry, but at the dawn of the new millennium, he was the only performer who'd joined the show in the 1940s still on the bill.

Hank Williams: June 1949

Early in 1949, Hank was in Shreveport working on the *Louisiana Hayride*. He'd been recording with intermittent success since 1946, but his record of "Lovesick Blues" had just knocked George Morgan's "Candy Kisses" from the top of the country charts when he was invited to Nashville. Though they didn't realize it at the time, Hank had already made his Opry debut.

Hank Williams greets some young fans backstage.

JUDGE HAY:

We were putting on a show at Montgomery City Auditorium. This would have been the late 1930s. A boy about fifteen came rushing up. He said, "Judge, just let me do one number, please." I said, "You walk around backstage and I'll listen to you." The show was going on, and I listened to him, and he did real well. I said, "Get up there and do a couple of songs." Found out later, that was Hank Williams, and it had to be ten years or more before he joined the Opry.

Hank's reputation preceded him, but the Opry finally decided that he was a risk they had to take on.

OSCAR DAVIS, *Hank's manager:*

I came to Jim Denny, and Jim said, "No we won't have Hank Williams. We talked about him with Harry Stone and he's got a bad reputation with drinking and missing shows." So I plead and plead with him, and finally he agrees to square it away.

In order to get Hank on the Opry, his producer and music publisher, Fred Rose, gave the composer credit on a song that he [Rose] had written to Harry Stone and Jack Stapp. That song, "Chattanoogie Shoe Shine Boy," became a big hit for Red Foley, Frank Sinatra, and others in 1949.

Red Foley (partly obscured with fedora hat) introduces Hank Williams on the Prince Albert Opry. Red Foley: "Well, sir, tonight's big-name guest is making his first appearance on Prince Albert Grand Ole Opry. He's a Montgomery, Alabama, boy. Been pickin' and singin' about twelve years, but it's been about the last year he's really come into his own, and we're proud to give a rousing Prince Albert welcome to the Lovesick Blues Boy, Hank Williams. Well, sir, we hope you'll be here for a good long time, buddy."

Hank Williams: "Well, Red, it looks like I'll be doing just that, and I'll be looking forward to it."

GRANT TURNER:

Hank brought that song "Lovesick Blues" to the Opry. They brought him in that first night and put him in the boss's office so he could relax, and when it came his time, they brought him down, and Red Foley introduced him. People loved that "Lovesick Blues" song so much, they kicked up the dust in the auditorium. The spotlights looked like they were picking up smoke, there was so much dust kicked up.

LITTLE JIMMY DICKENS:

The mystery of Hank Williams I have never been able to figure out: what the magnetism was that he had. Anytime you worked a concert with him, you didn't have to peep around the curtain to see if you had a full house. You knew it. He'd tell you, too. "I drew a full house, now go out there and entertain 'em." When he came onstage people would become unglued. The lyrics that would come out of his mouth. Unbelievable! He wasn't that well educated. Where did all this come from? It would scare you.

Whistlin' Dixie. From left: Hank Williams, Jerry Rivers, Sammy Pruett, Cedric Rainwater, and Don Helms; seated, Minnie Pearl.

CHET ATKINS, *Opry staff guitarist:*

Hank would come up to you at the Opry and say, "I got a new one for you, hoss." He'd get right up in your face and sing it, and the smell of bourbon would be pretty strong. Then he'd play something like "Mansion on the Hill," or one of those unbelievably great songs. Someone like Ernest Tubb or Hank Snow would be standing around, and they'd say, "I'd like to record that, Hank." Hank would narrow his eyes and say, "Naw, it's too damn good for you. I'm gonna record it myself." I think those were his test runs. If Ernest Tubb and Hank Snow wanted the song, Hank knew it was a hit.

Even the mainstream press was beguiled by Hank's enigma, especially after his songs, like "Cold, Cold Heart," "Jambalaya," and "I Can't Help It," became pop hits for Tony Bennett, Frankie Laine, Jo Stafford, and others.

RUFUS JARMAN, *journalist, in* Nation's Business:

He is a lanky, erratic country man who learned to play guitar from an old Negro named Teetot in his home village of Georgiana, Alabama. "You ask what makes our kind of music successful," he says. "I'll tell you. Just one word: sincerity. When a hillbilly sings a crazy song, he feels crazy. When he sings, 'I laid my mother away,' he sees her a-laying right there in the coffin. He sings more sincere than most because he was raised rougher than most. You got to know a lot about hard work. You got to have smelled a lot of mule manure before you can sing like a hillbilly. There ain't nuthin' queer at all about them Europeans liking our kind of singing. It's liable to teach them more about what everyday Americans are really like than anything else."

For a couple of years, Hank raced back to Nashville almost every Saturday night. He knew that the Opry was the most exclusive club in country music, and knew that he'd worked hard to get there. But that would eventually change as he grew more successful.

Hank Snow: January 1950

Hank Snow had recorded in Canada since 1936, but encountered only disappointment in trying to broaden his career into the United States. The

Opry was still signing artists like Jimmy Dickens and George Morgan, who didn't have hits, but the show's management was as resistant to Hank Snow as they'd been to Hank Williams. Snow, though, had a champion on the Opry in Ernest Tubb. The two shared a fanatical passion for Jimmie Rodgers, and Tubb promised to do his best to get Snow onto the show.

HANK SNOW:

I could hear the Opry in eastern Canada pretty well. I wrote to Ernest [Tubb] in care of the Grand Ole Opry and got a nice letter back, and we corresponded. Ernest said, "Hank it's all happening in Nashville. Nashville is the home of country music. If you want to advance your career you should be there. I'll do my best to get you on the Opry, but there's one problem: they won't sign anyone unless they have a hit record."

Tubb tried to interest Harry Stone in hiring Snow as a replacement for him while he was on the West Coast. According to Tubb, the conversation between Stone and himself went like this:

"Well, what do you think?"

"He sounds too much like you."

"Ah, don't gimme that stuff. I'm talking long distance and I'm spending my money. I'll argue with you when I get home. He sings like he's a Jimmie Rodgers fan, but with that Canadian brogue, he can't sound like me."

Hank Snow was working at the Big "D" Jamboree in Dallas when Tubb finally persuaded Jim Denny to take a chance on his friend.

HANK SNOW:

I got a phone call from Ernest. "Hank, I had a talk with Mister Denny. He thinks he'll be able to place you on the Opry." I was wondering how Ernest had convinced Mister Denny. After all, I still didn't have a hit record in the USA. Mister Denny didn't say anything about a tryout. He said he wanted me to start on January 7, 1950, at seventy-five dollars a week. I said many prayers during the few weeks before my Opry debut that I would be a success. God has his plan for all of us, even a little weakling from Nova Scotia, Canada.

On March 28, 1950, Hank Snow recorded his first American hit, "I'm Movin' On," and the Opry stage provided a ready-made audience of around ten million.

HANK SNOW:

All the years of frustration came together with just one song. Mister Denny confirmed my fears. He said, "A few weeks ago, Harry Stone heard you sing for the first time. He said, 'Who the hell is that out there trying to sing?' I can tell you now, 'I'm Movin' On' is a miracle if ever there was one. They were about to drop you." The Opry audiences changed overnight. They were completely indifferent one week, and the next week they were wildly enthusiastic.

From left, Jack Stapp, Hank Snow, and Jim Denny, backstage.

The new stars not only ensured that no other radio barn dance would eclipse the Grand Ole Opry, but the concentration of so many country stars in one place meant that the business would soon follow them to Nashville.

Hank Snow greets fans backstage at the Opry.

PROGRAM December 1, 1951

WARREN PAINT — 7:30 to 7:45

ROY ACUFF ....Crawdad Song
LEW CHILDRE ....Hang Out the Front Door Key
THE LE CROIX SISTERS ....Down On My Knees
OSWALD ....Foggy Mountain Top
HOWDY FORRESTER ....Fire In the Mountain

AMERICAN ACE COFFEE — 7:45 to 8:00

ROY ACUFF ....Just A Friend
UNCLE DAVE MACON ....That's Where My Money Goes
ROY ACUFF ....Glory Bound Train
THE JUG BAND ....I Like Mountain Music
JIMMY RIDDLE ....They Cut Down the Old Pine Tree

MARTHA WHITE — 8:00 to 8:30

ERNEST TUBB ....Tomorrow Never Comes
BILL MONROE ....Uncle Pen
MAMA MAYBELLE ....Keep on the Sunny Side
THE CROOK BROTHERS ....8th of January
NEAL BURRIS ....There's Been a Change in Me
JUNE CARTER ....Too Old to Cut the Mustard
CHET ATKINS ....Crazy Rhythm
ERNEST TUBB ....Bless Your Little Old Heart
BILL MONROE ....Truck Driver Blues
TERRY YOUNG ....Leather Britches

PRINCE ALBERT — 8:30 to 9:00

RED FOLEY ....Alabama Jubilee
COWBOY COPAS ......'Tis Sweet to Be Remembered
THE SQUARE DANCERS ....Here and There
RED FOLEY ....Farther Along
THE JORDANAIRES ....Search Me, Lord
COWBOY COPAS ....I Love You, My Darling, I Love You
STRING BEAN ....Lonesome Road Blues
RED FOLEY ....Old Home Down On the Farm
THE SQUARE DANCERS ....Sally Goodin

ROYAL CROWN COLA — 9:00 to 9:30

ROY ACUFF ....Thy Burdens Are Greater Than Mine
THE FRUIT JAR DRINKERS ....Cotton Eyed Joe
HANK WILLIAMS ....Cold, Cold Heart
DUKE OF PADUCAH ....Comedy
THE LE CROIX SISTERS ....Down Yonder
MOON MULLICAN ....Heartless Lover
LONZO AND OSCAR ....Why Should I Cry Over You
ROY ACUFF ....Don't Wait 'Til Judgment
HANK WILLIAMS ....Crazy Heart
OSWALD ....Late Last Night
HOWDY FORRESTER ....Turkey In the Straw

FORTUNE FEED — 9:30 to 10:00

CARL SMITH ....Let Old Mother Nature Have Her Way
LITTLE JIMMY DICKENS ....Cold Feet
ANITA CARTER ....I'm Crying
JAMUP AND HONEY ....Comedy
HANK SNOW ....Music Making Mama
THE 'POSSUM HUNTERS ....Peacock Rag
THE JORDANAIRES ....Read That Book
CARL SMITH ....If Teardrops Were Pennies
LITTLE JIMMY DICKENS ....It May Be Silly
HAL SMITH ....Sally Goodin

WALLRITE — 10:00 to 10:15

BILL MONROE ....I'm On My Way Back to the O...
THE OLD HICKORY SINGERS ....I Wa...
NEAL BURRIS ....If You Need Me, I'll Be
OLD JOE CLARK ....Sha...
BILL MONROE ....Get Down On Your Knee a...

DR. LE GEAR — 10:15 to 10:30

ROY ACUFF ....Who Broke ...
UNCLE DAVE MACON ....Rock
ROY ACUFF ....The Heart That Was Broken
ROBERT LUNN ....Talkin...
HOWDY FORRESTER ....Turkey in th...

JEFFERSON ISLAND SALT — 10:30 to 11:00

ERNEST TUBB ....Driftwood on t...
LITTLE JIMMY DICKENS ....L...
THE GULLY JUMPERS ....Mocki...
MOON MULLICAN ....Cherokee
THE JORDANAIRES ....Roll on
ERNEST TUBB ....I'm With A Crowd, But S...
JUNE CARTER ....Mommy Real P...
LITTLE JIMMY DICKENS ...If It Ain't One Thing ,It's ...
CHET ATKINS ....Spanish Fo...
MAMA MAYBELLE ....Wild
FIDDLE ....Ricketts H...

D-CON — 11:00 to 11:15

COWBOY COPAS ....Down in Nashville, T...
ANNIE LOU AND DANNY ....I...
LAZY JIM DAY ....Singing th...
COWBOY COPAS ....Shame, Shame
FIDDLE ....Bill Ch...

NIRESK — 11:15 to 11:30

HANK WILLIAMS ....Moaning th...
SAM AND KIRK ....While I'r...
AUDRY WILLIAMS ....Tightwad
HANK WILLIAMS ....I Can't
FIDDLE ....Bile Dem Cabbag...

SOLTICE — 11:30 to 11:45

HANK SNOW ....One M...
LEW CHILDRE ....Everybody's
THE CROOK BROTHERS ....Fishers I...
HANK SNOW ....Brand On M...
THE CROOK BROTHERS ....Trouble Among the Y...

11:45 to 12:00

CARL SMITH.................Part of My Heart Is ...
LONZO AND OSCAR ....Let's Live a Littl...
THE FRUIT JAR DRINKERS ....Cackl...
CARL SMITH ....Let's Live ...
THE FRUIT JAR DRINKERS ....Down...

GRAND OLE OPRY®

Chet Atkins

Margie Bowes

Carl and Pearl Butler

Archie Campbell

The Carlisles

Martha Carson

Mother Maybelle Carter
and the Carter Sisters

Johnny Cash

Cedar Hill Square Dancers

Cousin Jody

Wilma Lee and
Stoney Cooper

Skeeter Davis

Roy Drusky

The Everly Brothers

Lester Flatt and
Earl Scruggs

Lefty Frizzell

Don Gibson

Billy Grammer

Hawkshaw Hawkins

Goldie Hill

Ferlin Husky

Stonewall Jackson

George Jones

Rusty and Doug Kershaw

The LaDells

The Louvin Brothers

Rose Maddox

Benny Martin

Moon Mullican

Jimmy C. Newman

Webb Pierce

Ray Price

Jim Reeves

Marty Robbins

Jean Shepard

Carl Smith

Hank Snow

Red Sovine

Stoney Mountain Cloggers

Tennessee Travelers

Justin Tubb

Porter Wagoner

Kitty Wells

The Wilburn Brothers

Del Wood

Faron Young

7

DEPARTURES AND ARRIVALS

T he Grand Ole Opry had begun as just another show on WSM, but by 1950 it was bigger than the station itself. It was still heard on WSM, but more than 160 other NBC stations picked up part of the show, and it went out over Armed Forces Radio as well. People were beginning to say "Grand Ole Opry" when they meant "country music." Management of the show became a prize worth fighting for, and, in the early 1950s, a power struggle unfolded between Harry Stone and Jim Denny.

JACK DeWITT:

Harry Stone was a good radio man. When we, WSM, had contracts with the companies that advertised on the Opry, Harry was very good at dealing with them. Unfortunately, it got to the point where he was taking money from them, and that's when we fired him. Up to then, he completely refused to cooperate with me, and wouldn't have anything to do with reporting to

Harry Stone at the helm. In 1950, Judge Hay wrote, "Harry's hobby is his cruiser on the Cumberland River, in which he gains relaxation after a tough day at the office. He named his boat the Grand Ole Opry. Let us assure our audience that the job of managing one of America's largest broadcast stations is a big one, fraught with many diverse problems."

me. The interesting thing is that both Jim Denny and Harry Stone were very stricken with a girl named Dollie Dearman. Harry had this boat that he kept down on the river, and one of our announcers, Louie Buck, came to me one time with a picture of [Dollie Dearman] on that boat. She was all spread out with nothing on. I didn't know that Louie knew Greek mythology, but he said, "This is the one that launched a thousand ships." Anyway, Stone went out to Arizona, and Denny finally married her. His wife divorced him and he married her.

Harry Stone left WSM in August 1950 and, in January the following year, moved to KPHO in Phoenix, Arizona. Jim Denny and Jack Stapp now ran the Opry, but Jack DeWitt was determined to keep Denny on a short leash.

Dollie Dearman. Early in her career, Dollie had been a dancer with Roy Acuff and Minnie Pearl, and she entertained the troops on USO tours. After the war, she worked for the Grand Ole Opry selling songbooks.

Charlie and Ira Louvin, the Louvin Brothers: February 1955

In the late 1930s, when Ira and Charlie Louvin saw Roy Acuff near their hometown in northern Alabama, they were already perfecting the unerring sibling harmony that later influenced Emmylou Harris, the Everly Brothers, and many others. Working at various radio stations throughout the mid-South, their goal was always to join Acuff on the Grand Ole Opry.

CHARLIE LOUVIN:

We had a neighbor a mile away that had a radio. He owned a grocery store, and there were pretty good crowds in his living room on Saturday night, fifteen, twenty, twenty-five people, just to listen to the Opry. We'd stay until he'd say it's goin' home time, and someone ran us off. Mr. Acuff came to our neighborhood. It was the first year he came to the Opry. He was drivin' that car. Block and a half long. It was an air-cooled Franklin. Three doors on each side. There was places he had trouble going 'cause the car almost needed hinges to make the curve. It was ten cents for kids and twenty cents or a quarter for adults. We didn't have no money to get in, but it was warm weather and they had the windows up so we heard and seen the show as good as anybody. It looked like a good life. I was twelve years old, and from that point we earnestly prepared ourselves to be on the Opry.

Ten years later, Ira and Charlie decided it was time for them, too, to be Opry stars. Charlie Louvin's story of how hard it was to get on the Opry proves how crucial Opry membership had become.

The Louvin Brothers treat the audience to some of their close harmony singing on the Prince Albert Opry.

CHARLIE LOUVIN:

We were working Memphis, and every time we'd have a day off on the weekend we'd come to the Opry. We'd corral Jim Denny in what was known as the tool shed at the Ryman. We'd take him in there and sing him a song. We got that "Don't call us, we'll call you" for years. It got rough after I got back from Korea, so we called Ken Nelson at Capitol Records and said, "Do you know anybody at the Opry?" He said, "Well, I'm pretty good friends with Jack Stapp." I said, "Well, Ira and I, we decided that we're gonna quit the business if we can't get on the Opry." 'Cause we just weren't makin' a living, you see. I was on the street at a payphone. Ken Nelson called Mister Stapp and told him he had a duet that was on his label, and he'd like to have 'em on the Opry. Evidently, Mister Stapp give him a discouraging message, and Mister Nelson said, "Well, if you don't want 'em, the Ozark Jubilee does." And Mister Stapp said, "Now, wait a minute, we don't want no more people going up to the Ozark Jubilee. Tell 'em to show up this Friday." So we went up and we were introduced to Vito Pellettieri and Jack Stapp, and we were taken to Mister Denny's office. He totally ignored us for ten minutes. He talked to everybody in town that his secretary could find. Finally, my brother, who had a much shorter fuse than me, said, "Well, Mister Denny, we'll see you tonight on the Grand Ole Opry." Mister Denny pulled his half-glasses down to the end of his nose and looked up over what he wasn't busy at, and said, "Boys, you're in tall timber. You'd better shit and git it." My brother looked him in the eye and said, "We got the saws. Jus' show us where the woods are."

The Grand Ole Opry was not only drawing the top country stars to Nashville; it was drawing the music business in their wake. Record producers knew that their artists would be there on the weekend; song pluggers knew that the record producers would be in town; and bookers knew that they could pitch show dates to artists' managers. Many of the deals

The Louvin Brothers with their producer, Ken Nelson.

were done backstage at the Opry, or in the alley beside the Opry, or at what is now Tootsies Orchid Lounge across the alley. Before the Second World War, the hubs of the business had been Chicago, Cincinnati, Dallas, and Los Angeles, but within a few years the country music business centered itself in Nashville.

Roy Acuff and Fred Rose had started Acuff-Rose Publications in 1942, and its success inspired Jack Stapp to follow suit. The fact that Stapp went into partnership with a New Yorker shows the fast-growing impact of country music. Country songs like Pee Wee King's "Tennessee Waltz" and Hank Williams's "Cold, Cold Heart" (both published by Acuff-Rose) became hits for pop singers and gave others the idea that there was money in country music.

JACK STAPP:

Lou Cowan was my superior during the war in England. We were involved in propaganda broadcasting to Europe. He'd made a reputation in radio with shows like Stop the Music, Break the Bank, *and so on. We stayed in touch, and one day he called me from Chicago. "Jack, you're starting to make some noise down there with that country music." He had an idea for a country music show and he came down. After the audition we went across the street for a sandwich, and that's where the idea for Tree Music was born. Lou suggested it, thinking that with my contacts at the Opry and the station I'd be able to get a lot of songs recorded.*

Tree Music started in 1951, and Stapp's songwriters would eventually include Roger Miller and Willie Nelson. Jim Denny launched Cedarwood Music in 1953, and his company went on to sign Mel Tillis, John D. Loudermilk, and many others. But Acuff-Rose, which had been established almost ten years earlier, remained the major player in Nashville's music publishing scene with Hank Williams, Pee Wee King, Don Gibson, Marty Robbins, and later Roy Orbison and the Everly Brothers.

A few recording sessions had been held in Nashville in the 1920s, but Eddy Arnold's first-ever recording session at the WSM studios in December 1944 is generally reckoned to mark the birth of the recording business in Nashville. Almost three years later, several WSM engineers launched the first professional studio in Nashville. They located it near WSM in the Tulane Hotel, and named it the Castle Recording Laboratory because WSM was known as the Air Castle of the South. When Ernest Tubb and Red Foley recorded at Castle in August 1947, the recording business in Nashville was underway. Tubb and Foley recorded for Decca Records, and Decca's Paul Cohen relied heavily on WSM's musicians, especially pianist Owen Bradley, to arrange the sessions. Bradley would later take over from Cohen and sign Patsy Cline, Loretta Lynn, and many others to Decca.

The music industry in Nashville grew so quickly in the years after the Second World War that WSM announcer David Cobb coined the phrase "Music City U.S.A."

DAVID COBB:

I wish I could remember the exact date, but I'm sure it was circa 1950 because we celebrated Red Foley's fortieth birthday that same year. We originated some sustaining (that is, noncommercial) programs for the NBC network. One of them was The Red Foley Show, *and I was the announcer. One morning, I felt that my opening words would require something that placed a little more*

emphasis on Nashville, so one morning it came out. "From Music City U.S.A., Nashville, Tennessee, WSM presents The Red Foley Show." *It fell trippingly from the tongue and felt right, like a good billboard should. Right after the show I got word that Jack Stapp wanted to see me in his office. When I walked in, he was beaming. "Where did you ever get an idea*

The Red Foley Show, *where David Cobb (standing at mic) coined the name that stuck, Music City U.S.A.*

like Music City U.S.A.?" He thought it was the greatest thing since George Hay had named the Grand Ole Opry. From that day, whenever Jack Stapp wanted a catchy phrase, he would come to me for it, but I was never able to equal "Music City U.S.A."

In 1951, Harianne Moore in WSM's advertising department suggested bringing all of the disc jockeys around the country who spun records by Opry stars to Nashville for a celebration. Fewer than fifty came, but the event was enough of a success for it to become the annual Disc Jockey Convention, which itself metamorphosed into Country Music Week. It was a chance for the artists to thank the disc jockeys and for the disc jockeys to tape spots with the artists that could be played on their local stations.

Although the Grand Ole Opry represented the pinnacle of the country music business, the cast was rarely stable for long. Several artists from the show's earliest days, including Sam and Kirk McGee and Uncle Dave Macon, were still there; in fact, as Uncle Dave grew older, he worked fewer road dates and became the Opry mainstay he always said he'd been. He celebrated his eightieth birthday at the Opry, and passed away eighteen months later on March 22, 1952.

WSM press release:

Uncle Dave Macon, known to millions of radio listeners as "Dixie Dewdrop" of WSM's Grand Ole Opry, died at Rutherford Hospital after an illness of several weeks. He was 81 years old last October 7. He was one of the small group of

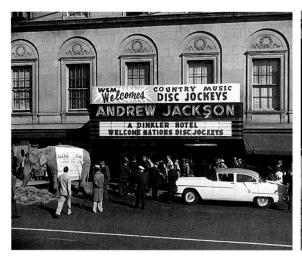

entertainers who, a quarter of a century ago, joined George Hay in the Grand Ole Opry, creating a new interest in folk and hillbilly music which today has grown nationwide, making Nashville known as the folk music capital of the country. His last appearance on the Grand Ole Opry was on Saturday March 1. He traveled with Opry road troupes until 1950.

Uncle Dave left mementoes to the entire Opry cast, and gave one of his banjos to Roy Acuff's Dobro player, Bashful Brother Oswald. The night he died, Hank Williams sang "Farther Along" in his memory. Hank's tribute to Uncle Dave Macon was only the second time he'd appeared on the show that year.

LEFTY FRIZZELL, *country star:*

[Hank] and me was on the road. I had "Always Late" and "Mom and Dad's Waltz" and "I Want to Be with You Always" on the charts. Hank said, "Lefty, what you need is the Grand Ole Opry." I said, "Hell, I just got a telegram from [music publisher] Hill & Range on having number one and number two, and I got maybe two more in there, and you say I need the Grand Ole Opry?" He said, "You got a hell of an argument."

For years, Hank's goal had been to reach the Grand Ole Opry, but after less than three years he came to the conclusion that the Opry needed him more than he needed it. He began to skip the Saturday night Opry and Opry-sponsored shows. The Opry planned to use Hank's popularity as leverage to secure a prime-time country music show on NBC-TV, but Hank became increasingly uninterested in the Opry's plans for him. His music was also sometimes not in line with the wholesome image of the Opry. When he performed "My Bucket's Got a Hole in It" on the show, he had to change "ain't got no beer" to "ain't got no milk." The mutual antagonism came to a head in August 1952.

ERNEST TUBB:

I came in one Friday to get my mail and I heard Jim Denny on the telephone. He said, "Hank that's it. You gotta prove to me. You call me in December, and I'll let you know about coming back to the Opry next year." When Jim hung up

Webb Pierce Disc Jockey Convention badge.

the telephone, he had tears in his eyes. He said, "I had to do it. I had to let Hank go." When I was in the parking lot, I ran into Mr. Craig. He knew, and he said, "What do you think, Ernest?" I said, "Well, I hate it, but I saw tears in Jim's eyes, and I know it was the hardest thing he ever had to do. He told me he was going to try and get Hank to straighten up." Mr. Craig said, "I'm sure Jim means well, but it may work the other way. It may kill him." I was feeling the same way.

JOHNNIE WRIGHT *of Johnnie and Jack, Opry stars:*

I was with Hank when he got fired. Jim Denny told him he was going to have to let him go. He had a check coming, about three hundred dollars. He said, "You cain't fire me 'cause I already quit." Jim asked Hank if anyone was there with him, and Hank said "Johnnie Wright's here." He said, "Tell Johnnie I want to talk to him." I got on the phone and Jim said, "Johnnie, he's got a check up here. You come by and pick it up." My brother-in-law had a Chrysler limousine and Hank had his trailer with Drifting Cowboys written on the side. We put all his belongings in the trailer and his reclining chair in the back of the limousine and put him in there. We got Hank in the car and went up to WSM. Roy Acuff was in Jim Denny's office. Roy said, "Have you got Hank out there?" I said, "Yeah." Owen Bradley said, "Let's go out and see him, Roy." They went out and I picked up his check. Then we took off to Montgomery. We went out Broadway, and there was a liquor store out there at 16th and Broad, and Hank said, "Johnnie, pull in there and get me some whiskey." So I pulled in and got him a fifth and cashed his three-hundred-dollar check. The guy that owned the liquor store said, "Is Hank out there?" I said, "Yeah," so the guy came out and spoke to him. We took him to his mother's house. We pulled his clothes off, put him to bed and talked to his mother 'til he woke up. Hank acted like he didn't care he'd been canned.

Hank had come to the Opry from the *Louisiana Hayride* in Shreveport, and in August 1952 he returned to the *Hayride*, but just four months later, he was dead. Opry artists played at his funeral, and the show reclaimed him in death.

HORACE LOGAN, *emcee of the* Louisiana Hayride:

Acuff was talking about "Hank's friends from the Grand Ole Opry . . ." Jim Denny was sat in front of me. He turned around and said to me, "If Hank could raise up in his coffin, he'd look up toward the stage and say, 'I told you dumb sons of bitches I could draw more dead than you could alive.' "

On January 4, 2003, Hank Williams Jr. and his son, Hank Williams III, performed on the Opry, commemorating the fiftieth anniversary of Hank Williams's death. Hank Jr. introduced the son of Rufus Payne, an African American street musician who'd taught Hank Sr.

Hank Williams wasn't the only star who conflicted with the Opry's zealously guarded "family values" ideals. Red Foley's private life gave the Opry as much concern as Hank Williams's no-shows. His wife, Eva, died of a reported heart attack on November 17, 1951, although her death was widely rumored to be suicide brought on by Foley's infidelities and drinking.

The following April, Foley was sued for one hundred thousand dollars by the husband of singer Sally Sweet, charging alienation of affection. That same month, Foley made headlines again.

Roy Acuff, Red Foley, Carl Smith and Webb Pierce sing at Hank Williams's funeral.

The Tennessean, May 1, 1952:

Clyde "Red" Foley, folk singer who was unconscious in Vanderbilt Hospital from an overdose of sedative was described by his physician as recovering in very good fashion. The physician, Dr. Crawford Adams, said the nationally known Grand Ole Opry star suffered acute depression with anxiety state resulting from the death of his wife last November and the filing of an alienation of affection suit against him. It was understood that Foley took a large dose of sleeping tablets at his home on Bear Road at approximately 9:30 a.m. Monday.

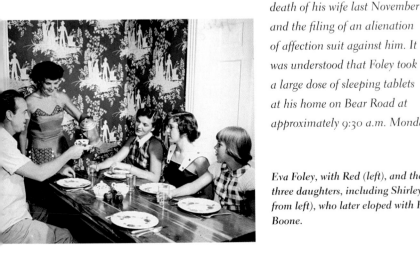

Eva Foley, with Red (left), and their three daughters, including Shirley (third from left), who later eloped with Pat Boone.

He then called someone at Vanderbilt, presumably his physician, and related what he'd done. An ambulance was summoned. The alienation suit was filed April 16 by Frank B. Kelton, husband of an attractive television singer known professionally as Sally Sweet, charging that she had been lured and enticed away from him by a certain well-known radio star.

GORDON STOKER *of the Jordanaires, Opry gospel group:*

He wanted to do better. He'd quit drinking, join a church, even talk about being a preacher. He really wanted to be a good Christian, but just didn't have the inner strength. He once said something that's become quite a cliché now, but back then was the first time I'd ever heard it. He said, "I'm my own worst enemy."

In April 1953, Foley stepped down as host of the Prince Albert Opry, but his behavior grew increasingly erratic. An unpublished memo in the *Nashville Banner* files from city editor Eddie Jones shows how close to the edge Foley had gone.

left: **Webb Pierce with fans and his manager Hubert Long (right).**

right: **Webb Pierce on the Opry stage with reporter Charlie Lamb. Announcer Grant Turner encourages the audience to applaud, while Jack Stapp stands to the right.**

Red Foley's three daughters have left home and have voluntarily placed themselves under full custody of Ernie Newton. Newton is a bass player on the Opry and apparently a clean straight operator. The story I got was that the children were fed up with Foley's new wife, Sally Sweet, and contacted a lawyer and gave him sufficient grounds. Foley is in New York today and due back in Nashville the middle of next week, after which he says he is going to California to live.

Hank Williams and Red Foley were gone, but the Opry was still attracting the top up-and-coming stars. Hank had

brought Ray Price onto the show shortly before he left, and Jack Stapp and Jim Denny recruited Webb Pierce, Faron Young, and Johnnie & Jack from the *Louisiana Hayride*, together with Johnnie's wife, Kitty Wells.

And out in Phoenix, Harry Stone discovered Marty Robbins and alerted the Opry. Like Jimmy Dickens and George Morgan, Marty had no hits, in fact no records, but the Opry took Harry Stone's word and gave him a guest spot on the Prince Albert show in June 1951. Marty didn't disappoint, and Opry made him a full member in January 1953. It was hard to get on the Opry without a hit, but it would never be impossible.

Acquisition of younger singers like Webb Pierce, Marty Robbins, and Ray Price meant that the Grand Ole Opry still had something for every generation. Singers who would soon revolutionize country and pop music, like Elvis Presley, Johnny Cash, and Jerry Lee Lewis, were listening dutifully every Saturday night. The show was still relentlessly fast-paced and still represented the pinnacle of the business, but the years immediately ahead would bring fresh challenges.

left: **Marty Robbins.**

right: *The lore of the Old West always intrigued and inspired Marty Robbins. His father was a Polish immigrant, but he always identified with his maternal grandfather, who'd been a Texas Ranger.*

123

MAN OF THE YEAR

Country music was slow coming to records because the manufacturers believed that even if "hillbillies" bought records, they really wanted pop or classical music rather than their own music. Similarly, radio stations didn't think "hillbillies" would support their advertisers until the Opry helped to prove them wrong. And country music was equally slow coming to television because the signal didn't reach rural areas . . . and because the sponsors didn't think that "hillbillies" would buy their products.

Network television started in 1949, and by 1954 more than half of American homes had a television set. WSM launched its television station in 1950 and produced a country music show for local consumption, but country music didn't come to network television until 1955. And the first networked country show wasn't the Grand Ole Opry.

After Red Foley left the Opry in 1953, he was approached by KWTO in Springfield, Missouri, to host a new radio barn dance, the *Ozark Jubilee*. From the beginning, the plan was to take the *Jubilee* to television, and on January 25, 1955, it went out on the ABC-TV network. Its success encouraged ABC to schedule three other television shows, *The Pee Wee King Show*, *The Eddy Arnold Show*, and the *Grand Ole Opry*.

Jean Shepard sings for the camera on the Purina Opry show, produced by WSM-TV for ABC.

Purina sponsored the Opry on ABC-TV, but rather than film the Saturday night radio show, Purina insisted upon staged sets with merry-go-rounds, hay bales, and noncountry guests such as Tony Bennett, Buddy Ebsen, and opera singer Marguerite Piazza.

The Purina Opry show went out in the 1955–56 season, but didn't return, while the *Ozark Jubilee* remained on ABC-TV until 1960. In a high-stakes game, the Opry had lost ground early on.

In the fall of 1954, the Opry had missed another opportunity. Less than three months after his first record was released, Elvis Presley played a guest spot on the Opry, and could have been signed to the show. Like many rock 'n' roll singers, he'd grown up listening to the Grand Ole Opry.

Elvis Presley: October 2, 1954

Elvis Presley's first single, "That's All Right"/"Blue Moon of Kentucky," was released in July 1954, and became enough of a sensation in and around Memphis for his record company, Sun Records, to pull a few strings and get him a guest spot on Hank Snow's portion of the Grand Ole Opry. "Blue Moon of Kentucky" was a song that Bill Monroe had written and recorded in 1946, and Elvis was worried that his rockabilly version would annoy the legendarily irascible Monroe.

BILL MONROE:

He come up to the Grand Ole Opry one time and come in the dressin' room where I was at. He apologized for the way he had changed "Blue Moon of Kentucky." I told him, "Well, if it give you your start, it's all right with me."

BUDDY KILLEN, *Opry bassist:*

I noticed a young man standing off to the side. He looked fearful and lost, shaking and pacing with his guitar on his back. "Hi," I said, "I'm Buddy Killen. I play bass on the Opry." "Hi," he sort of mumbled, "I'm Elvis Presley. If Sam Phillips would let me leave, I'd git out of here. These people are gonna hate me." Phillips was his record producer and the owner of Sun Records. "You'll do fine," I assured him, and hoped he would.

SCOTTY MOORE, *Elvis's guitarist:*

They wouldn't let us do but one song, and that had to be "Blue Moon of Kentucky" because it was a country song. The audience reaction was very slight. They applauded. They didn't go wild. There wasn't any booing or hissing. Just polite applause. It wasn't as bad as people have written it up to be. After we did the song and went offstage, Jim Denny, according to Elvis, made the comment, "You better keep driving the truck."

BUDDY KILLEN:

There was no earthshaking response. He didn't bring the house down and there was no encore. Years later, there was a motion picture supposedly portraying the event. In the film, Jim Denny suggested that Elvis not give up his day job. The truth of the matter is that Denny did nothing of the kind.

Before long, the checks for "Blue Moon of Kentucky" made their way to Monroe. "They was powerful checks," said Monroe. "Powerful checks."

Two weeks after his Opry tryout, Elvis joined the Opry's major rival, the *Louisiana Hayride* in Shreveport, and used the show as a springboard to success. In July 1955, he toured Florida with Hank Snow. By then, Eddy Arnold's former manager, Colonel Parker, was managing Snow through a jointly owned company. Using Snow's name to impress Elvis and his parents, Parker booked Elvis and eventually took over his management, edging Snow out of the picture in the process.

Colonel Parker and Hank Snow hired a publicist, Mae Boren Axton, who wrote songs as a sideline. In October 1955, Mae brought her songs to Nashville in search of a music publisher. The publisher usually tries to place songs with artists, but Mae already had an artist in mind for one song.

MAE AXTON:

I went to one well-known publisher, and said, "I've got a song here that will sell a million." One of his associates just laughed. That night at the Grand Ole Opry, I saw Jack Stapp. He said, "Mae, you never have offered me a song. Why?" "I've got one for you now, it's 'Heartbreak Hotel,' " I replied. "I'll take it," Jack answered. He's a busy man at the Opry, as you know. I came back in November for the Opry-sponsored disc jockeys' convention. I saw Elvis in the Andrew Jackson Hotel lobby. I told him, "Elvis, I got a song you are going to listen to right now." He said, "I can't do it, I've got to go to a meeting." But I insisted. We went to my room and played the song. He said, "Hot dog, Mae, play that again."

Still on Sun Records, Elvis was in Nashville at WSM's Disc Jockey Convention to showcase his act for RCA. Just a few days after the convention, RCA purchased his contract, and "Heartbreak Hotel" became his first RCA single . . . and first nationwide hit. The Opry made a point of signing the next major star on Sun Records, Johnny Cash.

Elvis at the 1955 Disc Jockey Convention.

Johnny Cash: July 7, 1956

BEN A. GREEN, *in the* Nashville Banner, *July 14, 1956:*

Tension gripped the big Ryman Auditorium stage as young Johnny Cash stepped forward to "achieve his life's ambition," and sing on the Grand Ole Opry. You could feel the charged atmosphere—some folks in the wings held their breath. All of the Opry people were pulling for this newest member of their family to score big with the 3,800 folks looking on and millions more listening in from coast to coast. He had a quiver in his voice, but it wasn't stage fright. The haunting words of "I Walk the Line" began to swell through the building, and a veritable tornado of applause rolled back. The boy had struck home. One onlooker told us, "He'll be every bit as good as Elvis Presley. Probably better, and he'll last a whole lot longer. He has sincerity, tone, and he carries to the rafters." Johnny Cash, just 11 months into his career, is one of the youngest stars ever to reach the Grand Ole Opry. What was his reaction? "I am grateful, happy, and humble," he said. "It's the ambition of every hillbilly singer to reach the Opry in his lifetime."

JOHNNY CASH:

I remember something Ernest Tubb told me in 1956 the first time I met him. It was a big-deal night. I'd just encored on the Grand Ole Opry, and now I was meeting Ernest Tubb live and in person. He looked at me and he said in that

left: **Johnny Cash and the Tennessee Two, Marshall Grant and Luther Perkins.**

right: **Johnny Cash signs autographs backstage at the Opry.**

grand, gravely voice I'd been hearing on the radio, "Just remember, son, the higher up the ladder you go, the brighter your ass shines."

DOLLY PARTON:

I waited for him in the Ryman parking lot. A man stepped out of the stage door and walked over to us. There was only me and Johnny Cash. I had never seen a man with such presence. Tall, lanky, and sexy with that trademark voice that cut through me like butter. Now I knew what star quality was. I was just a thirteen-year-old girl from the Smokies, but I would have gladly given it up for Mr. Cash right there in the parking lot. I found myself blurting out, "Oh, Mister Cash, I've just got to sing on the Grand Ole Opry." I know he must have heard that all the time, but he looked at me as if he was thinking, You know this kid is really serious.

In spite of the addition of Johnny Cash to the Opry roster, Elvis's continued success presented the Opry with the biggest challenge it had faced in its thirty-year history.

WESLEY ROSE *of Acuff-Rose Publications:*

"It was a very dangerous time. In all the years I've been in the business I'd say it was the most critical time for country music. Elvis Presley broke out. They were playing him on all stations. By playing rock artists on country stations, the country listeners began to tune out, and then the country programs began to disappear. We had six hundred stations playing country music, and it got down to around eighty-five stations."

Compounding the Opry's problems, there was a crisis within management. Edwin Craig and Jack DeWitt saw WSM's employees starting sideline businesses that relied to a great extent on their employment at WSM. Jim Denny and Jack Stapp owned music publishing companies, and three WSM engineers owned Castle Recording Laboratories. Under pressure from WSM, Jack Stapp gave up ownership of Tree Music, for a while at least. The engineers were offered roles at WSM-TV if they gave up the studio, and they accepted. Jim Denny was offered a pay raise and the job of formally managing the Opry if he gave up Cedarwood Music, and the situation came to a head on September 26, 1956.

JACK DeWITT:

Jim Denny's main objective was to take over the Grand Ole Opry. He was always running me and other people down. He thought he had enough strength to take it over, and I think he wanted to force me out. He was a strange man. A tough character. He had the worst rug, hairpiece, of any that I've ever seen, and he also carried a pistol, an automatic revolver. The big blowup came when I went to our board of directors and Edwin Craig, and they said, "You need to tell him that you will raise his salary to a certain figure if he will stay and run it for us, but if he's not interested, just fire him."

MARIE CLAIRE, *Jim Denny's assistant:*

Denny had met with DeWitt two or three times about Cedarwood, and had been warned to sell it or leave WSM. Denny came in late the morning it all happened. As soon as he got in, DeWitt wanted to see him.

JACK DeWITT:

I brought Denny into my office and told him, "Jim, we've got a choice for you. You can stay with WSM, which we'd like for you to do. We will raise your salary [if] you devote your entire time to WSM and the Artists Service Bureau, and making money for WSM and managing the artists so that they are happy with WSM." He said, "I don't want to do that." I said, "Well, Jim, I'm sorry, but we can't do otherwise." He said, "You'll have to fire me." He wouldn't even discuss the higher salary we were offering him.

MARIE CLAIRE:

Denny never returned to his office. He went straight to Cedarwood [one block away]. He came in a few hours later, gathered his things. He said simply, "DeWitt let me go."

KEN MARVIN, *George Morgan's sideman:*

I saw Jim standing in the elevator just as the door closed. All he was carrying under his arm was his Billboard Man of the Year award.

Both artist manager Hubert Long (left) and Jim Denny (right) encouraged Opry acts to leave the show.

JIM DENNY:

It's a strictly personal matter between DeWitt and myself in which DeWitt feels that no employee of the station should be better off financially than himself. DeWitt feels that when he makes decisions, whether they are right or wrong, no one should contest them. I know I shall be much happier as an independent operator than being handicapped by working under the supervision of someone who knows nothing about the country music business.

JACK DeWITT:

He tried to take over [the management and booking of] Roy Acuff, who wouldn't go with him. He tried to take over Ernest Tubb, who wouldn't go with him. He did take over Minnie Pearl, and I've never forgiven her. We brought in D. Kilpatrick, who was the first independent manager of the Opry. Denny thought he was the manager of the Opry, but he wasn't.

Walter D. Kilpatrick, known simply as "D.," was a tough-talking former Marine who'd been Capitol Records' first Nashville producer. He had just left Mercury Records when Jack DeWitt approached him. Jim Denny didn't leave the Opry alone, though. He promptly started the Denny Talent Agency and recruited several Opry stars, including Carl Smith and Little Jimmy Dickens, for a show he was assembling on behalf of Philip Morris. Structured like the Camel Caravan, the Philip Morris Caravan toured the United States for eighteen months.

LITTLE JIMMY DICKENS:

Jim took some of the [Opry] talent with him. I checked with [my manager] and we studied it over, and he—not me—decided that it wouldn't be feasible for the deal we had with Philip Morris for me to stay with the Opry. He thought that when we were through, we could come back to the Opry, so I took his and Mr. Denny's advice. But it didn't work out that way. Once I took that show, that cooled it for me with the Opry.

The lingering bitterness from Denny's departure meant that Jimmy Dickens wouldn't rejoin the Grand Ole Opry until 1975, almost twenty years later. Encouraged by the success of "Heartbreak Hotel," Jack Stapp left WSM and the Opry in July 1957. Meanwhile, Red Foley's *Ozark Jubilee* was posting excellent ratings on Saturday night . . . the Opry's night. Denny's successor, D. Kilpatrick, had to recruit artists to replace those who'd defected, and address the problem of declining attendance.

D. KILPATRICK:

Rock 'n' roll was the enemy, and I do mean the enemy. At the time Presley hit, we couldn't draw breath in the auditorium. We couldn't draw nothin'. I remember addressing a group of women voters and telling them that rock 'n' roll was the devil's workshop. I thought it was then, and I know for a damn fact it is now. The problem was that the country guys began sounding like the pop guys, and it got so you'd need a computer program to tell the difference. I didn't want to compete with rock 'n' roll or pop music. I said, "Let's do it our way, then we got something very distinct to sell." And yes, I'm the son of a bitch that wouldn't let them bring drums on the Opry stage. It was the principal instrument in rock 'n' roll. Why take the thing that's killing you and give in to it?

STONEWALL JACKSON, *Opry star:*

At the Ryman, you'd only have a few rows of people up front. This really hurt Ernest Tubb. It hurt him deep. He was like a man grieving, like he'd had a

D. Kilpatrick and the Everly Brothers at the 1958 Disc Jockey Convention. From right: Don Everly; Phil Everly; Kilpatrick; Ott Devine of WSM; songwriters Boudleaux and Felice Bryant (who'd written several of the Everlys' greatest hits, including "Bye, Bye Love" and "Wake Up, Little Susie"); Archie Bleyer, president of Cadence Records; and Jack DeWitt of WSM.

The Everly Brothers playing at the Disc Jockey Convention.

couple of kids die. The gravy got a bit thin there. It was the lowest ebb I've ever seen country music at. When Presley hit, it just preempted country to the lowest amount I've ever seen it preempted.

GRANT TURNER:

One Saturday night around Christmas, there was hardly anyone there. All the stars were home for Christmas, but no one was at the show to see 'em. I was worried about the Opry then.

The closest D. Kilpatrick came to rock 'n' roll was the Everly Brothers. Although they were only in their early twenties, the Everlys had been performing on country radio for more than ten years, and for a long time, they were the only successful rock 'n' roll act managed and produced in Nashville. Their country pedigree was just long enough to satisfy Kilpatrick.

BILL ANDERSON:

My mom and dad came to a convention in Nashville in 1958. It had been four or five years since they'd been there, when it was wall-to-wall people. They came back and told me that they'd been by the Opry on Saturday night, and they'd stuck their heads in the door, and they were amazed. It wasn't even half full. They said, "While we were standing there, a whole bunch of people came streaming in the door. They poured out of the little shops up and down Broadway and came running and screaming and standing at the door." It was because they'd introduced the Everly Brothers. My mom and dad said those people stood there and screamed while the Everly Brothers were onstage, and as soon as they went off, these people left. I remember getting a call from Hank Snow's manager asking me if I wanted to book him. He was coming through Commerce, Georgia, where I was a deejay. I thought, Goodness, we're probably talking thousands and thousands of dollars. His manager said, "I can let you have Hank and the band at a real good price." I said, "How much?" He said, "Two hundred and fifty guarantee." I was stunned, but that was the real low ebb.

HAL SMITH, *Ernest Tubb's booking agent:*

Things were on the decline, not to where we were starving, but certainly not doing as well as we had. TV was red-hot all of a sudden. Ernest came out to the office and we talked everything over. We came this close to concluding that the best thing to do was get out of the business. His brother was in the insurance business in Texas then, and Ernest said, "I could go into business with Bud, but this is all I've ever done." It was so sad.

Country music survived and prospered again, but the Opry's older stars, like Ernest Tubb and Roy Acuff, were sidelined. Eventually, they would be recognized as the music's elder statesmen, but in the 1950s they had to contend with lower personal appearance fees and lower record sales. The Opry itself had to walk a fine line between bringing in some of the newer stars that younger listeners wanted to hear without alienating the older audience.

Archie Bleyer, president of Cadence Records, presents the Everly Brothers with a gold record, while the Opry's Grant Turner looks on.

135

WSM
GRAND
OLE
OPRY

✱
✱ ✱
9

SURVIVING NASHVILLE

Replacing departed cast members, D. Kilpatrick kept it country. In November 1956, he signed an artist who accomplished something that no one had accomplished since the show's earliest days, and someone who definitely kept it country.

GRANT TURNER:

Judge Hay was still there. He was in charge of answering fan mail. [His official title was Audience Relations.] Someone had written a song, someone wondered what kind of mandolin Bill Monroe played, or what was Cousin Wilbur's last name. Did Uncle Dave Macon eat country ham three times a day? And he conducted auditions on Tuesday mornings around ten o'clock. The Judge would bow his head as if in deep thought, remove his glasses and put pressure on his nose with his thumb and forefinger. Finally, he would lift his head and look the singer full in the face. He'd say, "Friend, I want to thank you for coming by today. We have a full roster of singers just now, so let me ask you to go back home." But Stonewall Jackson was one Opry star that was hired in this way. I remember him standing in the corner of the studio with no microphone, and singing for the Judge.

The Grand Ole Opry cast, 1956, with Judge Hay in front.

Stonewall Jackson: November 1956

Stonewall had been farming in Moultrie, Georgia, and drove his farm truck to Nashville wearing his workday clothes. He had never performed on radio or recorded, and had no idea of what it usually took to get on the Grand Ole Opry. Driving up Franklin Road, he saw Acuff-Rose Publications and took a room across the street at the York Motel.

WESLEY ROSE:

One afternoon, we heard some guitar pickin' and singin' across the street in the motel. Then this guy came over and played songs for us. It was Stonewall Jackson. He was glad we liked the songs, but he said, "Mister Rose, I came here for just one purpose: to get on the Grand Ole Opry. Can you get me an audition?" I told him, "You can't get on the Opry unless you're on a record label. That's a rule." "Mister Rose," he answered. "You get me an audition, I'll end up on the Opry." He was so young and so country and so appealing. I said, "I'll try, but don't get your heart broke if they don't take you." It couldn't happen again in a million years. Back when we tried to get Hank Williams on the Opry, we had to work on it for three months, and he had hits at the time. Stonewall never had any records, but he just went down and knocked 'em out.

STONEWALL JACKSON:

The first phone call I ever got in Nashville was from Wes Rose. He'd got me an audition at the Opry. I went down and auditioned with Judge Hay the next morning at nine o'clock.

What happened next was both a fairy tale come true . . . and a bitter wake-up call for a young entertainer fresh off the farm.

D. KILPATRICK, *letter to WSM management, December 10, 1958:*

On October 19, 1956, Judge Hay requested that I personally audition Stonewall Jackson. The audition was around three p.m. and Stonewall was immediately employed on a temporary basis. I left for dinner around 5:30 p.m., and upon returning I observed a man named John Kelly talking to Stonewall in the entrance room of Studio B. It came to my attention that Stonewall signed a management contract with Kelly whereby Kelly would receive one third of Stonewall's gross income and revenue. On November 2, I had Stonewall and John Kelly in my office to explain that such a contract was prohibitive and not to the best interest of the artist or the Grand Ole Opry. I told Kelly that we didn't want to build an artist who was currently making little or no money, then to have the artist become a money-maker and be frustrated and bitter as a result of such a commitment made at an early stage of his career. This has happened to other Opry artists. If there ever was a greenhorn, it was Stonewall, but his natural simplicity and his extreme desire to sing, plus his ability to render a song charmed both Judge Hay and I. After much discussion, Kelly agreed to release Stonewall from his contract. Jim Denny stated to me that Kelly had caused him considerable trouble when he, Denny, was head of WSM's Artist Service. Denny stated that he had personally threatened to run Kelly out of town.

STONEWALL JACKSON:

I was wearin' patched khaki farm clothes and a beat-up hat. Ernest Tubb introduced me. He said, "Here's a brand-new guy, just got in town from Georgia in his pickup truck. We hear that he sings a good country song, and we're all gonna be rooting for him. Here's a brand-new singer, you've never heard tell of him before. Here's Stonewall Jackson from down in Moultrie, Georgia." Ernest could build you up. He could make you look like a star by the time you hit the

stage. The other artists were snickering. They thought the Opry had hired a new comedian, so they were ready to put the laugh on. I thought, "Man, this ain't workin' so good. It's now or never," so I just lit into it. I sang that sucker as good as I could sing, and the band got into it. Everybody got quiet. Ernest had to bring me back out four times. I felt accepted then.

An early Stonewall Jackson appearance.

Kilpatrick was on safer ground approaching Porter Wagoner at the Ozark Jubilee. Porter tried to position himself so that he could work both shows, but Kilpatrick forced the issue, and in March 1957, Porter moved to Nashville to join the Opry. Kilpatrick also hired Wilma Lee and Stoney Cooper from the Wheeling, West Virginia, Jamboree. Other new hirees during the 1950s included Don Gibson, Billy Grammer, the Wilburns, Hank Locklin, Bill Anderson, Skeeter Davis, and George Hamilton IV.

Some of the younger artists, like Johnny Cash and the Everly Brothers, quickly found it impossible to meet their Opry commitments. They were on coast-to-coast tours and couldn't afford to give up a lucrative Saturday night showdate to fly back to Nashville at their own expense to appear on the Grand Ole Opry. The Opry was still the dream of every country music performer, but the reality of membership led to persistent squabbles. Marty Robbins lashed out against the Opry's restrictions and quit more than once, but nevertheless saw the show's value in building a career and returned.

New Opry star Don Gibson with Minnie Pearl.

BILL MAPLES, *journalist, 1958, in the* Tennessean:

Robbins was fired last Saturday after his performance on the Opry's Prince Albert Show. A station official quoted Robbins as saying he did not need the Opry. Robbins said he did not say this, but did criticize management. But Robbins

Skeeter Davis, who joined in 1959, became best known for her 1963 crossover hit, "The End of the World."

and WSM patched up their quarrel and Robbins joined the Grand Ole Opry again. In returning to the Opry, Robbins will not benefit so much financially as he will from the prestige of the show and from its nationwide coverage by radio. Opry musicians are paid union scale which is $30 for leaders and $15 for supporting musicians.

When Marty Robbins topped the pop and country charts with "El Paso" the following year, the trouble resumed.

D. KILPATRICK *memo to Jack DeWitt, January 15, 1959:*

Robbins' demand that his vocal trio be used couldn't have been worse. Our acts use four musicians and sometimes less, so we can't allow Robbins to use eight other than himself. Before Roy Acuff's departure for Europe, Robbins personally berated Acuff for consistently plugging the Opry and WSM on personal appearances. Robbins' statement to Acuff was, "What the hell have they done for you?"

As hard as Kilpatrick tried to stand his ground, he knew that his bargaining position wasn't good. "Live" radio was fading into memory, and, one by one, the other radio barn dances folded. The Old Dominion Barn Dance closed in 1957, and the WLS National Barn Dance, together with the Ozark Jubilee and the Louisiana Hayride closed in 1960. Out in California, Home Town Jamboree closed in 1959 and Town Hall Party in 1961. The Opry lost its Prince Albert network sponsorship in 1960, but hung tough.

BILL ANDERSON:

The other shows didn't have the commitment from above. Edwin Craig was still there and he wanted to keep the Opry alive. The other thing that the Opry did, whether intentionally or not, was to be bigger than any individual star. Elvis was so big at the Louisiana Hayride, but when he left, the Hayride died. The Hayride was not bigger than Elvis, but the Opry was bigger than any of its stars.

Bill Anderson (seated) in his deejay days with (from left) Hawkshaw Hawkins; Hawkshaw's wife, Jean Shepard; Stonewall Jackson; and Marty Robbins.

BUD WENDELL, WSM *and Opry executive:*

Some felt that the Opry was no longer meaningful to artists' career longevity; that they were wasting their time to go with it, so there was a lot of turmoil. But the Opry was strong enough to survive and continue, and to be more accommodating and sensitive to artists' careers. The Opry had been run in a somewhat autocratic fashion, because it had been the only game in town: If you wanted to be a star you had to be on the Grand Ole Opry. So we went from that kind of posture to one that was much more sensitive to the needs of the artists. We had to recognize that there were other, very significant media equally as significant as the Opry in building a career; and we had to understand that Opry members could make a heckuva lot of money instead of being there on a Saturday night. It was still an important piece, but it wasn't the only way to get to the top. For many years, you could not be a major star without being a member of the Opry. Finally, the Opry woke up and realized that you could go around the Opry and become a superstar. So it had to kind of change its posture and change its relationships. Record companies were moving to Nashville, and managers were moving here, publishing companies were moving here, and we were trying to figure out how to reposition the Opry to keep it strong and make it attractive to artists of some stature to come in and play and walk away from those big dates.

It wasn't long before the Nashville music business realized that rock 'n' roll *hadn't* killed country music. In fact, rock 'n' roll had opened up pop airplay to such an extent that a country record could get played if it didn't sound too country. In Hank Williams's day, his songs had to be "covered" by pop artists if they were to get on the pop charts. It wasn't long before artists such as Jim Reeves, who'd been an Opry member since 1955, and Patsy Cline stripped away their Southern accents along with hard country instruments like the steel guitar and fiddle. In came faultless diction, the piano, vibraphone, electric guitar, chorus, and strings. Just as WSM announcer David Cobb stumbled upon the phrase "Music City U.S.A." to describe the industry moving to Nashville, so local magazine owner Charlie Lamb coined the phrase "Nashville Sound" to describe the changes that were overtaking country music.

BILL ANDERSON:

Country music came back, but it didn't come back as "Wreck on the Highway" or "In the Jailhouse Now." It came back as "I Can't Stop Loving You."

With several Nashville Sound pioneers in the cast, D. Kilpatrick decided to make another play for prime-time television. In April 1957, he

Jim Reeves.

helped write a proposal to ABC-TV. The Opry had been on ABC-TV briefly in 1955–56, but, with the advent of the Nashville Sound, Kilpatrick believed that it was time to try again.

WSM *proposal to ABC:*

The dividing lines between categories, eg. Pop, country, rock-and-roll, are vanishing. April 1957 is the month and the year of the "new formula" for hit songs. It is a formula composed of one part country, one part rock-and-roll, and one part pop. It is a formula whose mainstay is the country musician whose trademark is the small instrumental combination, and whose success is so certain that every recording studio in Nashville has been working night and day with recording stars and A&R men moving into the city from both coasts. Patsy Cline's "Walking after Midnight" sold 400,000 records in 14 days! And she is a country artist. The mastery of this new formula is precisely the trump card which has shot many Grand Ole Opry stars into even greater prominence.

ABC-TV didn't go for the Opry's pitch, but the Opry's attendance slowly increased as country music itself rebounded. And Kilpatrick had made his point: the Nashville Sound was okay; rock 'n' roll was not.

Journalist BILL MAPLES, *"Country Music Goes Country" in the* Tennessean, *May 18, 1958:*

The Grand Ole Opry may be one of the most persuasive forces in the revival of country music. In the first place, rock 'n' roll is not allowed there. Some time ago, the Wilburn Brothers came on-stage in tuxes and sang one of their latest releases. "Ooh Bop Shee Boom." After the performance, which was admittedly as good as rock 'n' roll gets, D. Kilpatrick told the boys not to sing that particular song on the Opry again. Later, he explained to me why he'd taken this stand. "I can show you a huge file of critical letters we've received after doing such songs on the Opry," he said. "WSM has operated very successfully with country music for 33 years. We figure that if we stay with country music, we'll be here another 33 years. Besides, when the crowd gets to the Ryman on Saturday night expecting to hear country music and it hears rock 'n' roll instead it's like a bunch of fans going to Sulphur Dell expecting to see a baseball game and finding a mumble-peg match instead."

The Nashville Banner, *November 10, 1958*:

Because the Grand Ole Opry lives:

(1) Nashville is Music City USA, trailing only Hollywood and New York in providing music for the world. (2) The community has some 3,000 or more residents who can trace their livelihood to the music industry. (3) Approximately $5,000,000 in fast-circulating tourist dollars come into this community every year with the 250,000 visitors attending the Opry.

FRIDAY NIGHT OPRY

FRIDAY, NOVEMBER 14, 1969

7:30-8:00— MINIT BURGER

BILL MONROE
STU PHILLIPS
CARL and PEARL BUTLER

8:00-8:30— GATES TIRE CO., SWEET SUE

WILLIS BROTHERS
WILMA LEE COOPER
STAN HITCHCOCK
JUSTIN TUBB

8:30-9:00—KROGER

ROY ACUFF
THE CARLISLES
DEL WOOD

9:00-9:30— BALTZ BROTHERS, FORD MOTOR CO.

TOMPALL and the GLASER BROTHERS
ERNIE ASHWORTH
COUSIN JODY

9:30-10:00— TRABUE TRANSMISSION, BEECHNUT CHEWING TOBACCO

LESTER FLATT
RAY PILLOW
DOTTIE WEST

10:00-10:30—COLEMAN SAUSAGE, CEE BEE FOOD STORES

JIM and JESSE
STRINGBEAN
MARION WORTH

Program Subject to Change Without Notice!

GRAND OLE OPRY

SATURDAY, NOVEMBER 15, 1969

1st SHOW

6:30-6:45—MRS. GRISSOMS

BILL MONROE
WILMA LEE COOPER
TOMMY JONES

6:45-7:00—RUDY'S

RAY PILLOW
DEL WOOD
COUSIN JODY

7:00-7:30—LUZIANNE

ROY ACUFF
ERNIE ASHWORTH
CAL SMITH
JUSTIN TUBB

7:30-8:00—STANDARD CANDY

STU PHILLIPS
STAN HITCHCOCK
MARTHA CARSON
THE CROOK BROTHERS
TENNESSEE TRAVELERS
THE FOUR GUYS

8:00-8:30—MARTHA WHITE

WILLIS BROTHERS
DOTTIE WEST
STRINGBEAN
JACK BARLOW

8:30-9:00—STEPHENS

TOMPALL AND THE GLASER BROTHERS
MARION WORTH
THE CARLISLES
RED SOVINE
THE FRUIT JAR DRINKERS

WE ARE PROUD TO SALUTE THE FOLLOWING NATIONAL LIFE AND ACCIDENT INSURANCE COMPANY REPRESENTATIVES CELEBRATING SERVICE ANNIVERSARIES:

Miss Gladys Mc Dowell—Gadsden, Ala.—40 Years
Mr. R. M. Breeden—Chicago, Ill.— 25 Years
Miss Joanna Hamilton—Tyler, Texas—20 Years
Mrs. Dorthy Wolski—St. Joseph, Mo.—20 Years
Miss Eleanor Staha—San Antonio, Texas—20 Years
Mrs. Louise King—Ft. Smith, Ark—20 Years
Mrs. Ann Gorney—Chicago, Ill.—20 Years

2nd SHOW

9:30-10:00—KELLOGGS

WILLIS BROTHERS
WILMA LEE COOPER
CAL SMITH
TOMMY JONES

10:00-10:15—FENDER GUITAR

THE FOUR GUYS
STRINGBEAN
JUSTIN TUBB

10:15-10:30—PURE OIL

ROY ACUFF
DEL WOOD
MARTHA CARSON

10:30-10:45—TRAILBLAZER

STU PHILLIPS
STAN HITCHCOCK
COUSIN JODY

10:45-11:00—BEECHNUT CHEWING TOBACCO

ERNIE ASHWORTH
JACK BARLOW
THE CROOK BROTHERS
THE TENNESSEE TRAVELERS

11:00-11:30—COCA COLA

RAY PILLOW
DOTTIE WEST
RED SOVINE
SAM and KIRK McGEE
THE FRUIT JAR DRINKERS

11:30-12:00—LAVA

TOMPALL AND THE GLASER BROTHERS
MARION WORTH
THE CARLISLES

GRAND OLE OPRY®

NEW MEMBERS: 1960s

BILL ANDERSON	JIM AND JESSE	DEL REEVES
ERNIE ASHWORTH	HANK LOCKLIN	TEX RITTER
BOBBY BARE	BOBBY LORD	JEANNIE SEELY
THE BROWNS	BOB LUMAN	CONNIE SMITH
PATSY CLINE	LORETTA LYNN	LEROY VAN DYKE
JIMMIE DRIFTWOOD	WILLIE NELSON	BILLY WALKER
THE FOUR GUYS	NORMA JEAN	CHARLIE WALKER
THE GLASER BROTHERS	THE OSBORNE BROTHERS	DOTTIE WEST
JACK GREENE	DOLLY PARTON	MARION WORTH
GEORGE HAMILTON IV	STU PHILLIPS	
SONNY JAMES	RAY PILLOW	

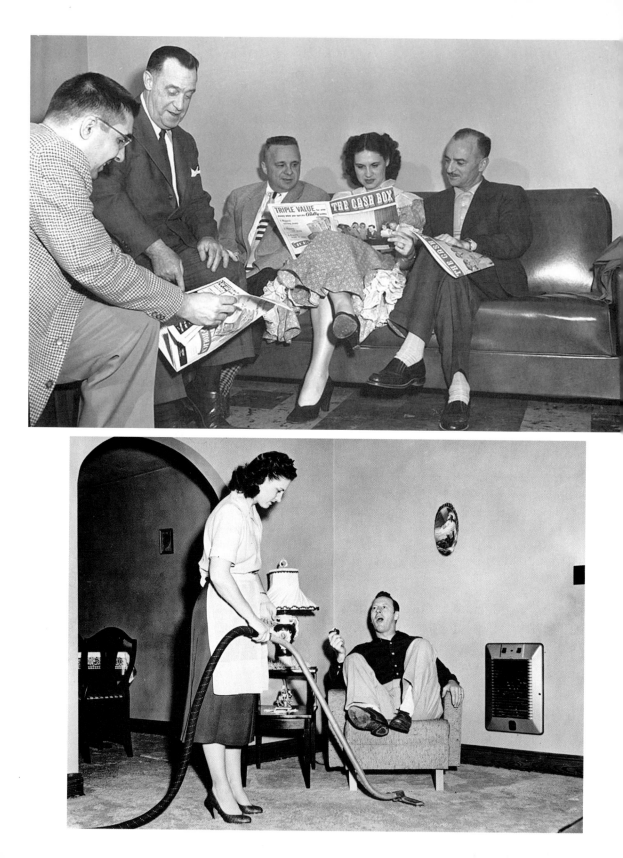

"A FRIEND OF A FRIEND OF MINE IS A FRIEND OF OTT DEVINE"

In 1959, D. Kilpatrick left the Opry to join Acuff-Rose. His replacement, Ottis "Ott" Devine, had been with WSM since 1935. In 1957, Devine had replaced Jack Stapp as WSM program director before taking over the Opry as well. The dust had settled. The Grand Ole Opry might not have been the force within the industry that it once was, but it was still the dream of everyone who sang country music. Ott Devine lowered the Saturday night commitment required for Opry membership, but held fast to that commitment. He managed the show for nine years, signing several artists who would become Opry mainstays, including Patsy Cline, Loretta Lynn, Bill Anderson, Jan Howard, Bobby Bare, Willie Nelson, Jim and Jesse, Connie Smith, Dottie West, and Jack Greene.

The Opry's cautious approach to change was never more apparent than in its attitude toward women. There had been women on the Opry from the very first night when Eva Thompson accompanied Uncle Jimmy Thompson, but the Opry's first female singing star was Kitty Wells. Kitty sang her finger-pointing hit, "It Wasn't God Who Made Honky Tonk Angels," in a very unthreatening way, and her below-the-

Kitty Wells made her living in a business overwhelmingly dominated by men . . .

. . . while projecting an image of domesticity.

knee gingham gowns remained her trademark. She was a reluctant star, and her husband, Johnnie Wright of Johnnie & Jack, managed her career and pushed her into the spotlight.

Kitty Wells: 1952

KITTY WELLS:

Roy Acuff once informed Johnnie that a woman should not be starred in a country act because they couldn't carry the show. Johnnie told Roy, "Well, we're just gonna try it."

Jean Shepard joined the Opry in 1955, and stayed. Aside from Kitty Wells and Minnie Pearl, the only other female solo act in the cast at the time was pianist Del Wood. Others came but didn't stay. Rockabilly queen Wanda Jackson made just one appearance, and Rose Maddox stayed only a few months. Like Jean Shepard, they'd launched their careers in western dance halls, but unlike her, they found the Opry to be a hard adjustment.

WANDA JACKSON:

I was just getting ready to go on in one of my new sexy little white and red fringe outfits, and Ernest Tubb said, "Are you Wanda Jackson? You're on next, hun." I said, "Okay, I'm ready." He said, "Well, you can't go on the stage at the Opry like that. You can't show your shoulders!" So I went back and I happened to have a pretty decent white leather fringe jacket that I put on, but I was near tears. I came out of there and I said, "I'll never come back to this place again!"

ROSE MADDOX:

I had a costume made for my record "Tall Man." Blue satin skirt with silver fringe, bare midriff, long sleeves with the silver fringe, boots, neckerchief, and cowboy hat. I thought the Opry would come apart. The bosses nearly come unglued. Whenever I saw Minnie Pearl after that, she'd say, "Every one of them Opry bosses jumped on me. 'Why'd you let her do that?' "

A December 1959 memo to performers from D. Kilpatrick confirmed that there really was a dress code, even if it wasn't very clear. "It is suggested that female performers dress more in keeping with the show," wrote Kilpatrick, "and, when possible, the use of a guitar or another instrument is suggested."

But a new addition to the Opry stage was soon to change the policy on attire for female performers.

Patsy Cline: 1960

OTT DEVINE:

I was standing onstage watching one of the performers when Patsy came up behind me and said a bit hesitantly, "Mr. Devine, do you think I could ever become a member of the Grand Ole Opry?" Of course I knew of her talent. I had heard her sing. She had a beautiful voice. And so I replied. "Patsy, if that's all you want, you are on the Opry."

Signing Patsy Cline seems like an easy decision, but when she joined the Opry in 1960, she'd had just one hit, "Walkin' after Midnight," and that was three years earlier. Her career was at its lowest ebb, and she told her family and booking agent to leave messages for her at the Opry because she couldn't afford the fifty dollars to get a phone connected. The following year, though, she signed with Decca Records, and her first Decca record, "I Fall to Pieces," became a number-one country hit.

Patsy Cline.

After Patsy joined the Opry, she went home and typed out her biography for the Opry's news service.

Married to Charles Dicks and have one little girl . . . Julia Simadore (Bible name). Living at 213 East Marthona Road . . . off of Old Hickory . . . out Gallatin Road . . . Madison Tennessee (buying home) Neighbor to Hank Snow. Husbnad [sic] . . . lineatype operator . . . he works. Curley Printing Co. I don't want to get rich . . . just live good.

Patsy gradually began to challenge the women's dress code. She didn't play guitar or other stringed instruments, and her fringed cowgirl outfits slowly gave way to sheath dresses and pantsuits.

DOTTIE WEST:

One night in '62 or '63, Patsy showed up in this gorgeous Nudie-designed pantsuit, and Ott Devine told her she couldn't wear it. You had to wear a dress back then.

MINNIE PEARL:

Patsy in her pantsuit caught inadvertently in a shot for an Opry sponsor.

Patsy was not coy by any means. This was unusual at the time, especially for a woman performing country music. Her sense of herself was evident in the way she sang and the way she moved, revealing her pain and deepest emotions. She never attempted to tone down her sexuality, but that was Patsy.

On June 14, 1961, Patsy was involved in a near-fatal car wreck near her home in Madison. "They thought I was gone twice during the sewing up and had to give me three pints of blood," she said later. On July 3, Patsy wrote to WSM employee Trudy Stamper.

If you can't read this letter, blame it on this splint. I'm doing lots better and my operation last Tuesday was a great step forward and the Dr. says after three months more, after this heals up and over good I'll go back for another operation and have these scars cut out and pulled together again. I'll be back to singing in between now and that operation even with the scars. Little make-up should make me presentable enough to stand me. I'm sure glad I had those new pictures made when I did. I've got to cut a single because there's not a song in the can at all.

Love,
Patsy Cline

PS. Many thanks to Ira Looney [Ira Louvin] who had all the artists sign two pages of autographs to me last Sat night. I'll always keep it. Sure made me feel great.

One month later, Patsy recorded her next single, "Crazy."

PATSY CLINE, *introducing "Crazy" on the Opry:*

I recorded a song called "I Fall to Pieces," and I was in a car wreck. Now I'm really worried, because I have a brand-new record, and it's called "Crazy."

GRANT TURNER:

Patsy had a lot of hard luck in her career. One time, they brought her out onstage in a wheelchair. She'd been involved in a very serious auto wreck. She was in the hospital for months, it seemed, and then they brought her out, not to sing but just to greet her fans.

PATSY CLINE, *from her wheelchair on the Opry stage:*

The greatest gift I think you folks could have given me was the encouragement you gave me right at the very time when I needed you the most. You came through with the flyingest colors. I just want to say you'll never know how happy you made this ol' country gal.

THE SECOND CARNEGIE HALL CONCERT

In November 1961, Patsy Cline joined the Grand Ole Opry cast in bringing the show back to Carnegie Hall for the first time since the 1947 concerts.

DOROTHY KILLGALLEN, *gossip columnist:*

You hipsters who have been planning a fall vacation might want to leave early. The Grand Ole Opry does a gig at Carnegie Hall this month. Remember when Carnegie Hall was associated with music?

UPI *wire service report:*

The Grand Ole Opry staged its show at Carnegie Hall last night, and, well sir, them yankees loved it. The jampacked audience was a little different from most Carnegie crowds. There were no dowager ladies in mink coats. But there were a lot of sideburns, and how those cowboy boots did shine. Audience reaction was a little different, too. Instead of applauding at the end of a number, they applauded as the songs started and they rhythmically clapped through the number. The crowd was made up of widely assorted groups including New

left: **The Opry at Carnegie Hall, 1961.**

right: **Grandpa Jones, Minnie Pearl, Faron Young, Bill Monroe, and Patsy Cline show off their keys to New York City.**

Yorkers, Tennesseans, and one lady from Paris who only said, "If slower they sing, I understand the words." Grandpa Jones got the only encore. His "Mountain Dew" could hardly be heard because everybody was singing along with it. Bill Monroe scored a screaming hit, especially when he played "Blue Moon of Kentucky," a Monroe song made famous by Elvis Presley. Minnie Pearl was the one who put her trip to its best use. She learned to dance the twist. Faron Young showed up in a powder blue sequined suit and Patsy Cline has certainly recovered from her auto accident. T. Tommy Cutrer tried to calculate how much hay he could store in the hall. Marty Robbins and Jim Reeves were begged for encores, but the group had to clear the stage by 11:30 p.m.

Stony Mountain Cloggers and Tommy Jackson on the stage at Carnegie Hall.

Marty Robbins plays for a full house at Carnegie Hall.

★   ★   ★

On March 5, 1963, Patsy Cline; her manager, Randy Hughes; Jean Shepard's husband, Hawkshaw Hawkins; and Hughes's father-in-law, Cowboy Copas, flew back to Nashville from Kansas City in a small plane that Hughes piloted. They had just performed at a benefit for the widow of a local deejay, "Cactus Jack," who had died in a car wreck.

BILL ANDERSON:

My phone rang about seven in the morning, which was highly unusual. A friend of mine called me and said, "Have you got your radio or TV on?" I said, "No." He said, "Hawkshaw Hawkins was killed in a plane crash." I thought an airliner went down, and I turned on the radio and heard Grant Turner and T. Tommy Cutrer give the news. They were breaking down. The emotion of it was unbelievable.

Nashville Banner,
March 6, 1963.

Though Bill at first had only heard about Hawkshaw, the news was even worse—there were no survivors of the crash. On March 7, there was a Nashville memorial service for Patsy Cline, whose remains were to be returned to Virginia. Among those scheduled to attend were Kitty Wells and her husband, Johnnie Wright, as well as Wright's singing partner, Jack Anglin.

BILL ANDERSON:

I was sitting right in front of Johnnie Wright and his wife, Kitty Wells, at Patsy's memorial service, and I turned around and spoke to them. Then, as we were leaving, I saw somebody take Johnnie by the arm and pull him aside.

JOHNNIE WRIGHT:

I was standing outside when my daughter Ruby got hold of Opry manager Ott Devine on the phone. She told Ott what had happened and then asked him to put me on the phone. Ott said, "Your daughter's on the phone, Johnnie, and it's very serious." She said, "Daddy, Jackson's dead." I couldn't believe it. We'd just gotten in off the road.

Johnnie's singing partner Jack Anglin had died in a car wreck just a few miles from the funeral home where the memorial service was held.

BILL ANDERSON:

Johnnie was sobbing as he went away and Kitty was just walking along behind. It almost defied description. It was almost surreal. What could possibly happen next? We were starting to wonder if we were jinxed.

OTT DEVINE, *leaving the funeral home:*

I just don't know. Jack Anglin's death on top of all the others. It's almost more than we can stand.

Two days later, Devine took the stage at the Grand Ole Opry, and said:

All of us were shocked and saddened this week when word was received from a hillside near Camden, Tennessee, that within the wreckage of a small plane the lives of four members of our Grand Ole Opry cast had ended. And then came Thursday's tragic automobile accident taking the life of Jack Anglin of the team of Johnnie and Jack.

What do we say when we lose such friends? We can reflect upon their contributions to us all through entertainment, their acts of charity and of love. We can think of the pleasure they brought to the lives of millions, and take some comfort in knowing that they found fulfillment in the time allotted to them. We can share the sorrow of the families in their loss, and appreciate the loss, not only to WSM and the Grand Ole Opry, but to their associates and the music industry, and especially to all of you, their friends. There is great significance that Patsy Cline, Cowboy Copas, Hawkshaw Hawkins, and Randy Hughes were

Ott Devine (at podium) leads the Opry cast in a remembrance of Patsy Cline, Hawkshaw Hawkins, Randy Hughes, Cowboy Copas, and Jack Anglin.

returning from a performance staged to help someone else. They will never be forgotten.

We ask that you in the audience stand and join us for a moment of silent prayer in tribute to them.

One minute of silence followed.

Thank you. Patsy Cline, Cowboy Copas, Hawkshaw Hawkins, Jack Anglin, and Randy Hughes never walked on this stage without a smile. They would want us to keep smiling and recall the happier occasions. I feel that I can speak for all them when I say, let's continue in the tradition of the Grand Ole Opry.

MINNIE PEARL:

Roy Acuff struck up his fiddle and played a number for them. I stood in the wings trying not to break down, but the tears were hard to hold back. Roy called me out and I tried to compose myself. I recall swallowing my tears. I said, though not very loudly, "Howdee, I'm just so proud to be here," but the rest is a blur. Grief and sorrow seem so alien to the Opry environment.

Some were beginning to say that the Grand Ole Opry was jinxed, and over the next two years there was a spate of accidents and fatalities involving current or former Opry members. Less than three weeks after Jack Anglin's death, Texas Ruby, who appeared on the Opry with her husband, Curly Fox, died in a trailer fire while Curly played the Friday Night Opry. On August 27, former Opry executive Jim Denny died of a heart attack; he was 52. And on November 16 that year, Ernest Tubb and Jean Shepard were involved in a wreck near Durham, North Carolina, in which the driver of an oncoming car was killed. On July 31, 1964, Jim Reeves died in a plane crash, and on June 20, 1965, former Opry member Ira Louvin of the Louvin Brothers died in a car wreck. Three weeks after Louvin's death, Roy Acuff was seriously injured in a car wreck near Sparta, Tennessee.

ROY ACUFF:

I'd sung "Wreck on the Highway" so many times, it flashed in my mind when I saw that car coming toward us. I just started to pray. I think the wreck was a warning that my luck—my traveling luck—was running out. Any game you play, you're gonna lose sometimes, and I've been traveling thirty years about a hundred thousand miles a year.

ERNEST TUBB:

Ol' Roy's retired five times. After that bad wreck in the summer of '65, he said, "Ernest, I'm quitting that road. You better get off it too before it kills you." I came back in that Christmas, and I didn't see Roy. I asked someone where he was, and they said, "He's up in Alaska."

The number of travel-related incidents was surprisingly low for a cast that traveled as a way of life. The road *was* a problem for the Opry, but in another way. Because most Opry performers made their living on tour, it was hard to meet the Opry's requirement of twenty-six appearances a year to retain membership. If an artist had a hit, managers and bookers insisted that they *not* work the Opry on the most lucrative night of the week, and it's a testament to the lure of the Opry that so many artists still wanted to be on the show anyway. Several artists, though, wanted to work the Opry on their own terms, and the conflict came to a head in December 1964.

CLARA HIERONYMOUS, *journalist, in the* Tennessean:

Twelve top country and western music stars will not appear on the Grand Ole Opry in 1965 and have been prohibited from using the Opry name in their outside billings, it was learned yesterday. Another entertainer, long-time favorite Minnie Pearl, has been given a leave of absence from the show for the coming year, but will continue to use the Opry billing in her current contracts. Others leaving the Opry roster were George Morgan, Don Gibson, Billy Grammer, Johnnie Wright, Kitty Wells, the Jordanaires, Faron Young, Ferlin Husky, Chet Atkins, Justin Tubb, Stonewall Jackson, and Ray Price. According to WSM officials, the move was in keeping with a longstanding Opry rule that performers must appear in 26 shows a year in order to be retained. "Nobody is mad at anybody," said WSM public relations director, Bill Williams, "it's just that periodically we have to take stock. These entertainers will be allowed to return any time they wish."

BILL ANDERSON:

That was a surprise. I'd never signed a contract saying that I would be in twenty-six times a year. I had the same manager as Faron and Ferlin, and I just felt that they made the choice to work the road. Hubert Long was our manager, and I remember him coming to me at that time and saying, "Do you realize how much money it's costing you to be on the Grand Ole Opry? I could book you out on the road and you're down there making eighteen dollars and seventy-five cents." I considered leaving, but my father, who knows nothing about show business but a lot about human nature, gave me as good a piece of advice as I've ever gotten. He said, "Son, look around you." The Opry was owned by National Life, and he said, "Maybe the Opry isn't at the very top, but these people haven't gotten to the level they're at by being stupid. They'll turn things around, and you'll be glad you stayed." I took his word and it's some of the best advice I've got in my life.

Johnny Cash had left the Opry in 1958. He returned in 1964, but was asked to leave the following year for a very different reason.

JOHNNY CASH:

The band kicked off a song, and I tried to take the microphone off the stand. In my nervous frenzy, I couldn't get it off. That was enough to make me explode in a fit of anger. I took the mic stand, threw it down, then dragged it along the edge of the stage. There were fifty-two lights, and I wanted to break all fifty-two, which I did.

CARLENE CARTER, *country singer and Johnny Cash's stepdaughter:*

He was banned from the Opry for a long time. He kicked out all the floor lights . . . the floodlights at your feet. I don't know what came over him. I don't know what upset him so much. I think he was just bein' Cash.

Johnny Cash on the Opry stage with Roy Acuff.

Ott Devine eventually relaxed the requirement to twenty weeks per year, and explained the situation in a letter to Earl Scruggs.

> *It has not been and never will be possible to stage the Grand Ole Opry as we know it and compete with the road shows in talent fees. The talent fees have doubled since 1962 and as you know, each weekend we schedule several times the number of musicians that a road show would carry. The number and cost of firemen, policemen, ushers, ticket takers, etc. we are forced to employ has increased each year.*

> *It was never our intention to ban for life those persons unable to meet our requirements as to the number of Saturday nights at the Opry House. We were not angry with them then or now. . . . Some felt we were too harsh in not allowing the acts to even guest with us in 1965. Some felt we were not strict enough. In my opinion, all were treated as fairly as possible. . . . We feel that the twenty week requirement settled upon last year is fair to the artist who wishes to remain a member of the Grand Ole Opry and fair to the audience which travels hundreds of miles to see you here in Nashville. We will continue maintaining and improving the Grand Ole Opry, and hope that you will continue to appreciate its value to you.*

The Opry still had an irresistible allure for many up-and-coming stars.

JEANNIE SEELY:

The Opry might not have been as important to the industry as it had been, but all of us grew up listening to it, and we grew up wanting it. In fact, the Opry was the biggest reason I moved to Nashville. Once I got a record that charted, I wanted the Grand Ole Opry. I was out in California. I met Dottie West out there. I said, "Dottie, I don't know enough to try for the Grand Ole Opry yet." She said, "Jeannie, that's where you learn." Boy, was she right. I had a record climbing the charts, and they were calling me saying, "We took over this market and that market," and I said, "Well, did anyone talk to Mr. Devine yet?" 'Cause I wanted the Opry.

Another of the Opry's new hires, Willie Nelson, came to Nashville in 1960. He'd made plenty of records, but everyone around Nashville thought of him as a songwriter because none of his own records had sold as well as other artists' recordings of his songs, like Faron Young's record of "Hello Walls" or Patsy Cline's "Crazy" or Ray Price's "Night Life" or Jimmy Elledge's "Funny (How Time Slips Away)." All were Willie Nelson hits, but not for him.

WILLIE NELSON:

November 28, 1964, was when I made my first appearance on the Grand Ole Opry, for which I was paid thirty-five dollars. And I cohosted a television show with my old hero, Ernest Tubb. The whole enterprise was supported by my songwriting royalties. But I love the Opry. The family tradition there is very similar to the family tradition I grew up with. It's very important to keep family units together, and that's the kind of life that the Opry was trying to set an example for. The show represents the people to themselves.

Ott Devine welcomes Willie Nelson to the Opry.

Ott Devine faced yet another problem: in September 1963, after twenty years at the Ryman Auditorium, the Opry's parent company, National Life, had to decide whether to leave the family home, or buy it.

DAVID HALL, *journalist, in the* Tennessean:

The Opry's lease expired. National Life said it was considering a move to the Fairgrounds. The difficulty had been over price. WSM had sought to rent the Ryman for one year at a price of $30,000 with four one-year renewal options at an annual increase of $1,000.

JACK DeWITT:

The people who ran the Ryman, including Horace Hill and the others, decided that the thing to do was to sell the Ryman Auditorium to us. I was on a committee to deal with Dan May, who was in charge of selling the Ryman. We'd meet and we'd trade a whole lot of jokes back and forth, and they started out at $700,000, and we got them down to $220,000, and bought it. It took weeks and weeks to get the deal done. The problem was, how do we cool the place in summer? In the wintertime it was cold, but we could take care of that with the furnace they had in there. Summertime was just unbearable. I had fans put in the windows to try to cool it off some. I got a price from an air-conditioning outfit, but they said there was no place to put the equipment. The roof wouldn't hold it, and we didn't have the land around there to put it outside.

After purchasing the Ryman Auditorium, WSM officially renamed the building the Grand Ole Opry House. Stoney and Wilma Lee Cooper, George Morgan, unknown, Roy Drusky, Loretta Lynn, Bill Carlisle, and Roy Acuff watch as Ott Devine hangs a temporary banner.

From the beginning, the Grand Ole Opry had been part of WSM and WSM had been part of National Life, but by the 1960s the Opry was slowly distancing itself from both. The managers who took over after Ott Devine's departure in 1968 saw a future for the Opry that had nothing to do with insurance or even radio.

HAL DURHAM, *Opry announcer and later manager:*

For many years, the Opry manager was a part of the radio station staff, and the Opry was simply another program of the radio station. It was not a separate entity. It was just another live music program. Up until the 1960s, WSM had live classical music, live pop music, and the Opry. The manager of the Opry was also a program staff member of WSM. Only after Bud Wendell took over the management of the Opry in 1968 did the Opry become a separate entity. Then the manager of the Opry reported to the president of National Life.

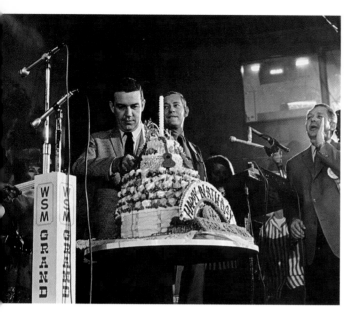

Bud Wendell cuts the Opry birthday cake, 1969.

JACK DeWITT:

Bud Wendell was my executive assistant. When I retired in 1968, Irving Waugh took over as president of WSM. He fired Ott Devine as manager of the Grand Ole Opry, and he made Bud Wendell in charge of the Opry. Irving was always afraid of Bud Wendell. He was afraid that I would make Bud president of WSM, but I didn't do it because Irving had been vice president and ought to be promoted. Bud called me and said, "Jack, I've been put aside. I'm in charge of the Grand Ole Opry. What should I do?" I said, "Bud, it's the best thing in the whole company. Just hang in there and do it," and he became very good at it.

JEANNIE SEELY:

Bud Wendell developed a vision for the Opry, a very important vision. Bud had a strong business background, but he came to understand what made it click between us and the audience. He was easy to work with. During that time, we had the credit system where you had to work a certain number of dates at the Opry to earn credits or be suspended. One year, Jack Greene and I were out on the road together. We were both on the charts, and we were working all the time. I got to figuring out what we had on the books and we were going to come out a credit and a half short. I went in to talk to Bud and asked him if we could make up this credit after the first of the year. He just listened and raised his eyebrow, and he said, "You tried, and I think we can bend the rules here. We'll see what next year brings." He knew that sometimes you couldn't go strictly by the rule book, and he knew we were sincere.

Bud Wendell's vision would take the Opry into the twenty-first century, but, one month after he took over, the man who'd had the original vision for the Opry died. On May 11, 1968, at 10:00 p.m., Opry announcer and Hay protégé Grant Turner, along with the rest of the Opry, paid tribute to founder George D. Hay, who had passed away three days earlier.

GRANT TURNER:

George Hay not only created the Opry out of the fabric of his imagination, he nurtured and protected it during its formative years. He heard the heartbeat of a nation in the country music he loved. He taught us to measure our music by this golden yardstick: it must be eloquent in its simplicity. He called himself the Solemn Old Judge. If he was solemn, it was only to the face of those who sought to change or corrupt the purity of the barn dance ballads he sought to preserve. We, the performers and friends of the Grand Ole Opry, salute the memory of one whose influence is felt on the stage of the Opry tonight—the Solemn Old Judge, George D. Hay.

Among other contributions to the country music community, Bud Wendell (left) launched Fan Fair.

Five months later, on October 8, Judge Hay's longtime nemesis, Harry Stone, died. The last years weren't good for either of them. Judge Hay felt that the Opry had turned its back on him and his concept of the show. He left Nashville and died in Virginia. Harry Stone had returned to Nashville to help start the Country Music Association, but was working as an advertising salesman for a magazine published by the Tennessee Electrical Cooperative Association at the time of his death.

And then, on June 26, 1969, WSM's founder, Edwin Craig, died. The three men who had steered the Opry through its earliest years had died within thirteen months of each other.

11

"ALL MY HIPPIE FANS"—
THE BLUEGRASS REVIVAL

O pry stars like Bill Anderson and Marty Robbins were in the pop charts, and the "Nashville Sound" was on everyone's lips. No one quite knew what the "Nashville Sound" was (producer Chet Atkins famously rattled his change when asked), but everyone knew what it *wasn't*. It wasn't bluegrass.

Country music had irrevocably changed, but bluegrass hadn't and wouldn't. Until the mid-1950s, bluegrass records had been played alongside other country records and bluegrass stars toured alongside country stars, but, as country music changed, bluegrass held fast to its old ways and distanced itself from country music. Several bluegrass artists, including the Stanley Brothers, lost their major-label deals, and the music retreated to smaller record labels, smaller stations, and smaller venues. Only Flatt and Scruggs were doing well, while Bill Monroe struggled along with everyone else.

KENNY BAKER, *Bill Monroe's fiddler player:*

There was a few years there, about the time this rock 'n' roll came in. It wasn't only bluegrass music, but all of country music shot its wad. Why they just disbanded left and right there in

Lester Flatt (left) and Earl Scruggs (right) on stage for Martha White with announcer T. Tommy Cutrer.

Nashville. Bill kept an outfit going, but he damn sure didn't make no money with it.

BUCK WHITE *of the Whites, Opry stars:*

I saw Bill Monroe in Wichita Falls right around that time. He could only afford to bring two men. We got a boy from the Light Crust Doughboys to play banjo with him, and you gotta believe he played a different kind of banjo. But Bill put on a show. He never complained. He was sufferin' along with a lot of others.

RALPH RINZLER, *musicologist and later Bill Monroe's manager:*

Bill Monroe was in the dumps because of rock 'n' roll. Another factor was that Flatt and Scruggs had cornered the market on what was left. Bill was left behind because he stuck hard with what he believed in, and he had no business organization behind him. Mrs. Scruggs managed their business and gave the impression that bluegrass began and ended with Flatt and Scruggs.

Although it was commonly believed that Bill Monroe hadn't spoken to Flatt and Scruggs since the duo left his employment in 1948, they'd worked together in the early 1950s, and it wasn't until Flatt and Scruggs's sponsor, Martha White Flour, began pressing for the duo's inclusion on the Opry that the fallout occurred.

JAKE LAMBERT, *bluegrass musician:*

Knowing WSM always paid attention to the amount of mail a group could pull, Cohen Williams [of Martha White Flour] collected a huge mail bag full and took it to WSM. He dumped it out on the office floor of Jack DeWitt. Either they put Flatt and Scruggs on Martha White's half hour of the Opry or he would pull his company's advertising off the station.

Bill Monroe's case was that the Opry wouldn't hire someone who sounded like Roy Acuff or Ernest Tubb, so they shouldn't hire another bluegrass act. He tried to get up a petition to keep Flatt and Scruggs off the Opry, and insisted that his sidemen not talk to Flatt and Scruggs or

Surviving Nashville. Bill Monroe on WSM-TV with host Smilin' Eddie Hill to his left.

their sidemen. It wouldn't be the last time Bill Monroe acted in that way, but while others like Flatt and Scruggs edged the music in new directions, Monroe kept it pure and simple for future generations.

RICKY SKAGGS:

If it hadn't been for Bill Monroe and his tenacity, bluegrass music might have died. He set his face like flint. He kept it alive. Flatt and Scruggs took the music onto television, but Bill Monroe's hang-in-there-like-a-rusty-fishhook attitude really kept the music alive. He survived rock 'n' roll, and he survived Nashville.

In the late 1950s, few would have given good odds on the survival of bluegrass; it was hard to find on the radio and on records. But it not only survived; it found an entirely new audience, an audience that most Opry stars hadn't even thought about.

RALPH EMERY, WSM *deejay:*

Sonny Osborne told me that there used to be eleven thousand bluegrass fans in the United States. I asked him how he knew, he said, "We recorded bluegrass for years and we sold eleven thousand copies every time out."

169

"All My Hippie Fans"—The Bluegrass Revival

Look *magazine, August 27, 1963:*

Serious students of folk music, always seeking genuine ethnic sources, are rediscovering the spirited "Blue Grass" style, which is perhaps closer to the majority of Americans than any other musical form.

DOUG GREEN *of Riders in the Sky, Opry stars:*

I was in college in the sixties, and we played bluegrass. There was something so plaintive and approachable about it. When you're nineteen, you haven't seen your share of honky-tonks and broken hearts. The country music experience you find in those kind of songs is remote, but songs about the mountains, missing home, and the straightforward honesty of the emotions resonated with a lot of college-age kids.

SHARON AND CHERYL WHITE *of the Whites, Opry stars:*

The kids weren't about materialism. They looked for something honest and real, and bluegrass was it. You can't help but be drawn to it. The purity of it. Louise Scruggs managed Lester Flatt and Earl Scruggs, and she was the one who began booking Lester and Earl into campuses. They said it couldn't be done, but she was right.

D. Kilpatrick was still in charge of the Opry in 1959 when Louise Scruggs called him because she'd received some interest from college campuses. Opry stars had never played campuses; in fact, never even thought of playing there.

D. KILPATRICK:

Louise told me that Davidson College in North Carolina had called them and wanted to schedule a performance on campus, and she wanted to know if they should do it. I said, "What do you mean whether?" She said, "Well, we don't want anyone laughing at us." I said, "They're not going to laugh at you." It wasn't three months and they were over at Duke University. Then before long that Esquire magazine article came out on them.

The *Esquire* article by folklorist Alan Lomax appeared in October 1959. Lomax coined the phrase "folk music in overdrive" to describe bluegrass. Late the previous year, the Kingston Trio had taken an old mountain song, "Tom Dooley," and made an international pop hit out of it. "Tom Dooley" ignited a folk craze on campus, and Lomax's article refocused interest on bluegrass as a repository of American folklore. At first listen, bluegrass appeared to have been unaltered for hundreds of years; in fact,

Lester Flatt (left) with Louise and Earl Scruggs.

of course, Bill Monroe had formulated the style just fifteen years earlier. Some of the songs were ancient, but many more were modern. Flatt and Scruggs sensed an opportunity, and on LPs like *Folk Songs of Our Land*, began tailoring their repertoire to their new audience. For one thing, college students bought LPs, not singles, and quite suddenly bluegrass LPs didn't sell only eleven thousand copies anymore.

Bill Monroe felt slighted, and when Ralph Rinzler, then a student at Swarthmore College, asked him for an interview, he snapped, "If you want to know about bluegrass, ask Louise Scruggs." But Rinzler persisted and eventually took over Monroe's management.

RALPH RINZLER:

Recognition for bluegrass and for Flatt and Scruggs as its significant exponents began with Scruggs' 1959 appearance at the Newport Folk Festival, followed by Flatt and Scruggs' joint appearance in 1960. It was February 1963 that Bill made his first college appearance at the University of Chicago Folk Festival, followed by his first New York concert appearances and his first folk club date at the Ash Grove in Los Angeles. Bill Monroe became the patriarch of bluegrass just as his rural and urban followings began to come together at festivals and concerts, united tenuously by their love for his music.

SHARON WHITE *of the Whites:*

Those festivals started, and you could tell that there were many bluegrass groups that Bill wasn't approving of. It worried me. I thought, If he doesn't let go of this music, he'll choke it to death.

RALPH RINZLER:

That he didn't smile on LP jackets is wholly consistent with his personality and symbolizes the degree to which he held himself apart from those around him, musically, socially, and personally. A man more easily persuaded would likely not have succeeded in so formidable an undertaking as bucking the rushing cultural and economic tide of the country music industry.

Flatt and Scruggs's career received a considerable boost from the television series *The Beverly Hillbillies.* They backed Jerry Scroggins on the show's theme song, "The Ballad of Jed Clampett," and their version became a hit single. The show's writer/producer later brought them onto the show for cameo appearances, boosting their profile yet again.

Lester Flatt with Granny in a Beverly Hillbillies *publicity shot.*

LESTER FLATT:

That song wasn't our favorite, but we learned to love it when it hit number one on the trade charts. Working with Beverly Hillbillies *is different from what we're used to. On our own TV show for* Martha White, *we cut three or four shows as fast as we can. Out there, it takes them a week to cut a thirty-minute film.*

A new record producer wanted them to record Bob Dylan songs and other contemporary material. Scruggs embraced the challenge; Flatt did not. Success had enabled Flatt and Scruggs to set aside their artistic differences . . . for a while.

PAT WELCH, *journalist, in the* Tennessean:

On the night of February 22, 1969, when [Flatt and Scruggs were] supposed to perform at 10:15 on the Grand Ole Opry, Flatt simply walked out without consulting Scruggs. Since that occasion, Flatt has not spoken to Scruggs, and the next information Scruggs had concerning him was on February 25 when he was advised that Flatt was trying to obtain bookings through an agency in violation of his contract with Scruggs Talent Agency. Scruggs charged that Flatt lived on his [Flatt's] farm in Sparta, Tennessee, since 1960 and devoted a minimal amount of time to the business of the partnership. On some occasions, Scruggs said he had to use tapes on road trips to familiarize Flatt with the new material.

After Flatt and Scruggs broke up, Earl Scruggs formed a revue with his sons Gary (left) and Randy (right).

After the rift, Lester Flatt returned to traditional bluegrass, and, in 1971, set aside long-standing differences with Bill Monroe. Although they both played on the Opry, they had managed to avoid speaking to each other since 1953, but backstage at the Opry one night Monroe sent his son, James, to ask Flatt if he would play at Monroe's Bean Blossom Festival. Marty Stuart, who had joined Flatt as a thirteen-year-old mandolin player, recalled the historic reunion.

MARTY STUART:

Bluegrass festivals were becoming a big thing. You'd see the Woodstock generation, mom and pops, bikers. Bean Blossom was a major event, and Lester played there in 1971. Everyone knew there had been a row, but then Lester came out and did a duet with Bill Monroe on "Will You Be Loving Another Man." The crowd went berserk. John Hartford told me he watched it and bawled like a child.

Lester became a rock star. We started working college campuses a lot. The first show was Michigan State. Gram Parsons and Emmylou Harris opened for us. The Eagles were out touring with "Desperado" then, and Bernie Leadon wanted

173

"All My Hippie Fans"—The Bluegrass Revival

to meet Lester. Lester said, "Aw, this ain't gonna amount to nothin'." But it did. I don't really know what Lester thought about that crowd. He and Earl had played for a lot of hippies in the sixties. It wasn't brand-new to him. The hippies loved him. He didn't get what they were about, but he understood applause and he understood ticket sales and he understood encores.

Ten years passed without much, if any, communication between Flatt and Scruggs.

Lester Flatt with Marty Stuart and the Osborne Brothers, 1975.

MARTY STUART:

Spring 1979, Bob Dylan was playing Nashville. When I was introduced to him, he said, "Aren't you the kid that plays mandolin with Lester Flatt?" I said yes. Dylan asked, "How is Lester, anyway?" I said, "He's dying." He wondered if Lester and Earl talked anymore. I told him I didn't think so. He said this was sad because Abbott and Costello were always going to speak, but they never got around to it before one of them died. Dylan kind of left it at that, but I went up to a payphone and called Earl and asked him if I could come talk with him. When I got there, I told him that the end was real soon for Lester and I wished he would consider going to see him one last time. Scruggs did, and that's just one more reason why I love him.

The bluegrass revival broadened into a revival of traditional country music. At the forefront of this revival was the Nitty Gritty Dirt Band's three-LP set, *Will the Circle Be Unbroken,* which paired the rock 'n' roll band with traditional artists and songs. Although Bill Monroe pointedly refused to be a part of the album, it succeeded in reconciling rock musicians with heritage artists like Roy Acuff. At the same time, there was a growing acknowledgment of the Opry's role in preserving and showcasing vintage country music. Most nights at the Opry, fans could still see the entire history of country music represented.

Other older artists—often to their surprise—found a new audience within the counterculture.

ERNEST TUBB:

When the hippies first started coming up to me, I was a little apprehensive, but they've turned out to be some of my biggest fans. These kids are looking for down-to-earth realism. They're looking for something our country's lost over the years. They're sincere, and they could be more right than a lot of the rest of us. I don't mind long hair as long as it's clean, and all my hippie fans have been clean and well-behaved.

GRAND OLE OPRY

WELCOME

Every Friday and Saturday evening fans from across the nation and many foreign countries travel to Music City U.S.A. to see the Grand Ole Opry. This world famous Country Music Show is the oldest continuing radio program in existence. It has never missed a broadcast in over half a century. And no matter where you live, the Grand Ole Opry is as close as your radio on WSM Clear Channel 650. We hope you enjoy the show and will come again often.

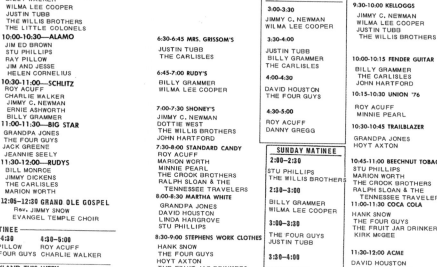

FRIDAY, JULY 14, 1978

6:30-7:00—BALTZ
JIM ED BROWN
RAY PILLOW
JIM & JESSE
HELEN CORNLIUS

7:00-7:30 DOAN'S PILLS
DEL REEVES
BILLY WALKER
WILMA LEE COOPER
ERNIE ASHWORTH
THE LITTLE COLONELS

7:30-8:00—CRACKER BARREL
ROY ACUFF
CHARLIE WALKER
STU PHILLIPS
JUSTIN TUBB
THE WILLIS BROTHERS
MARION WORTH

8:00-8:30—ODOM SAUSAGE/ WRANGLER
GRANDPA JONES
JIMMY C. NEWMAN
JACK GREENE
JEANNIE SEELY

8:30-9:00—KROGER/SUNBEAM
BILL MONROE
THE FOUR GUYS
JIMMY DICKENS
THE CARLISLES
BILLY GRAMMER

9:30-10:00—BEECHNUT TOBACCO
BILLY WALKER
WILMA LEE COOPER
JUSTIN TUBB
THE WILLIS BROTHERS
THE LITTLE COLONELS

10:00-10:30—ALAMO
JIM ED BROWN
STU PHILLIPS
RAY PILLOW
JIM AND JESSE
HELEN CORNELIUS

10:30-11:00—SCHLITZ
ROY ACUFF
CHARLIE WALKER
JIMMY C. NEWMAN
ERNIE ASHWORTH
BILLY GRAMMER

11:00-11:30—BIG STAR
GRANDPA JONES
THE FOUR GUYS
JACK GREENE
JEANNIE SEELY

11:30-12:00—RUDYS
BILL MONROE
JIMMY DICKENS
THE CARLISLES
MARION WORTH

12:05—12:30 GRAND OLE GOSPEL
Rev. JIMMY SNOW
EVANGEL TEMPLE CHOIR

FRIDAY MATINEE

3:00–3:30	3:30–4:00	4:00–4:30	4:30–5:00
JACK GREENE	BILL MONROE	RAY PILLOW	ROY ACUFF
JEANNIE SEELY	BILLY WALKER	THE FOUR GUYS	CHARLIE WALKER
JIMMY DICKENS			

APPEARING AT OPRYLAND THIS WEEK

JULY 17— LESTER FLATT • JULY 18— LARRY GATLIN
JULY 20— THE OSBORNE BROTHERS

SATURDAY, JULY 15, 1978

6:30-6:45 MRS. GRISSOM'S
JUSTIN TUBB
THE CARLISLES

6:45-7:00 RUDY'S
BILLY GRAMMER
WILMA LEE COOPER

7:00-7:30 SHONEY'S
JIMMY C. NEWMAN
DOTTIE WEST
THE WILLIS BROTHERS
JOHN HARTFORD

7:30-8:00 STANDARD CANDY
ROY ACUFF
MARION WORTH
MINNIE PEARL
THE CROOK BROTHERS
RALPH SLOAN &
THE TENNESSEE TRAVELERS

8:00-8:30 MARTHA WHITE
GRANDPA JONES
DAVID HOUSTON
LINDA HARGROVE
STU PHILLIPS

8:30-9:00 STEPHENS WORK CLOTHES
HANK SNOW
THE FOUR GUYS
HOYT AXTON
THE FRUIT JAR DRINKERS

SATURDAY MATINEE

3:00-3:30
JIMMY C. NEWMAN
WILMA LEE COOPER

3:30-4:00
JUSTIN TUBB
BILLY GRAMMER
THE CARLISLES

4:00-4:30
DAVID HOUSTON
THE FOUR GUYS

4:30-5:00
ROY ACUFF
DANNY GREGG

SUNDAY MATINEE

2:00—2:30
STU PHILLIPS
THE WILLIS BROTHERS

2:30—3:00
BILLY GRAMMER
WILMA LEE COOPER

3:00—3:30
THE FOUR GUYS
JUSTIN TUBB

3:30—4:00
ROY ACUFF
THE CARLISLES

9:30-10:00 KELLOGGS
JIMMY C. NEWMAN
WILMA LEE COOPER
JUSTIN TUBB
THE WILLIS BROTHERS

10:00-10:15 FENDER GUITAR
BILLY GRAMMER
THE CARLISLES
JOHN HARTFORD

10:15-10:30 UNION '76
ROY ACUFF
MINNIE PEARL

10:30-10:45 TRAILBLAZER
GRANDPA JONES
HOYT AXTON

10:45-11:00 BEECHNUT TOBACCO
STU PHILLIPS
MARION WORTH
THE CROOK BROTHERS
RALPH SLOAN &
THE TENNESSEE TRAVELERS

11:00-11:30 COCA COLA
HANK SNOW
THE FOUR GUYS
THE FRUIT JAR DRINKERS
KIRK McGEE

11:30-12:00 ACME
DAVID HOUSTON
LINDA HARGROVE
THE DUKE OF PADUCAH

WSM is an affiliate of the National Life & Accident Insurance Co. ● In Case of Emergency, Notify Your Area Hostess for Assistance ● Program Subject to Change Without Notice

GRAND OLE OPRY®

NEW MEMBERS: 1970s

JERRY CLOWER

LARRY GATLIN AND
THE GATLIN BROTHERS

TOM T. HALL

DAVID HOUSTON

JAN HOWARD

BARBARA MANDRELL

RONNIE MILSAP

JEANNE PRUETT

DON WILLIAMS

TAMMY WYNETTE

"THE OPRY WAS A COMFORT"

Often, in the late 1960s and early 1970s, it seemed as if the nation was polarized to the point that it might disintegrate into civil war. An institution such as the Grand Ole Opry had to take its stand. In November 1969, President Nixon made a televised speech about Vietnam. Concluding, he called upon "you, the great silent majority of my fellow Americans," and the Opry would entertain that silent majority. It would conjure up images of a more harmonious time and place, and its adaptation to social and musical changes would be measured.

BILL ANDERSON:

The Opry wasn't cutting edge. It wasn't designed to be cutting edge. The Opry was comfort. It took people's minds off protests and riots. It was a refuge for people who weren't caught up in the upheaval that was going on.

Charley Pride at WSM's forty-first birthday celebration in 1966.

MINNIE PEARL:

In an insecure world, the Opry doesn't change. Our jokes, many of our songs, and the customs we portray stay the same. People like it because it gives them a sense of security, a happy recollection of the way they were told things used to be in the good old days.

Nevertheless, change made its way to the Opry's door. Charley Pride became country music's first African American star since DeFord Bailey, and several groups, including the Byrds and Flying Burrito Brothers, blended sixties' rock with traditional country music. Just as Elvis gave the Opry audience of October 2, 1954, a sneak preview of rock 'n' roll, so the Byrds provided the Opry audience of March 15, 1968, with a preview of country rock. No one in the audience or even onstage could have foreseen it, but the Byrds and Burritos would influence the Eagles and many southern-rock bands, and those bands in turn influenced country music in the 1990s and beyond.

In March 1968, the Byrds were in Nashville to record what many regard as the first country-rock album, *Sweetheart of the Rodeo*. They asked for a guest spot on the Opry, believing the audience would embrace their music.

Opry band members Jimmy Capps and Hal Rugg observe as the Byrds—Kevin Kelley, Gram Parsons, Roger McGuinn, and Chris Hillman—make their Opry debut.

ROGER McGUINN, *leader of the Byrds:*

[Group member] Gram Parsons figured we could win over the country audience. He figured that once they dig you, they never let you go. So we were shooting for the Opry. We even played there. First rock group ever to do so. Columbia Records had to pull some strings to get us on the bill.

EMMYLOU HARRIS, *Opry star and Gram Parsons's duet partner:*

Gram wanted to be a country artist. He really wanted to bring country music to his generation and he wanted to

be accepted. There was that country boy yes-ma'am, no-sir about him. I think he wanted to be accepted by the Grand Ole Opry because it meant a lot to him. But he never got accepted. They were just too rock 'n' roll.

RANDY BROOKS, *journalist, in the* Vanderbilt Hustler:

The Byrds of "Mr. Tambourine Man," "Turn, Turn, Turn," and "Eight Miles High" fame were in last minute preparation for their Grand Ole Opry debut. An unidentified man suggested that, for the sake of public relations, they use the current number one song, "Sing Me Back Home," for their encore. The boys had other ideas, and even after the MC introduced that song, guitarist Graham [sic] Parsons began to play "Hickory Wind," a very pretty and very country tune. In performance the Byrds were a far cry from their earlier days. The unbearable volume of amplified instruments, which has impaired the hearing of stalwart Byrds fans in the past, was gone. In its place was the lazy twang of steel guitar and three very pleasant voices, actually audible over the accompaniment. Both "Hickory Wind," and "You Ain't Goin' Nowhere" drew polite but unenthusiastic response from an audience which only minutes before has cheered heartily for the Glaser Brothers and displayed unabashed adoration for Skeeter Davis. Following their appearance at the Opry, the Byrds came to Vanderbilt. The studios of WRVU were crowded with onlookers as each member of the group played disc jockey and answering service during an informal interview conducted by Gary Scruggs and Speed Hopkins. In reply to a telephoned question, Parsons said that he feels that the next sound in pop music will be an "exploitation of country music." One caller who accused the Byrds of being "dirty Commies" turned out to be group member Chris Hillman phoning from downstairs.

Less than one month later, Opry audiences were forced to confront the turmoil of the late 1960s head-on. On April 4, 1968, Martin Luther King was killed and riots erupted spontaneously in 130 cities.

The Tennessean, *April 6–7, 1968:*
Opry to Miss 1st Live Program in Past 43 Years

The 7 p.m. curfew imposed by Mayor Beverly Briley interrupted the normal routine for thousands of the city's residents, and brought complaints from both negro and white. Several persons who phoned the Nashville Tennessean *complained that they were frightened to go home from work because police officers were given the authority to stop anyone on the street for questioning. One man called to say that the closing of bars and taverns put him on the wagon for the weekend. Briley proclaimed a civil emergency existed in the city as a result of scattered violence in North Nashville. For the first time in 43 years there'll be no live Saturday night Grand Ole Opry. Instead of a live show, radio listeners will hear tapes of past performances. The Opry would have performed for the 2204th consecutive time tonight.*

Of course, the Opry had been canceled or preempted several times in its history, but this was the first and only time it was canceled because of civil unrest.

BUD WENDELL:

Nashville was closed down. You just were not allowed out. The streets were to be cleared. I called [the mayor] and I said, "I understand all this, but you must mean for everybody except for us," and he said, "No, you're included." So we had no alternative. We couldn't get artists together, bands together, even if we had wanted to do something. There was no way for people to get out. So we did the best thing we could. It was during that period of time that we had bomb scares. People would call schools and businesses and say a bomb was going to go off in ten minutes, so we had a standby tape that we made ahead of time, and we played that tape. It was a sad night, but we survived it.

Roy Acuff addressed the fans, many of them from out of town.

Friends, can I have your attention a minute. There's something I'd like to say. We all know there's a curfew on in Nashville. It starts at seven o'clock, and there's not going to be an Opry tonight. It seems a shame that so many people have come in from out of town and won't be able to see it. Let's see if we can't find a place and give them a show.

Roy Acuff brought the crowd to his museum on Broadway. Upstairs in a square dance hall, Acuff's impromptu Opry started at 2:00 p.m.

At a time when many believed that the country was drifting toward anarchy, the senselessly brutal slaying of Grand Ole Opry and *Hee Haw* star David Akeman, known as Stringbean, on November 10, 1973, seemed to bring the era's troubles inside the Opry House itself.

BUD WENDELL:

String and Estelle had been there on Saturday night. I had coffee with them sitting around some of those little ol' drugstore tables I had put in there. These guys were out there ransacking the house and listening to the Opry knowing that they weren't going to get caught because they could hear Stringbean pickin' on the show. I remember one thing String said. He and Grandpa Jones were discussing their hunting expedition, and String looked at me and he said, "How y'all gonna make it around here next week with both of us gone, Bud?"

GRANDPA JONES, *Opry star:*

The next morning, I was all packed for hunting and went over to pick up String. As I drove up the lane, I thought I saw a coat lying about seventy-five yards in front of the house. When I got closer, I saw it was a person. I stopped the car and went over. It was Estelle; she had been shot in the back and in the head. I felt her, and she was cold. I rushed to their little house and hollered for String. His banjo he had played the night before was sitting on its side on the little porch. I opened the screen. The other door was already open. String was lying in front of the fireplace. Shot in the chest. The phone had been pulled off the wall, so I jumped in my car, drove to my house and called the Metro Police Homicide Division.

Stringbean.

Stringbean had come home to find the robbery in progress and entered his house shooting.

BILL HANCE, *journalist, in the* Nashville Banner:

Stringbean was shot once and fell dead in the living room. Police said Estelle attempted to flee but was gunned down about forty yards away, near a wooden cattle guard. The couple had lived on the farm 17 years and were extremely happy and content living the simple life. They could have had more, but didn't want more. Stringbean never drove a car; his wife did all the driving. Roy Acuff stood staring at the little house where his longtime friend had been a shot a few hours earlier. "You know," he said, "String would sit in that chair over there and be content for hours just to look up at the top of the mountain watching the birds, squirrels, and rabbits. I'll tell you what the trouble is, the damn laws are too lax. The judges are too lenient with criminals, and because of this the country is unsafe."

There had been rumors that Stringbean didn't believe in banks and kept a large amount of cash in his home, but the thieves found nothing, nor did the police. John A. Brown and Marvin Douglas Brown were charged, and in October 1974, they were convicted of Stringbean's and Estelle's murders. In 1996, twenty thousand dollars in cash was discovered behind a brick in the chimney of the Akemans' home. Marvin Brown died in jail in 2003, and John Brown was denied parole that year.

Lawlessness, civil rights, and Vietnam were just some of the issues that divided the nation in the late 1960s and early 1970s. "Women's lib," as it was called at the time, was another. Tammy Wynette's 1968 hit, "Stand by Your Man," became a polarizing record. Tammy, who had five husbands, might not have stood by her men for very long, but she certainly gave voice to those who did. When she sang her song on the Opry stage, she was speaking for millions of women who weren't burning their bras, and for their husbands, who weren't burning their draft cards. Even so, the Opry had to confront the issues raised by the women's movement. Change would be subtle and measured, but it would come.

Loretta Lynn: 1962

Patsy Cline had changed the way women dressed on the show, and some of her songs hinted at a sexuality that might have shocked or surprised earlier generations of Oprygoers, but Patsy didn't live to see her protégé, Loretta Lynn, address burning social issues head-on. Loretta not only saw a lot of changes on the Opry and in the entertainment business, but ushered in some of them. Newly signed to Decca Records in 1960, she was billed as the "Decca Doll from Kentucky," but within a few years no one would ever be billed like that again. In 1966, at the Third Annual Conference on the Status of Women in Washington, D.C., the National Organization for Women was formed to campaign for equal rights. Two years later, protesters demonstrated in front of the Miss America pageant. Loretta, though, brought controversial issues down to a personal, nuts-and-bolts level, allowing her listeners to make up their own minds.

EMMYLOU HARRIS:

Well you know she lived it, and she told it like it was. When she was upset with her husband, she'd write "Fist City." When she was tired of having babies, she [sang] "The Pill," and she just wrote with just such honesty, but there wasn't any real anger. You can almost visualize her voice. Her head almost visualizes itself coming out of your car radio. There's so much presence in her voice. Loretta and Kitty Wells may not have wanted to call themselves feminists, but I think that they were what feminists would hope to be, which is your own woman. Totally comfortable in their own skin, and not giving a hang what anybody else thinks.

LORETTA LYNN:

I wasn't trying to change anything. I was just singing how I felt about things. I like to be on the woman's side, but I never went out to put a man down.

Dolly Parton: January 1969

Dolly Parton left a hardscrabble life in Sevierville, Tennessee, immediately after graduation in 1964, and came to Nashville. She'd already guested on the Opry and made a few records, but her early years in

left: Ernest Tubb's Midnite Jamboree would often take a chance on untested artists, such as Loretta Lynn. Loretta Lynn: "Ernest had his choice of women singers when he did a duet album, but he chose me after I'd had just a couple of hits. He said I was an 'honest country performer who sang with heart and soul.'" Loretta first appeared on the Midnite Jamboree promoting her first record on September 17, 1960.

right: Ott Devine breaks the news to Loretta Lynn that she's a member of the Grand Ole Opry. Minnie Pearl: "It was a man's world when I came here, and it was a man's world when Miss Kitty and Loretta came in, but Loretta battered down those barriers."

Dolly and Porter on the Porter Wagoner Show. *Dolly Parton first hit the* Billboard *charts with the song "Dumb Blonde," and then proceeded to show the world she is anything but.*

Nashville would have sent anyone less resilient back home. Then, in 1967, Opry star Porter Wagoner made her a regular on his syndicated television show and got her on RCA. By the time she joined the Opry in 1969, she was portraying female sexuality in a more daring way, and getting away with it because she lampooned it at the same time. And just as Loretta augmented her exposure on the Opry with appearances on the Wilburn Brothers' syndicated television show, so Dolly used her appearances on the Opry and Porter's show as a springboard to success.

The number of women on the Opry grew steadily. In came Dottie West, Jan Howard, Skeeter Davis, Connie Smith, Barbara Mandrell, and Jeannie Seely. Before long, they were asking why women never hosted Opry segments.

BARBARA MANDRELL:

When I was asked to become a member I asked the question, "What must one do to be able to host a segment of the Opry?" and I was told, "You must have gained enough status and you must be a man."

JEANNIE SEELY:

It never made any sense to me that a woman couldn't host a segment of the show. The first Opry manager to want to change that was Bob Whittaker. He said, "We're wasting fifty percent of our artist pool." I used to go up to Bob's predecessor, Hal Durham, and I'd say, "I know you've told me before why women can't host, but won't you tell me one more time." He'd rock from side to side and jingle his change and say, "It's tradition, Jeannie." I'd say, "Oh, it's tradition. It just feels like discrimination." Back then, they'd introduce women onstage with

"Here's a cute little girl, got on a pretty little outfit, put your hands together and make her feel welcome . . ." An introduction is when you tell the people about the person you're introducing. Something they can relate to. They'd never mention that I'd won a Grammy. Just "Here's a cute little girl, got on a pretty little outfit." As far as dress goes, Patsy changed things a little. She got rid of the cotton ruffles. Dottie West hedged a little. She wore the cotton ruffles, but she put some sequins on them. I'd never seen the Opry before I appeared on it, and I came from Southern California where everyone was wearing miniskirts.

There were some holdouts, of course, but most men on the Opry eventually came to see that things had changed irrevocably, and embraced those changes. On the occasion of the Opry's sixtieth birthday in 1985, a television special featured an all-woman segment, but most of the women on the Opry didn't want all-woman segments. Just parity.

Jeannie Seely, 1968.

Dottie West chats with Opry manager Bud Wendell, 1968.

the shield news

THE NATIONAL LIFE and ACCIDENT INSURANCE CO.

VOL. 6, NO. 30 | OPRYLAND GROUND BREAKING ISSUE | July 22, 1970

500 Invited Guests Attend Historic Event

GROUND IS BROKEN FOR OPRYLAND, USA

With the help of two mules and a plow, ground was broken June 30 in the home office city of Nashville for "Opryland, USA," WSM, Incorporated's entertainment-recreation complex which will surround the new home of the Grand Ole Opry.

A shirt-sleeve crowd of approximately 500 invited guests attended the historic ceremonies under sunny noontide skies.

The Opryland Park, scheduled for completion in spring of 1972, will be located approximately six air miles from downtown Nashville on 400 acres of gently rolling countryside.

On hand for the ceremonies, in addition to officials of National Life and WSM, Inc., were a host of state and city government officials; among those, the Honorable Buford Ellington, governor of the state of Tennessee, and the Honorable Beverly Briley, mayor of Metropolitan Nashville and Davidson County. Candidates for state political offices in the upcoming November elections in Tennessee and stars of the Grand Ole Opry also were in attendance.

After the invocation by the Rev. James Henry, minister of the Two Rivers Baptist Church in Nashville, veteran Opry announcer Grant Turner stepped to the microphone and briefly outlined the history of the Grand Ole Opry.

Turner said, "The story of the Grand Ole Opry is being written in two volumes: the first volume taking place over the past 45 years; and you who are present here today are helping us write the preface to the second volume—and this should be the biggest volume."

Irving Waugh, president of WSM, Inc., discussed the history of the Opry and the reasons for selecting the Pennington Bend area in Nashville for the site of the Opryland Park.

"Forty-five years ago WSM commenced broadcasting and very quickly started a country music program that grew into the phenomena that we know as the Grand Ole Opry," Waugh said.

"As country music grew and its appeal spread throughout the United States, more and more people came to Nashville and more and more demands were placed on the home of the Grand Ole Opry. We became increasingly aware of the inadequacies; the dressing room facilities, prop storage areas, and of course, the building was not suitable for air conditioning or any television production in any modern television age."

The president of WSM, Inc., went on to say, "We regrettably began to look seriously at the state of the old Opry house nearly three years ago. We began to seriously think about going to a new location and building a new home

Tennessee Governor Buford Ellington and Nashville Mayor Beverly Briley join forces with National Life President William C. Weaver, Jr., G. Daniel Brooks, chairman of the board, and Irving Waugh, president of WSM, Inc. behind the plow with Bashful Brother Oswald during the historic Opryland, USA ground breaking ceremonies in the home office city.

for the Opry. It was a tough decision—not just a financially tough decision, but it was a tough decision to break with a house that had really become a home that was identified all over the world with the Grand Ole Opry."

Selecting A Site

Waugh then cited the reasons the Pennington Bend area in Nashville was selected as the site of the Opryland Park, saying, "We finally settled on the spot where we now stand for many reasons: the beautiful stretch of the Cumberland river; many lovely trees; and when the Briley Parkway here is finished we will have easy access from interstates to the Parkway to this location." He added, "Here we have sufficient acreage to enable us to do many things that we want to do now and to expand down through the years as country music and the Opry continue their growth."

Mr. Waugh then introduced the chairman of the board of National Life and WSM, Inc., G. Daniel Brooks. Mr. Brooks added a word of welcome to the gathered guests, recognized the large number of dignitaries present, and introduced the Honorable Buford Ellington, governor of the state of Tennessee.

Governor Ellington said, "Last year I had the privilege of serving as chairman of the National Governors Conference. There were always two things that they wanted to discuss outside of those things on the agenda. One of those things was the Grand Ole Opry and I think that's wonderful—it's good for Tennessee."

Ellington then turned to Metropolitan Nashville and Davidson County Mayor

Beverly Briley and said, "I thank my stars and my Lord that I had the opportunity of working just a little bit with the Metropolitan government, with Dan Brooks and the others of the Grand Ole Opry. I would like to thank all of these men and those involved in the state level for making this day possible."

A Proud Possession

Mayor Briley approached the microphone and said, "I have watched the many people of National Life who conceived the innovative idea of developing and bringing into the modern world the thing that is sacred to the people of this whole generalized area, and that is our music.

"The progressive history of the Grand Ole Opry and of Opryland is one of the proud possessions of all of us in the Metropolitan Nashville and Davidson County area."

At this time, a beautiful plaque was presented to Mrs. Edwin W. Craig, widow of the late Edwin W. Craig, former National Life board chairman, by Mr. Waugh.

The plaque, which will be placed in the new home of the Opry, listed the roster of the entire company of the Grand Ole Opry as it was constituted on June 30. The inscription on the plaque read: "The Grand Ole Opry will stand as one of the outstanding attractions of all time in the field of entertainment."

These were the words of the late Mr. Craig who was the father of WSM and who through the early lean years of WSM gave unyielding support to

broadcasting to WSM, the Grand Ole Opry and country music.

C. A. Craig, II, vice president and chief agency officer, accompanied his mother to the microphone and responded, "On behalf of my mother and my entire family, we are grateful to accept for safekeeping this beautiful plaque."

The Company's president, William C. Weaver, Jr., called the event, "a mighty happy occasion for all of us in the WSM and National Life organizations."

He said, "We wouldn't be here today if a lot of people hadn't already invested a lot of work and a lot of cooperation in this project."

Mr. Weaver thanked all those associated with the Opryland project and turned his thanks to the "real stars of this show—the people, both living and dead, who have made the Grand Ole Opry what it is today—the stars of the Grand Ole Opry."

Old-Fashioned Way

Mr. Weaver then introduced Roy Acuff, who the Company's president called the "senior statesman of country music."

Acuff glanced around the crowd and said, "I see a man who has been a friend to me and to all of us in country music. That man is Mr. Eldon Stevenson (consultant to the Company and former honorary vice chairman)." Acuff continued, "I am glad to see you here, sir. I am sorry that other great gentleman, the late Mr. Edwin Craig, could not be beside you today."

"I am sorry that Mr. Craig and the man I am representing, The Solemn Ole Judge, George D. Hay, could not be here for this occasion. To me, Judge Hay was the originator of the Grand Ole Opry."

Acuff then held up the horn that was presented to him by the late Judge Hay and said, "Judge Hay presented this to me a long time ago. It is the old steamboat whistle that started the Grand Ole Opry performances."

Acuff and his Smoky Mountain Boys then performed their rendition of the "Wabash Cannonball," after which time Pete (Bashful Brother Oswald) Kirby, Acuff's dobro guitarist for 33 years, led two mules from behind the platform for the historic ground-breaking ceremonies. Messrs. Ellington, Briley, Brooks Waugh and Weaver grabbed the harnesses along with Brother Oswald and at Acuff's signal ground was broken for Opryland, USA.

Mr. Weaver said, "The Opry has always been close to the soil, so we felt an old-fashioned technique for this groundbreaking ceremony was appropriate."

13

OPRYLAND

The generation that had grown up with the Grand Ole Opry returned to it, perhaps, as Minnie Pearl said, because it represented a refuge from the music, social unrest, and divisive politics of the late 1960s and early 1970s. Opry attendance rose, but in the years after National Life bought the Ryman Auditorium, the building's shortcomings became increasingly apparent, especially as people became accustomed to air-conditioning. Moreover, Nashville's downtown core was disintegrating.

JACK HURST, *journalist, in the* Tennessean:

In 1971, for the first time, the Opry's attendance rose above 400,000. "I'd like to remind the Chamber of Commerce that the Opry crowd is Nashville's biggest convention of the year, and it happens every weekend," said Bud Wendell. He said that over the past five years the Opry's annual attendance has risen consistently at a rate of 6% a year.

The Shield News, *July 22, 1970.*

The Tennessean, *October 14, 1973:*

Eighty-eight percent of the persons polled indicated that the Grand Ole Opry was the main reason for their coming to Nashville. 63.2 percent say that it's "very likely" they will visit the Opry again. Asked "How would you rate the auditorium where you saw the Grand Ole Opry?" over 40 percent called the Opry House "poor" and another 31 percent said "only fair."

BILL ANDERSON:

The area around the Ryman had gotten really seedy. It had gone downhill pretty far pretty fast. The Ryman itself was in a terrible state of repair and the porno businesses had moved into Lower Broadway. You didn't want to spend a whole lot of time in that part of town.

BUD WENDELL:

I've always felt that the Johnny Cash television show [filmed at the Ryman for ABC-TV, 1969–1971] was really the start of Nashville as a tourist destination. So all of a sudden we found ourselves just inundated at the Ryman. The Opry had always had good, strong attendance, but all of a sudden it was just inundated with people wanting to come in: ticket requests, tour operators, and that whole thing. At the same time, downtown Nashville deteriorated. We were having shootings across the street. Where the convention center is now, there was a string of bars. Panhandlers harassed the people in line for the shows. The major retail businesses had left downtown and we had the same problems as many urban centers were having at that time. Well, here we are, owned by an insurance company; very sensitive to its public image. So, they said to us, "If the Opry is going to continue, we have to find a new home for it." We sensed that there was a real opportunity for major television exposure if we had first-class television production facilities, but we also realized that we had all these people coming down to see the Opry; coming from an average of 450 miles. Well, we had to have a hotel to take care of some of these people who've come these great distances, because they're going to spend the night.

Shortly after an initial decision in favor of a hotel and park, there were gasoline shortages.

BUD WENDELL:

National Life was a little timid about going ahead with plans for the hotel. They said, "If people can't drive 450 miles they're not going to need this hotel. We've already got the park, so we're stuck with it." We put the hotel on hold, but as those energy problems and gasoline shortage problems eased, we went ahead with our plans on the hotel and finally convinced ourselves that more people would come to the park than we anticipated, so we could build as much as a six-hundred-room hotel. I hired Jack Vaughn to develop that property. He said, "You all are going the wrong direction. You're talking about building overnight motel accommodations. There's an opportunity for Nashville to become a convention destination and instead of building this motel that charges $49.99 a night, we could build a major convention facility, attract organizations, build major exhibit space, and make Nashville a real convention destination." He convinced us of that and he said, "We need to build one thousand rooms." The insurance company, which had never been in this business before, said, "Whoa! No way are we going to build one thousand rooms, but we'll let you build the six hundred rooms and overbuild the exhibit areas and the restaurant space, the retail area and the public areas," so that we could eventually add the four hundred rooms. But with the six hundred rooms it got to be so successful that we had to add more ballrooms and more exhibit space, so to that extent the plan didn't work out. Then we added another thousand rooms and then another thousand rooms. The whole plan worked very nicely because we got the Opry House built and open and we were able to utilize all of those wonderful television facilities at a time when the networks still had prime-time variety shows, entertainment shows and all of those specials. There was still wonderful exposure for the artists in Nashville, Tennessee, but it also gave us a wonderful facility for the CMA awards show.

WSM press release, July 1, 1970:

Ground was broken yesterday—with a mule and a plow—for construction of the Grand Ole Opry's new home in the Pennington Bend area. The late Edwin Craig, longtime head of National Life and founder of the Opry [who had died on June 26, 1969], was honored at the ceremony, as were the stars of the Opry, both living and dead. The $25 million entertainment center which will occupy 369 acres along the Cumberland River is scheduled for opening in the spring of 1972. The seating in the new Opry House will be 50% bigger, increasing from 3,000 seats to 4,400.

IRVING WAUGH, *WSM president:*

The Opry House wound up costing fifteen million dollars instead of the five million we'd projected. If we'd known that at the beginning, we would never have done it. I've got this to say about National Life, though: while waves of nausea swept over [president] Bill Weaver at times, he backed us all the way.

The rides and attractions of Opryland USA opened in May 1972. In January 1974, Bud Wendell became vice president of WSM and the Grand Ole Opry and appointed former Opry announcer Hal Durham as Opry manager. Durham oversaw the move from the Ryman to the new Grand Ole Opry House on March 15 and 16, 1974.

WSM press release, January 22, 1974:

The grand opening and first performance of the Grand Ole Opry in WSM's new $15 million Opry house will take place March 16 before a capacity audience of regular Opry fans and music industry, civic, business, and government notables from across the nation. The last Saturday evening performance of the Grand Ole Opry in the 84-year-old Ryman Auditorium, will be March 9, and the last Friday evening performance will be March 15. The new 4,400-seat air-conditioned Opry house has been under construction since November 12, 1971. It is the world's

The new Grand Ole Opry House, September 1974.

largest broadcasting studio. It will be the first building to house the Opry that was specifically designed and built for the 48-year-old radio show. The new Opry house has the world's most advanced acoustical and lighting systems, 12 dressing rooms, a band rehearsal room, and more than 12,000 feet of storage space. Television shows can be produced in the auditorium or in the separate television production studio that has a seating capacity of 250. The new Opry house is the centerpiece of Opryland U.S.A., National Life and Accident's $26 million "theme" park.

BASHFUL BROTHER OSWALD:

We was all hatin' to leave. Roy Acuff figured it would be better to be out at Opryland. He said, "Boys, you're gonna like it out there," and they didn't all believe him. He said it would keep growing and be bigger all the time. He said, "Opryland will draw a lot of people to the Opry." But the Ryman had the best sound of anywhere I've ever played in my life. Course it didn't have no dressin' rooms or anything, but that was all right. Saturday nights, I couldn't wait to get down there and see all the boys. You'd go backstage and you'd talk. Someone would say, "I didn't make any money last week out on the road," and someone else would say, "Now I made a little. I'll let you have some." They don't do that now.

GRANT TURNER:

The Opry is like an old department store with the stuff stacked in the aisles. You can move it to a nice new building, but will the people still come? Nobody goes to a building, you know.

BARBARA MANDRELL:

I'm so very thankful I became a member of the Opry just before we moved into the big, beautiful Opry House. At the Ryman, the girls had the restroom as a dressing room. Here were these huge stars . . . Dolly Parton, Tammy Wynette, Loretta Lynn . . . sitting on toilets and visiting. We would all be perspiring so bad; it was so hot in there. But we were full of love and passion for our music and the people who would come to see us.

JEANNIE SEELY:

Oh, it was ungodly hot in the summer. One night, I guess it was August, I'd rolled my hair, fixed my makeup, and I walked down the ramp, and, with the humidity and the perspiration, I could feel my hair flattening and my makeup running. I was mad as hell. I stopped just short of the stage, and I said, "I've found out who you have to screw to get on the Grand Ole Opry, now who do you have to screw to get off?" But we all got to know each other. You'd bring a minimum of stuff with you 'cause there was just no room, and you'd share stuff. The bond between the Opry artists might never have been formed this closely if we hadn't been in the Ryman. It was like a big family in a little house.

ROY ACUFF *to the last house at the Ryman, March 15, 1974:*

Certainly there are memories of this old house that will go with us forever. Not all of them are good. Not all of them. Many of them are. But some of them are punishment. Punishment in the way we ask you to come visit with us and then we sit you out in the audience here and in the hot summer we sell you a fan for a dollar. You do your own air-conditioning. And some of you, we sell you a cushion to sit on because the seats are just not the most comfortable they can be. But out in Opryland when you come see us, we'll furnish the air-conditioner. We'll furnish the cushion seats.

HAIRL HENSLEY, *Opry announcer:*

George Morgan, Lorrie's father, was the star of the last portion of the Opry from the Ryman. The last song was his theme song, "Candy Kisses."

After "Candy Kisses," the entire cast assembled to sing "Will the Circle Be Unbroken." Garrison Keillor, then an arts columnist for the *New Yorker*, was in the auditorium that night. As a child, he'd heard the Opry in Minnesota.

GARRISON KEILLOR:

The best place to see the Opry that night, I decided, was in the [broadcast] booth with my eyes shut, leaning against the back wall, the music coming out of the speaker just like radio. That good old AM mono sound. The room smelled of hot radio tubes, and, closing my eyes, I could see the stage as clearly as when I was a kid lying in front of our giant Zenith console. It was good to let the Opry go out the same way it had first come to me, through the air in the dark. After the show, it was raining hard, and the last Opry crowd to leave the Ryman ran.

Inspired by the Grand Ole Opry, Keillor returned to Minnesota, and, on July 6, 1974, launched *A Prairie Home Companion* on Minnesota Public Radio. Like the Opry, it ran on Saturday evening and featured a mix of comedy and music. It was later syndicated via NPR.

JEANNIE SEELY:

When we moved, a lot of people asked me, "Aren't you afraid you'll lose something?" Well, of course, leaving the Ryman was sad, but I believe very much in a torch being passed and a responsibility being passed along with it. It was our responsibility to make the new building mean what the people before us had made the Ryman mean.

BILL ANDERSON:

I felt instantly at home. I felt like this was where we were meant to be, and where we were going to be for the next many, many years. I appreciate the Ryman. I

The boards of directors
of
WSM, Incorporated,
and
The National Life and Accident Insurance Company
cordially invite you
to the dedication of and
first performance in
the new Grand Ole Opry House
in Nashville, Tennessee,
on Saturday, the sixteenth of March,
beginning at six P.M.
Central Daylight Time

R.S.V.P.

*Invitation to the
Opry House opening.*

loved everything that was down there, but if you were ever there on a hot night in July with thousands of people blocking the entranceway to the building, and the temperature about 950 degrees backstage and no air-conditioning, then you appreciate what we've got at the new Opry House.

JEAN SHEPARD, *Opry star:*

We done the Friday night Opry from the Ryman and the Saturday night Opry from Opryland. That Saturday night it sounded like an Apache raid on a Chinese laundry. The sound was terrible. I come off the stage, and someone said, "Jean, how do you like the new building?" I said, "I don't like it at all." But it's gotten an awful lot better, it really has.

HAL DURHAM:

The last show at the Ryman was a matter of people grabbing up souvenirs and whatever they could find to remember the building. The thought then was that it would be torn down. We got to the new building on Saturday and realized that we knew nothing about it. We didn't know where the restrooms were or the backstage was, and the first show involved a visit from President Nixon. Of course, television was there, and the national press. Roy Acuff and his group opened the show, then we got to the part where he invited the president to come down, and then we invited Opry members to come onstage.

President Nixon sat down at the piano and played "Happy Birthday" and "My Wild Irish Rose" to his wife, Pat, and then tried to yo-yo with Roy Acuff.

PRESIDENT RICHARD M. NIXON, *on the Opry stage, March 18, 1974, to Roy Acuff:*

I'll stay here and try and learn to yo-yo, and you go be president for a while. Friends, country music speaks of family, our faith in God, and we all know that

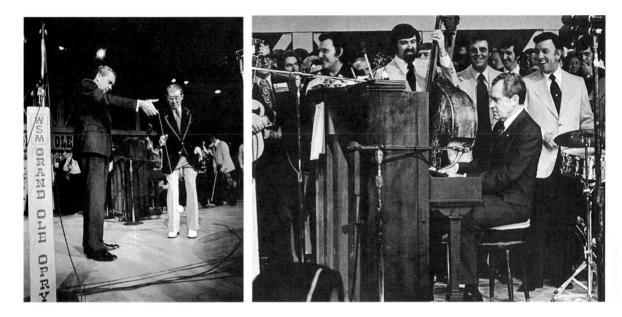

country music radiates love of this nation, of patriotism. Country music, therefore, has those combinations that are essential to America's character at a time when America needs character. Your music makes America better, and we come away better after hearing it.

left: **President Richard Nixon gets yo-yo lessons from Roy Acuff.**

right: **While many sitting presidents have visited the Opry, only Richard Nixon has actually played the Opry.**

ROY ACUFF *to President Nixon:*

He is a real trouper as well as one of our greatest presidents.

BILL ANDERSON:

I was standing onstage when Mr. Acuff and the president were out there playing with the yo-yos. I was next to Ernest Tubb, and I thought, Well, here's a man who's been at the Grand Ole Opry since 1943, and I turned to him and said, "Ernest, did you ever think you'd live to see the day when the president of the United States would come to the Grand Ole Opry?" He looked at me and said, "No, but I wish it had been another president."

The Opry crowd was quite possibly the last friendly audience that Richard Nixon encountered during his term in office. He had been named a co-conspirator in the Watergate break-in by a federal grand jury

President Nixon waves to the Opry audience.

the day before his appearance at the Opry. On August 8, he announced that he would resign.

HAL DURHAM:

You've probably seen those pictures of President Nixon playing piano, and all the Opry people backstage, but when I look at that photo I see many non-Opry people with no connection to the show who somehow got into the group. The first show ran forty-five minutes late. It was a cold night in March, and the second-show crowd was waiting outside to come in. We finally just ran the show straight through, emptied the house, and let the second-show crowd come in without actually having an intermission. The show ended that night about an hour and twenty minutes late.

Among those performing the first show at the new Opry House were Sam McGee, who, with his brother, Kirk, first performed on the Opry in 1926.

SAM McGEE:

There's people here now, I tell 'em how it was back in the early days, and they don't even believe me. There's only seven or eight of us original members left now. We had no idea when we started that [the Opry] would make such a go of it. I felt for a while that when our music was over, when we were gone, why that'd be the end of it. But it seems lately that people are getting interested in our music again. This Opry House is fine. It's the finest thing that could happen to the Opry. It's a place to show off. You can't sell barbecue without setting it out and saying, "That's barbecue, folks."

Among those returning to the Opry in the months after the move was DeFord Bailey. On the occasion of his seventy-fifth birthday in December 1974, he was brought onstage by Roy Acuff, who had worked with him in the late 1930s.

The move to Opryland was more than justified by the increased attendance. In 1974, the Opry drew 482,178 people; in 1975, attendance reached 751,546. The cost for National Life had been more than anticipated, but

WSM president Irving Waugh reasoned that the Opry was still a benefit to National Life in its battle with bigger insurers.

The move had been exhausting, but once the Opry was installed in its new premises, the question remained of what to do with the Ryman Auditorium. Early on, the prevailing opinion was that it should be demolished. National Life brought in a consultant, Jo Mielziner, who'd staged a production of *Romeo and Juliet* at the Ryman in 1935. Mielziner told the board that the Ryman was "full of bad workmanship and contains nothing of value as a theater worth restoring. In its latter life as part-time housing for theatrical presentations, there is absolutely not an item of true value because of the total inadequacy of this structure for this kind of operation." Only a few benches and signs should be saved, concluded Mielziner, and perhaps after the Ryman had been torn down, a modern concrete hall could be built to stage theatrical productions.

Roy Acuff to DeFord Bailey, December 16, 1974: "I guess DeFord traveled with us about six or seven years. I used him whenever I wanted to draw a crowd. DeFord would play and then I'd go on and try to hold their attention."

ADA LOUISE HUXTABLE, *the* New York Times, *May 13, 1973:*

In the name of reasonableness, the company [National Life] has sponsored studies that have come up with the not surprising news that preservation is "economically unfeasible." [But] there was probably no landmark rehabilitation that was not called economically unfeasible before it was successfully done. The latest study is by Jo Mielziner, who is not the most qualified expert on old building renovation, to put it mildly. . . . Destroying the Ryman is more than demolishing a touchstone of Nashville's past; it means abandonment of a neighborhood that needs help, and speeding the death of downtown. That's fine for the kind of redevelopers who wait like vultures to produce sterile new urban pap.

ROY ACUFF:

The Ryman's going to fall down anyway, so why not tear it down, then people wouldn't go down to that part of town. The old Opry house attracts persons who become potential customers for the massage parlors and other adult businesses.

It might be sad to some to tear it down, but I'm not that way. It would be a wonderful idea to take the bricks and build a chapel or church at Opryland. If they did that, I'd start going back to church. That plan would show the most respect for the building and Christianity. The Ryman served its purpose and served it well, but if they want to restore it, I'm doubtful anyone could get it done before it falls down. You can't heat it. I've stood on that stage doing a matinee, and you could see the sky. It's a fire hazard and the bricks are falling off the walls. Some crank or fanatic could throw a firebomb in there, and it would be gone in an hour.

DEL WOOD, *Opry star:*

The Ryman is the Carnegie Hall of country music. That's the problem with this country. Anything old is discarded to make way for the new. The Ryman is part of our heritage. To keep it doesn't take anything away from the new Opry House.

SKEETER DAVIS, *Opry star:*

I was one of the people who fought, and I will say fought, because we went to the historical boards, people like that to save the Ryman. Two people who raised

At one point, National Life officials proposed using some of the bricks and pews from Ryman to create "The Little Church of Opryland." The idea really never made it past this sketch, perhaps in part because of the ridicule from the New York Times: *"First prize for the pious misuse of a landmark, and a total misunderstanding of the priciples of preservation. Gentlemen, for shame."*

their voices to save it were Bob Dylan and Joan Baez. I really didn't want to go to the new building in the middle of a park. I still love the old Ryman, and I'm glad we saved it. Neil Young used to be in the wings of the Ryman when no one knew who he was. Andy Warhol came. I remember sitting there talking to him, and later Roy Acuff asked me, "Who was that freak?"

And so the National Life board deferred a decision on the Ryman Auditorium. It sat empty for years, long enough for downtown Nashville to be reborn around it.

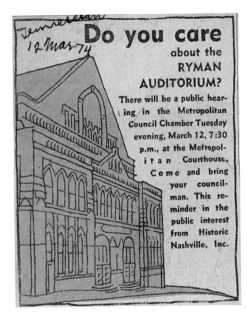

Ryman public hearing notice, March 12, 1974.

GRAND OLE OPRY

FRIDAY, MAY 16, 1986

FIRST SHOW

6:30-7:00—Block Drug

Porter Wagoner
Skeeter Davis
Roy Drusky
The 4 Guys
Boxcar Willie

7:00-7:30—Cat's Paw Rubber Co.

Ricky Skaggs
Jack Greene
Jan Howard
Riders In the Sky
Charlie Louvin

7:30-8:00—Cracker Barrel

Roy Acuff
Wilma Lee Cooper
Jimmy Dickens
Minnie Pearl

8:00-8:30—Nabisco, Taco Bell

Bill Monroe
Tom T. Hall
Jean Shepard

8:30-9:00—Kroger, Po'Folks

Hank Snow
Bill Anderson
Connie Smith
The Osborne Brothers

SECOND SHOW

9:30-10:00—Music Valley Drive Merchants

Ricky Skaggs
Lorrie Morgan
Jimmy C. Newman
Billy Walker
Ray Pillow

10:00-10:30—Goody's Headache Powder

Roy Acuff
Jeanne Pruett
Bill Anderson
Boxcar Willie
Carlisles

10:30-11:00—Red Man Tobacco

Porter Wagoner
Tom T. Hall
Stonewall Jackson
Jeannie Seely

11:00-11:30—Luck's Foods

Hank Snow
The Osborne Brothers
Jean Shepard
Jimmy Dickens
Connie Smith

11:30-12:00—Heinz

Bill Monroe
The 4 Guys
Johnny Russell

12:05-12:30—Grand Ole Gospel

Rev. Jimmy Snow
Evangel Temple Choir

DON'T MISS THE 15th INTERNATIONAL

COUNTRY MUSIC FAN FAIR

JUNE 9 - 15, 1986 — NASHVILLE, TENNESSEE

For Further Information Write:
COUNTRY MUSIC FAN FAIR
2804 OPRYLAND DRIVE, NASHVILLE, TN 37214

SATURDAY, MAY 17, 1986

FIRST SHOW

6:30-6:45—Mrs. Grissoms

Porter Wagoner
Boxcar Willie

6:45-7:00—Rudys

Tom T. Hall
The 4 Guys

7:00-7:30—Shoneys

Ricky Skaggs
Lorrie Morgan
Ray Pillow
Johnny Russell

7:30-8:00—Standard Candy

Roy Acuff
Jan Howard
Stonewall Jackson
Jean Shepard
The Crook Brothers
The Stoney Mountain Cloggers

8:00-8:30—Martha White

Bill Monroe
Skeeter Davis
Jimmy Dickens
Riders In the Sky
Billy Walker

8:30-9:00—Music Valley Drive Merchants

Hank Snow
Del Reeves
Jack Greene
Jeanne Pruett
Jimmy C. Newman

SATURDAY MATINEE
Brought to you by
TOYOTA

3:00-3:30
Porter Wagoner
Charlie Louvin

3:30-4:00
Stonewall Jackson
Lorrie Morgan

4:00-4:30
Ray Pillow
The 4 Guys

4:30-5:00
Jack Greene
Amy Sue Macy
Carlisles

SECOND SHOW

9:30-10:00—Dollar General Store

Tom T. Hall
Wilma Lee Cooper
Boxcar Willie
Charlie Louvin

10:00-10:15—Little Debbie Snack Cakes

Ricky Skaggs
Jeannie Seely

10:15-10:30—Sunbeam

Roy Acuff
Carlisles

10:30-10:45—Pet, Inc.

Bill Monroe
Roy Drusky

10:45-11:00—Heil Quaker

Del Reeves
Jean Shepard
The Crook Brothers
The Stoney Mountain Cloggers

11:00-11:30—Coke

Hank Snow
Justin Tubb
Jimmy Dickens
Riders In the Sky
Billy Walker

11:30-12:00—Quincy's

Jack Greene
Jimmy C. Newman
Jeanne Pruett
Johnny Russell

Continue the Opry Experience by seeing the special new exhibit, "The Grand Ole Opry: The First 60 Years," at the Country Music Hall of Fame and Museum with more Opry stars, more Opry history, and all the golden memories of America's longest-running radio show.
Open Daily, 9-5. For more information, call 256-1639

The Kimball Grand is the official piano of The Grand Ole Opry.
In case of emergency, notify your area hostess for assistance.
Program subject to change without notice.

GRAND OLE OPRY®

BOXCAR WILLIE

ROY CLARK

JOHN CONLEE

HOLLY DUNN

PATTY LOVELESS

MEL MCDANIEL

REBA MCENTIRE

LORRIE MORGAN

RIDERS IN THE SKY

JOHNNY RUSSELL

RICKY VAN SHELTON

RICKY SKAGGS

MELVIN SLOAN DANCERS

B. J. THOMAS

RANDY TRAVIS

THE WHITES

WHO'S GONNA FILL THEIR SHOES?

Hal Durham managed the Grand Ole Opry from 1974 until 1993. He was the first to allow a full drum kit on the Opry stage, and he relaxed the number of performances needed to retain membership. But even with the vastly increased attendance at the new Opry House, Hal Durham and Bud Wendell knew that there was a problem on the near horizon: the show's stalwarts, Roy Acuff, Minnie Pearl, Bill Monroe, Ernest Tubb, and Little Jimmy Dickens had joined the Opry in the 1930s and '40s. Even the lead announcer, Grant Turner, had been there since 1944. When John Conlee was made an Opry member in 1981, he was the first new member since Larry Gatlin joined five years earlier.

HAL DURHAM:

We must face the fact that some of the present members of the Opry will either want to retire, quit, or whatever. We, like any business, can't close the door to young entertainers who want to join. Right now, we have 55 members and about 40 show up on Friday and Saturday nights. A lot of people tend to regard the Opry as something that's the same as it was in 1950 or 1935,

Hal Durham welcomes Ricky Skaggs to the Grand Ole Opry.

but the truth is that the Opry has changed through all these years, and now the Opry must reflect what's happening in country music today.

When Hal Durham expanded membership in 1982, it was to newer artists rooted in traditional music, Ricky Skaggs and the Opry's first "alternative" country group, Riders in the Sky. New artists might have been a necessity, but Hal Durham was always conscious of the Opry's audience and heritage.

RICKY SKAGGS:

When I worked with Emmylou Harris, I had an album called Sweet Temptation. *It was on a smaller label, Sugar Hill Records, but a song from that album, "I'll Take the Blame," was number one for six weeks on KIKK radio in Houston. They sung my praises to Columbia Records, and Columbia signed me. I came out to do a couple of guest appearances at the Opry, but I hadn't had my first number-one record. Then I got the phone call from Hal Durham. He wanted to take me out for the big lunch. About midway through the salad, Hal said, "Son, you're settin' the woods on fire. What would it mean to you to be a member of the Grand Ole Opry?" I about swallowed my fork.*

Ernest Tubb (right) and Hal Durham (second from right) become born-again cowboys with Riders in the Sky.

DOUG GREEN *of Riders in the Sky:*

I guess we were the first purely western group on the Opry. The Willis Brothers dressed western, but they did all those truck driving songs. And of course Tex

Ritter was a member before us, and half the stuff Marty Robbins sang on the Opry was cowboy songs, but we were the first western group. We didn't have a hit record or the ghost of a chance of having one, but Hal Durham probably thought that we were refreshing and funny, and we had a different sound. We were acoustic but we weren't bluegrass. He saw value in what we did as curators of a tradition and creators within that tradition. The cast made us welcome. We didn't feel like the new freaks on the block.

Another sign that the Opry was relaxing the way it did business came when Hal Durham allowed Marty Robbins to make the last portion of the show into a personal concert that very often ran overtime. His squabbles with the Opry long forgotten, Marty became one of the show's mainstays, but his passion was stock car racing, and he would often compete before coming onstage.

BUD WENDELL:

What happened was that none of the artists wanted to do the 11:30 show, 'cause it was late at night. But from a clear-channel radio standpoint, the signal was the strongest. The later at night it was, the stronger the signal and the greater the reach. Marty realized that, so he wanted to do the 11:30 show whenever he did the Opry. Typically, Marty would arrive at the Opry from the racetrack dirty and smelly. On at least one occasion when he was leading a race he just pulled his car off, parked it, and jumped in his automobile to make sure he did the 11:30 show, so it worked well and he built up that tradition. Even when we split the Opry into two shows, we never asked him to do the first show, because he wanted to race and he wanted to do that 11:30 show when nobody else wanted to do it. Ultimately, it turned out that he was pretty smart to do that 11:30 show. Other artists asked to be on his show.

HAL DURHAM:

He began to take liberties with time. Instead of running over five minutes, he'd run over fifteen minutes. When he started closing the show, we were still doing live commercials with jingles provided by our artists. The sponsor for that last segment was Lava Soap, and the Willis Brothers did their jingle, so when Marty ran late they'd have to wait around to sing that last commercial. Finally, we put the commercials on tape.

A BRAND-NEW BAG

One of Hal Durham's bolder moves backfired, and proved that the Opry cast and audience would only tolerate just so much change. On March 10, 1979, he brought soul music star James Brown to the show. The idea was Porter Wagoner's, but the fact that James Brown embraced it shows that the Grand Ole Opry's influence went far beyond country music.

PORTER WAGONER:

If James Brown was on the Opry, I thought we could get worldwide attention. Once in a while that's helpful, even if you're Coca-Cola or the Grand Ole Opry. You can be like Old Man River, just rolling along, but it's nice to have a shot in the arm every once in a while.

GRAND OLE OPRY *audience survey:*

Among the audience sample, country music rated the widest approval. Soul music was top of the "Do not like at all" rating with classical and rock running close behind.

CONNIE SMITH, *Opry star:*

When James Brown was on the Opry, and he said that when he was in Atlanta, he used to shine Little Jimmy Dickens' boots. He said from that time he always wanted to be on the Grand Ole Opry.

BUD WENDELL:

I met him at the old RCA studio on Saturday afternoon. I talked to him, gave him some guidance on what to do or how to do it on the Opry . . . that it was a live show and don't use any four-letter words, you'll have four or five minutes and it's a timed show, and that we didn't have all night.

JUSTIN TUBB:

George D. Hay would be turning over in his grave.

JAMES BROWN:

They treated me like I was a prodigal son. They treated me so nice, I felt guilty. I felt I got as much praise as a white man who goes into a black church and puts a hundred dollars in the collection plate.

The mail that followed included this from the "Greater" Memphis Citizens Council, dated March 15, 1979.

We consider it almost sacrilegious [sic] that the Grand Ole Opry stage (the last bastion of Southern white culture) should be open to soul singer James Brown, as well as other blacks who are not a legitimate part of country music. . . . We protest this infiltration of country music, which represents white roots—white culture. For, if blacks are allowed to move into country music, it will lead to its demise. What has made it special to white people will no longer exist.

Hal Durham replied:

Your letter concerning the recent appearance of James Brown on the Grand Ole Opry has been brought to my attention.

Since Mr. Brown's appearance represented neither an endorsement of his music by us, nor indicated any change in the direction of the Opry, one wonders why some were so affronted by it. The list of non-country acts that have appeared on the Opry is quite lengthy, and includes Perry Como, Dinah Shore, the Pointer Sisters, and Ivory Joe Hunter. We don't anticipate any change in this policy of occasionally introducing these non-country performers who are internationally acclaimed in their field.

Obviously, the Grand Ole Opry does not determine who enters the field of country music, nor did it ever. The Opry reflects, to some extent, the broad spectrum of country music, from the traditional sounds of the Crook Brothers to the modern music of Larry Gatlin and Barbara Mandrell. We have never considered the Opry the "last bastion of southern white culture." The Opry is a 53-year-old radio show that features country music (with occasional non-country guests). Nothing has happened recently to alter that fact, despite efforts by some who would create controversy where there is none.

Hal Durham.
March 20, 1979

top: *Porter Wagoner welcomes James Brown to the Opry as his special guest.*

below: *James Brown performed "Your Cheatin' Heart," "Georgia on My Mind," and "Tennessee Waltz" before launching into a five-song medley of his hits, including "Papa's Got a Brand New Bag."*

★   ★   ★

Running overtime, Marty ate into Ernest Tubb's Midnite Jamboree.

He would talk to Ernest on the air. "Just a couple more songs, Ernest, then we'll turn it over to you." One night, we taped a thing with Tubb so that when Marty said that, we'd punch in a tape with Tubb saying, "Okay, Marty, you've had your time. Now it's my turn." Eventually, we'd punch in a closing of Marty singing "El Paso," and went to sign-off. At the Opry House, they'd still be watching a Marty Robbins concert, but the radio station would switch over to Tubb.

Hal Durham's fears for his aging cast were soon realized. Marty Robbins's health was more precarious than anyone knew, and he died of a heart attack on December 8, 1982, at just fifty-seven years old. On August 14 that year, Ernest Tubb made his last appearance at the Grand Ole Opry and the Midnite Jamboree. His voice had shrunk to a croak and he couldn't move without an oxygen tank. Too sick to work, he retired, and died on September 6, 1984.

LORETTA LYNN, *Ernest Tubb's former duet partner:*

The Grand Ole Opry has never been the same. Today, everybody wants to be Ernest Tubb. All those boys try to look like him. Those hats, those boots, singing about how their ex's live in Texas.

Bill Monroe was hospitalized with colon cancer in 1980, prompting a reconciliation with Earl Scruggs. Roy Acuff's wife, Mildred, died in June 1981, and in April 1983 he moved to a house on the Opryland grounds.

ROY ACUFF:

Someone said, "Roy, you ought to get Bud Wendell to move out of his office on the top floor of the Roy Acuff Museum at Opryland, and make it into a home." Bud said, "Better than that, Roy, we'll build you a home." I had nothing to do with it. If I'd designed it, it wouldn't have cost so much. I was leading a very lonely life in a big house all by myself. I came in at night and it was lonely. I woke up in the morning and it was lonely. Now I'll be someplace where there's people. I can straighten out my life and get out of this loneliness I live in. I sit on the bench in front of my house and sign autographs, then I go back in the house and rest a while. You can't let 'em [tourists] in the house. If I let one in, they'd go tell the others, and I'd end up makin' enemies rather than friends. The house belongs to Opryland. I'm just a lifetime tenant. When I die, the key will be in the door with no strings attached.

The Opry was doing right by its long-serving artists, but the problem of replacing them was more urgent than ever. Hal Durham and Bud Wendell also knew that they must attract younger fans, redoubling the need to bring in younger artists. At the same time, the new artists mustn't alienate the longtime fans. It was a delicate balancing act, and a solution would come when country music went in search of its roots. In the meantime there was some urgent business that consumed everyone's attention: the Grand Ole Opry was for sale.

Nashville Banner

Nashville, Tennessee ☐ **Friday afternoon, July 1, 1983.** ☐ Vol. 109, No. 71 ☐ Music City Media ☐ 42 pages ☐ First edition

Gaylord to purchase Opryland

By Bill Fletcher
and Joseph White
Banner Staff Writers

Gaylord Broadcasting Co. was preparing to sign a letter of intent today to purchase Opryland USA from the American General Corp. of Houston, sources confirmed.

The purchase price was not disclosed but the price tag for the huge entertainment and hotel complex had been set at $270 million.

Gaylord is an Oklahoma-based firm with holdings that include two Oklahoma City newspapers

and the syndicated television show *Hee Haw.*

American General officials were planning to announce the sale later this afternoon on the stage of the Grand Ole Opry House.

The office of Ed Gaylord, president of the firm, said today a press release was being prepared.

"It is a letter of intent," the source told the *Nashville Banner.*

Gaylord is also planning an announcement from their Oklahoma City offices later today.

Expected to be included in the

sale is the Grand Ole Opry, affectionately known as the "mother church of country music," the Opryland USA theme park, the luxurious Opryland Hotel, WSM-AM and WSM-FM radio stations, the Nashville Network, the cable television operation with country music-related programming and Opryland Tours.

Besides *Hee Haw* and the Oklahoma City newspapers, Gaylord owns television stations in Tampa-St. Petersburg, Dallas-Fort Worth, Houston, Milwaukee, Seattle-Tacoma, Cleveland and New Orleans.

The firm also owns a number of radio stations and a newspaper in Colorado Springs.

Oklahoma Broadcasting is a subsidiary of Oklahoma Publishing Co., a privately-held conglomerate with sales of $200 million during fiscal 1981-82. The broadcasting division accounted for half of the parent company's sales during 1982.

American General became the owner of the Opryland complex in November

The $13 billion Houston insurance giant stated it would sell off properties which did not fit its

main financial business, including Opryland.

About 25 companies expressed interest in acquiring parts or all of the Opryland properties, including the Marriott Corp. of Washington, D.C., Bally Manufacturing Corp., Kroger Co., Gulf + Western Industries Inc. and Anheuser-Busch Corp.

American General set a price tag of $200 million to $300 million on the properties, and turned down a bid in March from a local group headed by former NLT Chairman Walter M. Robinson Jr.

First Boston Corp., a nationally

known acquisitions-expert firm which aided American General in taking over NLT, acted as American General's agent in the sale.

Other Nashvillians which attempted to bid on the properties included Nashville's Ingram Industries, headed by E. Bronson Ingram, and a group of investors headed by local attorney Larry D. Woods.

During the negotiations, American General Chairman Harold Hook said the sale would also take into consideration Opryland's position in "Tennessee's cultural heritage."

Ed Gaylord said perfect man for job

By Joseph White
and Bill Fletcher
Banner Staff Writers

Edward L. Gaylord, the man whose company is expected to take over the Opryland properties, is considered by associates and friends as the perfect man for the job.

Sam Lovullo, the producer of *Hee Haw* syndicated TV show owned by the Gaylord Broadcasting Co., said the Gaylord family "are beautiful Southern folks."

"They're very easy to work

with," Lovullo said. "The chemistry of this acquisition is just perfect between Opryland and the folks at Gaylord Co.

"Since the Gaylords already own *Hee Haw*, we see this as a marriage of *Hee Haw* and the Opry," he said.

Gaylord, 64, is a veteran newspaper publisher and broadcaster. Gaylord Broadcasting Co. owns television stations WVTV in Milwaukee, Wis., WTVT in Tampa, Fla., KSTW in Tacoma, Wash., and KHTV of Houston.

Gaylord Broadcasting, a pri-

vately held and family-dominated company, has roots dating back to 1903, when Edward King Gaylord came from Colorado and bought the *Daily Oklahoman* in Oklahoma City. It was four years before Oklahoma was admitted to the union.

He later purchased the *Oklahoma City Times.* E.K. Gaylord died in 1974 at the age of 101, but the family is still involved in the newspapers. Ed Gaylord is listed as editor of the two papers.

Jack Zimmerman, assistant managing editor of the *Daily Ok-

lahoman* and the *Times*, called Gaylord "a very low-key guy, where editorial is concerned."

Other business sources in Oklahoma City said the company is run as a family business, paternalistic but generally fair.

Gaylord's son, Edward K. Gaylord III, is also involved in the management of the newspapers.

Gaylord received his undergraduate degree from Stanford University in 1941. He is a graduate from Oklahoma City University's Law School. He is married to the former Thelma Feragen and

has four children.

Nashville broadcast executive George Gillett, owner of WSMV-TV Channel 4, described Opryland's new owner as a "wonderful businessman who has built a huge company."

Gillett said, "I know his reputation in the newspaper and television business is of the highest order. Nashville is fortunate in that if we are going to have someone other than a Nashvillian buy it, I couldn't think of a better buyer."

Gillett bought WSMV-TV from the NLT Corp. before American

General took over the Nashville insurance holding company. NLT sold the station to pursue its interest in the booming cable television market.

"He (Gaylord) is a member of the board of directors of the Cowboy Hall of Fame in Oklahoma City, and I understand he has been very supportive there, both personally and economically," Gillett said.

Mack Sanders, a former Midwesterner who owns WJRB radio station here, said Gaylord is "a very professional broadcasting

✦ ✦ ✦
15

UNDER NEW MANAGEMENT

In 1968, National Life became part of NLT Corporation. The following year, WSM's founder, Edwin Craig, died. In 1982, a rival insurer, American General Corporation in Houston, launched a hostile takeover. The board of NLT went as far as trying to convince investor Warren Buffett to buy NLT to ensure its independence from American General. Then NLT tried to turn the tables on American General by launching a hostile bid, but that only had the effect of ratcheting up the price that American General eventually paid. The debt incurred in purchasing NLT ensured that American General would place National Life's entertainment properties on the block.

MARGARET ANN ROBINSON, *daughter of WSM founder Edwin Craig:*

It was the biggest blow I have ever survived and the biggest blow my family has ever survived. It was a terrible, crushing personal blow because we were so closely involved with the people who worked at National Life and their families. National Life was run like a family.

top: **Nashville Banner, July 1, 1983.**

below: **Bud Wendell and Ed Gaylord announce the sale of the Opryland properties to Gaylord Broadcasting.**

"It's the mother church of country music," says Tom T. Hall. "Who goes and sells off your church?" The answer is American General Corp. of Houston. Minnie Pearl, who has been bemoaning her ill-fated attempts to "ketch a feller" since 1940 sees little humor in the proposed transaction. "It's our Opry, our womb, our cocoon. We're like children who've always had the same babysitter." But American General says it needs to drum up between $400 million and $700 million to help offset debts that triple to $950 million with the $1.5 billion NLT purchase. Besides, "businesses that are off our main thrust probably don't fit," says Harold Hook, chairman of American General. Whether the locals like it or not, it will be hard to find a parent as attuned to the Opry as NLT's National Life.

When American General spun off WSM, the Grand Ole Opry, Opryland, and its other media properties in July 1983, it was to Gaylord Broadcasting of Oklahoma City, a company very much attuned to the background and core values of National Life's entertainment group. Gaylord was already producing *Hee Haw* at the Opryland complex.

BILL ANDERSON:

American General couldn't have cared less about the Grand Ole Opry. All they wanted to do was get rid of it. Mister Gaylord had gotten involved in Nashville through Hee Haw, *and I wouldn't be a bit surprised if some of the* Hee Haw *stars, like Roy Acuff and Minnie Pearl, didn't twist his arm a little bit.*

The turmoil came just as Bud Wendell was finalizing a bold plan to take National Life's entertainment group into cable television.

BUD WENDELL:

Ultimately as WSM, Inc., evolved into Opryland, we became bigger than National Life. We felt that there really was an opportunity to create a cable channel of country music. Cable was in its infancy, but we were watching it very closely and we just felt that there was an opportunity, so we went to our owners at National Life and said to them, "This is a high-risk proposal; a very high-risk proposal." The business plan we put together [indicated] that if we did as well as

we thought, it would take us five years to turn a profit, and in that five years we
were going to lose about sixty million dollars. But if it worked the way we
thought it would, from that point on it was going to be fabulously successful.
And they believed us, so they said, "Okay. Go ahead." So we built The Nashville
Network, and we added one thousand rooms to the hotel. We were building the
network and spending the money when National Life was taken over. American
General saw what was going on and it scared them to death, so they put us up
for sale. At the same time, I had been acquainted with Ed Gaylord, because we
were producing Hee Haw *for him . . . so as soon as American General said that*
they were going to sell us, [Gaylord's] people came to me and said, "We really
would be interested in looking at this."

BILL FLETCHER, *journalist, in the* Nashville Banner:

American General handed the reins of the huge Opryland complex to Ed and
Thelma Gaylord, but WSM Inc. chairman Bud Wendell will remain in the
driver's seat. A well-placed source said the sale price is "in the neighborhood of
$270 million." The source said that only American General and top Gaylord
officials know the actual price. Dignitaries from Houston, Oklahoma City, and
Nashville filled the Grand Ole Opry House. It was already decided that the
destiny of the Opryland complex, including the Grand Ole Opry, the theme
park, the Opryland Hotel, the tours, and the new Nashville Network will remain
in the hands of local people. Gaylord pledged to become "one of the best
corporate citizens in the Nashville area."

TNN made its debut on March 7, 1983, and, on April 13, 1985, *The*
Grand Ole Opry Live began as a thirty-minute show on the network.

HAL DURHAM:

When we put the Opry out on TNN, a lot of people who were not familiar with
the Opry could see what it was. After the NBC network dropped the Prince
Albert show, we'd only been on WSM-AM, but with the addition of television
we were able to be in homes all across the country, as we once had been at the
height of network radio. And, as you might expect, there was additional exposure
for the artists on the show. There was some reluctance at first, but we found that
all the artists wanted to be on the televised portion because they've seen the
results of what that exposure can do for them.

BILL ANDERSON:

If you look at some of the very earliest Opry television shows from the 1950s, you'll see merry-go-rounds and things like that on there that were no part of the Opry then or any other time, but when they finally decided to televise the Opry just like it was—warts 'n' all—that's when the Opry began to succeed on television. The broadcasts on TNN had an enormously positive impact. In fact, a lot of people began thinking that the Opry was a television show. Television put a face on the Grand Ole Opry and took it to places where it had never gotten during the later years of AM radio.

In June 1986, Opryland branched into another area of the music business when it bought Acuff-Rose Publications from Wesley Rose and Roy Acuff. The price was not revealed, but Acuff-Rose was valued at around twenty million dollars at the time. The company had begun in 1942 when Acuff guaranteed Fred Rose twenty-five thousand dollars.

The Nashville Network arrived at a turning point in country music history. In 1981, at the height of the *Urban Cowboy* craze, country music accounted for fifteen percent of record sales, but by 1984, its share had dropped to ten percent or less. Just as the Opry had to solve the problem of its aging cast, country music itself needed new performers and new direction. The Opry's problem was highlighted when seventy-three-year-old President Ronald Reagan visited the Friday Night Opry to celebrate Roy Acuff's eighty-first birthday.

JIM O'HARA *and* ED CROMER, *journalists, in the* Tennessean:

A toe-tapping, singing Ronald Reagan brought his upbeat re-election campaign to the stage of the Grand Ole Opry. It coincided with Roy Acuff's 81st birthday celebrations. Lee Greenwood broke into a rendition of "God Bless the U.S.A.," with Reagan and others on stage and many in the crowd singing along as confetti dropped from the ceiling. The words to the song, which is featured in a Reagan television commercial, were printed on the backs of old-fashioned church fans passed out among the crowd.

PRESIDENT RONALD REAGAN:

We're here today to celebrate the eighty-first birthday of the King of Country Music. And, Roy, the other day I met with some senior citizens in the White

House, and I told them the only way I could sum up my feelings about older folks is to greet them by saying, "Hi, kids." I was thinking on my way down here in the plane: All of you are aware, I think, that there's a great resurgence of patriotic feeling sweeping the country. And it's heartening, and I've been moved by it. You could see it during the Olympics, how the crowds out in Los Angeles would wave the flag and sing along to "The Star-Spangled Banner." Now, there are a lot of reasons, I guess, why this good spirit has returned to our land. But it got a lot of encouragement from Nashville. It's the people of this city who never forgot to love their country, who never thought patriotism was out of style. And I know you were just expressing how you felt; you didn't know that you were doing your country a great service by keeping affection for it alive in your songs. But you were doing it a service, and I don't know if anyone has ever thanked you. But if not, thank you. People like you make me proud to be an American.

Now, the [Democrats] keep saying the answer to all [our] success is to start another old round of tax and tax and spend and spend. I think we all better remember that the [Democrats'] promises are a little like Minnie Pearl's hat—they both have big price tags hanging from them.

And nostalgia played a large role in the Opry's sixtieth anniversary show in November 1985. CBS-TV taped a special that aired on January 14, 1986. A segment of the show was given over to the Opry's veterans back home at the Ryman. Even Roy Acuff had become a little sentimental about the Ryman after ten years away.

MINNIE PEARL:

We reminisced a lot that night. When Roy Acuff walks out on that stage singing "The Wabash Cannonball," and I stand in the wings and watch him, it's as if I'm with him playing in rural Alabama on a rainy Monday night in the 1940s. To me, his voice hasn't changed in its rendition, in his fervor, and in his love of that audience. And when I walk out onstage, I feel something special. The Opry audience is different from any other audience. They've sent in for those tickets and have come here especially for the show. The majority of them are there because they care. "The Ryman Remembered" is my favorite part of the

Roy Acuff decorated his dressing room door in honor of President Reagan's visit.

show. We had such a feeling of déjà vu. I love the new Opry House, but back in the Ryman I felt the ghosts. I thought about what kind of person I was back then. I said to Roy while they were changing a camera angle, "What are you thinking about?" He was looking off so far away. He said he was thinking about all the people that had sat there in the Ryman in those old pews and what their hopes and dreams were.

President Ronald Reagan wishes Roy Acuff a happy eighty-first birthday.

Returning to the Ryman only emphasized how integral the Opry had once been to country music. It was still the most important stage in country music, but now the show's managers had to find its new role.

MICHAEL McCALL, *journalist, in the* Nashville Banner:

A typical live Opry broadcast in 1957 might feature current hits by Kitty Wells, Hank Snow, Ray Price, Jim Reeves, Faron Young, Webb Pierce, Marty Robbins, the Everly Brothers, and a dozen other leading hit-makers. [This year] 1987, a Saturday night roster at the Opry bears little resemblance to a Top 40 chart. On February 7, for instance, the line-up included only one act — the Whites — that had achieved a major hit in the 1980s. Today, with television, video, and other means of promoting a new act, live radio does not carry the same strength. And the discrepancy between the Opry's modest stipend and the income from a solo concert has grown ever larger.

The Ryman Remembered. From left: Pee Wee King, Roy Acuff, Bill Monroe, Minnie Pearl, Grandpa Jones, Little Jimmy Dickens, and Grant Turner.

HAL DURHAM:

Of course, the Opry doesn't have the impact on careers that it once did. At one time, the Opry represented the only game in town. Today, the artist has a lot of other doors open to him or her, mainly through the business of records. When the Opry was booming in the 1930s and '40s, the record business, especially country records, was very limited. Very few stations played country records, except at odd times, like five o'clock in the morning. Today, with thousands of country radio stations, it has opened the doors to so many people, and the Opry, as a live music place, is rare. So the Opry isn't the only game in town any more, but it is the only game in town that can offer that tradition, going back to the roots. Hank Williams, Patsy Cline, Red Foley, Roy Acuff. My experience has been that, at every show at the Opry, those spirits are there.

BUD WENDELL:

When road dates got so lucrative, you couldn't ask an act to come in and play the Grand Ole Opry for $100 or $200 when they were making $20,000 or $30,000, and now they're making $100,000, so it now becomes a situation, in my judgment, where, if they really want to be part of the tradition or the family, they'll cut out enough dates, or balance their schedule, where they'll be there on Saturday nights and make it worth their while and worth the Opry's while.

In the late 1980s and early 1990s, country music and the Grand Ole Opry were reinvigorated by artists with a deep respect for all that the Opry represented. Emmylou Harris and Ricky Skaggs had kept tradition-based music alive through some lean times, but suddenly they were joined by Randy Travis, Reba McEntire, Vince Gill, Clint Black, Patty Loveless, Alan Jackson, Marty Stuart, and Garth Brooks. These new artists didn't *need* the Opry as earlier generations had, but *wanted* it for all it symbolized.

RICKY SKAGGS:

Mister Acuff said something to me the night I joined the Opry. He said, "Yeah, we'll make you a member, but you'll never show up. You'll be like all the rest of 'em." And I said, "I'm gonna make you eat those words." And so every weekend I

Ricky Skaggs picks with Roy Acuff backstage.

was at the Opry, I'd knock on his door, and I'd say, "Hey, Mister Acuff, I'm here again." Finally, it got to a point where he said, "I don't want to hear it anymore."

STEVE BUCHANAN, *president of the Grand Ole Opry Group:*

There was one time that Vince Gill played on Roy Acuff's portion of the Opry. Vince was singing "When I Call Your Name," and Roy Acuff was sitting off to the side on a stool. Roy was listening so intently to Vince, and tears were running down his cheeks. It spoke to his love of the music. He was very unselfishly engaged in the song. To me, that perfectly symbolizes the Opry, handing it down from generation to generation.

Garth Brooks joined on October 6, 1990, the same night that Alan Jackson first appeared on the show. Introduced by Johnny Russell, Brooks performed "Friends in Low Places," "If Tomorrow Never Comes," and "The Dance."

CAROL LEE COOPER, *Opry star:*

Garth Brooks said that when he went out there it was so touching to stand in that circle where all of these people had stood before, people that are no longer with us, and he said that all he could do was stand there and cry. Johnny Russell was the one who introduced him that night, and Garth said, "I'll never forget Johnny Russell for this. He hugged me, and put the microphone down at his side where no one could hear what he said, and he said, 'Just enjoy it. Enjoy the moment.' "

HAL DURHAM:

There was an occasion in the 1960s at the Ryman when the audience reacted to a performance by Johnny Cash. They stomped their feet on those wooden floors, and the sound of a full house stomping their feet on those floors was

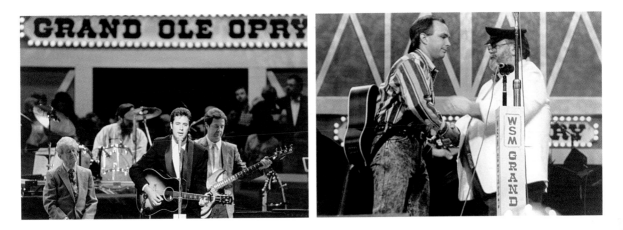

unbelievable. When we moved to Opryland with its concrete floors, it was a whole different sound. But there was one time when Garth Brooks appeared. He'd been on the Opry for a good while, but he had a period of achieving great success very suddenly. And he came back to the Opry for the first time after maybe a couple of big records, and the noise in the Opry House reminded me of the noise I'd heard at the Ryman in the 1960s.

left: **Roy Acuff looks on as Vince Gill performs.**

right: **Johnny Russell inducts Garth Brooks.**

ROY CLARK *to the Opry audience, following Garth Brooks:*

Twenty years ago, your mothers used to scream like that for me.

The new members joined the Opry just in time for the older members to pass the torch. Grant Turner died on October 14, 1991, and the following year the Opry lost one of its most iconic performers.

JAY ORR, *journalist, in the* Nashville Banner:

On its 67th anniversary broadcast Saturday night [November 30, 1992], the Grand Ole Opry family mourned the passing of a stalwart and celebrated the arrival of an exciting new member. A holiday weekend capacity crowd joined the Opry in marking the passing of Opry legend Roy Acuff and in welcoming new member Marty Stuart. Opry manager Hal Durham said, "This is an evening of great personal sadness for us all. For the first time in 54 years, the Grand Ole Opry will be going on without Roy Acuff. It will simply never be the same without him, and there is no way to replace him. But while we will miss his presence, his music and his spirit will forever be a part of this show." Jimmy

Dickens presided over the evening's brightest moment, the televised induction of Marty Stuart as the 70th [active] member of the Grand Ole Opry. He was announced as being the 71st member before Acuff's death.

MARTY STUART, *press conference, November 1992:*

There's a brand-new crop of country fans that haven't a clue about the Opry. I think it's our job to recruit 'em and introduce them to how great the Opry can be. I worked the Opry with Lester Flatt, but I left the show when Lester died in 1979. I called Hal Durham and told him that the prodigal son was ready to return. I've talked to Saturday Night Live bandleader G. E. Smith and Letterman bandleader Paul Shaffer, and I'm finding that people like that have always died to play the Opry, but never had a reason or been asked. Hal's agreed to let people like that come out and sit in with me.

Minnie Pearl had suffered a stroke in 1991; she died on March 4, 1996. Her husband didn't tell her of Acuff's passing.

When Bill Monroe was asked "Who will lead bluegrass music into the twenty-first century?" he replied without a moment's hesitation: "I will." He knew, though, that his prodigious energy was failing, and he died on September 4, 1996, knowing that the music he'd done more than anyone to create was more popular than at any time in its history.

BILL ANDERSON:

Mister Monroe mellowed a lot. I think he finally found that what he'd created was accepted and honored. He realized that it had all been worthwhile and was

An all-star bluegrass band, including the Osborne Brothers, Earl Scruggs, Jim and Jesse, Bill Monroe, the Whites, Ricky Skaggs, and Patty Loveless.

justified. That served to mellow him tremendously. It was a complete metamorphosis, and it was fun to watch. In earlier days, I'd pass him in the hallway backstage and I'd say hello and he'd walk right by you, but it got to where he'd kid with you, and he'd put a quarter in your hand after you'd performed. He could put aside some of the old animosities.

SHARON *and* CHERYL WHITE *of the Whites:*

Ricky [Skaggs] played commercial country music but tried to show the bluegrass influence. He was competing with whatever was on the radio, but he had Bill Monroe in the videos, and Bill began to appreciate that. Then when the Kentucky Headhunters did his song "Walk Softly on This Heart of Mine," the royalty checks made a believer out of him. It showed you could take bluegrass and make something commercial out of it, just like Elvis had done thirty years earlier. They put us in a dressing room with [Bill] at the Opry. We were on MCA Records then, and he'd pitch songs to us. He'd say, "Listen to this. Sing with me." We'd never heard it before! But when Bill Monroe says, "Sing with me," you try. We'd watch his mouth, and try our best.

RICKY SKAGGS:

Seeing people like me and others showing him respect really started to break down some of the walls he'd put up for protection. He was a very shy and very lonesome person, and I just pushed my way into his life. I think the love that I and Marty Stuart, Vince Gill, Patty Loveless, and others showed him began melting a lot of the coldheartedness he'd had. Then he had open-heart surgery, and that'll get your attention. I'd go over to his place, and we'd just play for three or four hours. He'd listen to me and he'd see that the music was going to live. Before he died, I promised him that I would tell the story of him and his life and his music. He was able to rest after that. I told him that the music was much bigger than him.

His funeral was a sad day but a happy day. It was at the Ryman, and it was one of those moments that only seem to happen at the Ryman. There's a scripture in the Bible which says that if the seed does not die and fall to the ground, it cannot produce fruit some thirty, some sixty, some hundredfold. Me and Marty and Vince Gill had been out to sing "Angel Band," and we came backstage. There was a digital clock backstage, and I looked at it. It had 11:11 on it. That number

*Roy Huskey, Jr.,
Patty Loveless, Vince
Gill, and Marty
Stuart bid farewell to
Bill Monroe.*

*has followed me. So many times, I'd look at a clock
and it would be 11:11. The way a digital clock reads, it
looks like a scripture. Eleventh chapter, eleventh verse.
There was an illumination around it, and I felt that
my heart was being pulled toward that. I said to
Marty, "That's a scripture. I'm gonna look that up."
God is trying to tell all of Mister Monroe's seed
something. We'd sung all these somber songs—"Angel
Band," and so on—and Marty looked at me, and said,
"Don't you think we ought to send him home with a
celebration?" I said, "Absolutely." He said, "Let's do
'Rawhide,' " and I said, "Yeah!" We got out there and
played "Rawhide" at six hundred miles an hour. I said
to everyone, "If you have a problem with this, get over
it. This is to honor Bill Monroe." The place came
unglued. It was like you'd put an electric shock in
every seat. It was a holy experience. When I got home,
I got my Bible out, and looked at different scriptures. I
looked at Isaiah, chapter 11, verse 11. It says, "And it
shall come to pass in that day that the Lord shall set
his hand again the second time." Second time, you
see. You can look, but from 1996, bluegrass music has
turned somersaults. It has grown and become so
popular. People say, the revival in this music started
with [the film O Brother, Where Art Thou?]. Wrong! O Brother didn't fire up
our music. Our music fired up O Brother. When Mr. Monroe died, I felt that it
was time for me to give up my career in country music and take my place at the
table to play this music I'd grown up playing.*

VINCE GILL:

*He loved that music so much, and he created it. Who else can say that they
defined a genre of music? It was Earl [Scruggs'] banjo and much else, but he put
it together, and that's a prideful thing and he was a prideful man. But it comes
back to the songs, and they're his songs. They're the common denominator. "Can
you play 'Molly and Tenbrooks' "? "Can you play 'Rose of Old Kentucky'?" The
legacy of great songs goes beyond his popularity as a singer. It's like Hank
Williams in that regard. I sang at Bill's memorial, and I was doing okay until*

the bagpipes played my song, "Go Rest High on the Mountain." Then I lost it. I didn't know it was coming. I was so honored that a song of mine was played at his memorial.

Hank Snow died December 20, 1999, and at the beginning of the new century, Little Jimmy Dickens was the only regular remaining cast member from the 1940s. The older generation was now the stars who'd come to the Opry in the 1950s, artists like Jimmy C. Newman, Wilma Lee Cooper, Porter Wagoner, Stonewall Jackson, and Jean Shepard.

JEANNIE SEELY:

They changed the Opry in their day and we changed it with drums and violins and in other ways. Their Opry has gone away, and now our Opry is going away because it's supposed to be going away. It's supposed to change, and it's changing as it's supposed to change.

As the new century dawned, country music was second only to rock as the most popular type of music in the United States, but once again the landscape was changing. Online radio, satellite radio, and music downloads were on the near horizon, changing an industry that once thought solely in terms of analog radio and records. Again, the Opry had to adapt or risk obsolescence.

FRIDAY, November 22, 1996

7:30-8:00 - Cracker Barrel
Porter Wagoner
Jimmy Dickens
Skeeter Davis
Oswald & Charlie
Ricky Skaggs

8:00-8:30 - Kraft-Maxwell
House/Rudys
Jimmy C. Newman
Bill Carlisle
Charlie Louvin
Stonewall Jackson

8:30-9:00 - Opry Book/
Fairfield Nashville
Grandpa Jones
Holly Dunn
Ray Pillow

9:00-9:30 Fiddlers Inn-Ramada
Inn/Williamson Dickey
Jim Ed Brown
Osborne Brothers
Wilma Lee Cooper
Riders In The Sky

9:30-10:00 - Dollar Store
Bill Anderson
Jack Greene
Jan Howard
Alison Krauss

10:00-10:30 Sheplers
Western Wear
Jeannie Seely
Jean Shepard
Jeanne Pruett
Daryle Singletary

10:30-11:00 Georgia Boot
Johnny Russell
Stu Phillips
The Whites
Billy Walker

6:05-6:30
Vietti/Goldkist
Opry Warm-Up Show
Kyle Cantrell, host

SATURDAY, November 23, 1996

FIRST SHOW

6:30-6:45 - GHS Strings
Mike Snider
Skeeter Davis

6:45-7:00 - Joggin In A Jug
Grandpa Jones
Trace Adkins

7:00-7:30 - Shoneys
Ricky Skaggs
Bill Carlisle
Holly Dunn
Jimmy C. Newman
Jeannie Seely

7:30-8:00 - Standard Candy
Marty Stuart
Jean Shepard
Alison Krauss
Travis Tritt

8:00-8:30 - Martha White
Bill Anderson
Daryle Singletary
Jeanne Pruett
Vince Gill
Opry Squaredance Band/
  Melvin Sloan Dancers

8:30-9:00 - Kraft Velveeta
Shells & Cheese
Jack Greene
Del Reeves
Rider In The Sky
Charlie Walker

SECOND SHOW

9:30-10:00 - Dollar General Store
Ricky Skaggs
Oswald & Charlie
Jeanne Pruett
Travis Tritt

10:00-10:15 - Massey-Ferguson
Grandpa Jones
Alison Krauss

10:15-10:30 - Opry Book
Jim Ed Brown
Jean Shepard

10:30-10:45 -Purnell's Sausage
Bill Anderson
Vince Gill

10:45-11:00 - Opry Book
Mike Snider
The Whites
Opry Squaredance Band/
  Melvin Sloan Dancers

11:00-11:30 - Coke
Marty Stuart
Daryle Singletary
Holly Dunn
Trace Adkins

11:30-12:00 - Loreal Haircare
Johnny Russell
Del Reeves
Jeannie Seely
Jimmy C.Newman

The Baldwin Grand is the official piano of the Grand Ole Opry

GRAND OLE OPRY®

NEW MEMBERS: 1990s

CLINT BLACK

GARTH BROOKS

BASHFUL BROTHER OSWALD
(PETE KIRBY)

DIAMOND RIO

JOE DIFFIE

VINCE GILL

ALAN JACKSON

HAL KETCHUM

ALISON KRAUSS

EMMYLOU HARRIS

MARTINA McBRIDE

JOHNNY PAYCHECK

CHARLEY PRIDE

MIKE SNIDER

MARTY STUART

TRAVIS TRITT

STEVE WARINER

TRISHA YEARWOOD

✫⋆✫
✫16✫

FACING THE FUTURE

I n the mid-1970s, the chance of Nashville's seedy downtown core being reborn
looked no brighter than the Ryman's chance of avoiding the wrecker's ball, but by
the late 1990s, weekend crowds thronged downtown as they had in the 1940s. Jo
Mielziner, the theatrical designer who'd called for the Ryman to be demolished, died
in 1976 and didn't live to see the Ryman become not only a centerpiece of Nashville's
downtown renewal but one of the country's premier live-music venues. Even the
Grand Ole Opry returned there for limited runs.

STEVE BUCHANAN, *president of the Grand Ole Opry Group:*

The Ryman had been open for daily tours and there were some segments of television shows
and movies shot there. In 1991, Emmylou Harris recorded an album at the Ryman with a
small audience and it really got people thinking about what we could do with it. Then, in
1992, we staged a special performance to celebrate the one hundredth anniversary of the
Ryman, again with a relatively small audience. It was a magical night with performances by
Emmylou Harris, Vince Gill, Ricky Skaggs, Bill Monroe and Connie Smith. It reminded

Passing it on. Vince Gill and Loretta Lynn, August 18, 2001.

everyone of what an extraordinary place the Ryman is to hear live music. At the same time, the city was starting to focus on downtown redevelopment, so the time seemed right to bring the Ryman back to life.

RICHARD BENNETT, *coproducer of Emmylou Harris's* At the Ryman:

The safety code meant that total admissions were restricted to something like two hundred a show, and we planned out the set list and recorded the same set three times in three days. All the reverb is natural there. It's just a marvelous room for recording. I think everyone had forgotten just how good.

EMMYLOU HARRIS, *liner notes to* At the Ryman:

It's more than the size and shape of that cornerless room. More than the wood used to build the curve in the Confederate Gallery, and more than the distance that a bass note has to travel to hit that back wall with those stained glass windows where the light sometimes came streaming in to illuminate the heart and soul of it all. It's the hillbilly dust.

Garrison Keillor and Chet Atkins on A Prairie Home Companion *at the Ryman. Keillor would eulogize Atkins at his funeral, held at the Ryman in 2001.*

MARY HANCE, *journalist:*

Opryland's parent company, Gaylord Entertainment, invested more than $1 million [eventually $8.5 million] in 1989–1990 to clean, stabilize, and restore the exterior of the Gothic structure and re-roof the Ryman Auditorium. The renovation and expansion (the construction of a 14,000 square foot support building on the north side) is set for completion by June 1994, in time for Fan Fair. The project will return the revered auditorium as a performance venue with 1,500 seats instead of the original 3,200. [The final capacity would be just over 2,300.] The total Ryman site size has tripled to 1.1 acres with the land Opryland is purchasing through the Metro Development and Housing Agency.

The official reopening was slated for June 4, 1994. The first show held there was Garrison Keillor's *A Prairie Home Companion,* the radio program inspired by the last night at the Ryman twenty years earlier.

In January 1999, the Opry returned to the newly refurbished Ryman for a three-show run. The following year it spent all of January there, and has since made the Ryman its winter home.

Porter Wagoner stars at the Opry's return to the Ryman, 1999.

BILL ANDERSON:

From an artist's point of view, it's wonderful for the half hour or so that you're onstage back at the Ryman. But then you have to park across the street in good or bad weather. There are no lockers so you can't leave your instruments or costumes or anything. There's not as many dressing rooms. But there's something awfully magical about walking out onto that stage. That said, after four months I'm ready to come back out to the new Opry House.

In January 1998, Opryland amusement park closed. In May 2000, the Opry Mills shopping mall opened on the site. The mall doesn't draw as many tourists as the park once did, and without the park as a "feeder," the Grand Ole Opry now relies more heavily upon its artists. At the same time, it has embraced new media, and in addition to its traditional home on WSM-AM, it can be heard over the Internet and on satellite radio. Parts of the show are also seen on American Forces television and on Great American Country cable television.

Hal Durham retired in 1996 and Bud Wendell in 1997. Bob Whittaker replaced Hal Durham. He'd joined the Opryland amusement park in 1971 and produced shows for the park before moving to the Opry in 1993.

BOB WHITTAKER:

I was a frustrated singer, but no one ever paid a dime to hear me sing, nor should they. I think the music and the industry dictate the changes at the Opry. It hasn't lasted because some general manager came in and decided to do something. It has lasted because we've been responsive to the industry and the fans.

We ask Opry members to do twelve appearances a year, but flexibility is the name of the game. Marty Stuart will walk in and ask if there's any room on the show. Vince Gill, too. One of the charms of the Opry is that it's not a tightly formatted show.

Bob Whittaker retired in 1998, and the Opry is currently in the hands of Steve Buchanan, president of the Grand Ole Opry Group, and Pete Fisher, vice president of the Opry Group and manager of the Grand Ole Opry.

PETE FISHER, *Opry vice president and general manager:*

The legacy alone is motivation enough to make you want to do your best for the Opry. When I first came here, I didn't want to do anything that would evoke a reaction, like scheduling James Brown, but I've come to realize that the Opry is so diverse that reaction is good. If people aren't saying, "Well, I loved it," "Well, I hated it," then we're losing some of the magic. Just because we're here to celebrate country music doesn't mean that we always have to preach to the converted.

People say the top stars are either on the road, in the studio, or on vacation, but there are many artists, many top artists, who share the special connection with the Opry and will make it a priority in their career. It brings context to what they do. They know where the music's been and they visit with the people who forged it. They see new artists who give us a hint of where the music might be going, and they reconnect with their place in the whole scheme. What we have to do is stay out in front of contemporary performers who are still building their careers. We want to return the Opry to being a star-making machine in country music, and we want to nurture the people who will still be in country music thirty years down the road.

STEVE BUCHANAN:

When you're entrusted with an iconic institution like the Grand Ole Opry, you can't help thinking of how the decisions you make today will impact the Opry in ten or twenty years. We not only want to build relationships with artists at an early point in their careers, but we want to build relationships with the music industry in general. Then, as a young artist's career builds, we're hopeful that they'll want to continue the relationship with the Opry and make the show part of their future. There are wonderful rewards and dividends conferred by Opry membership. Many of them are emotional and speak to the relationships among the artists. The Opry has never been about financial compensation, but we want the show to play a role in developing careers on different levels. Opry membership confers recognition that you simply don't get elsewhere.

PETE FISHER:

You don't persuade artists to join the Opry. If it takes persuasion, they're probably not right for us, nor we for them. In some artists, it's just inherent to respect all that the Opry stands for, and there is value for them in appearing on the show. The great thing about country music is its connection to where it comes from, and that continuum is a powerful factor. You measure the health of the Opry by the attendance of artists from all generations and customers from all generations. My dad stocks trout in his ponds and he says that to keep the ponds healthy you need a little stream of water coming in and a little stream going out, and that's how it is with the Opry.

John Dennis (Adkins's management company), Steve Buchanan, Jimmy Dickens, Trace Adkins, and Gaylord Entertainment President and CEO Colin Reed pose backstage the night Adkins was invited to join the Opry cast.

Among longtime cast members, there is some resentment that the newer artists don't appear regularly, but the Opry is attracting top new stars, such as Dierks Bentley and Brad Paisley, who are on the road up to three hundred days a year. In fact, the Opry—in the person of Marty Stuart—had to catch up with Dierks in Los Angeles to ask him to join. (Ironically, Dierks had been a researcher for TNN earlier in his career, and spent so much time backstage that Opry manager Pete Fisher asked him to back off.)

left: **Brad Paisley and Bill Anderson, October 2001.**

right: **Opry members Patty Loveless and George Hamilton IV (right) are joined by Opry general manager Pete Fisher in welcoming Del McCoury to the Opry cast. Looking on are Rob McCoury and Jason Carter.**

RICKY SKAGGS:

Some members of the Opry don't show up much as I'd like. I know the dollars are out there, and it's hard to give up those weekends. But one day, those weekends won't be there, but the Opry will still be here, and it'll be nicer to come back if you've invested. My son and I have this thing we call our love bank. Every time I hug or kiss him we make a deposit in the love bank. It's kind of like that with the Opry. Every time I come here on weekends, I feel like I'm depositing something. It's the history of the future.

BILL ANDERSON:

If I'm in Nashville on a Friday or Saturday night and I'm not at the Opry, I feel like I'm playing hooky and I keep waiting for the truant officer to come and throw me in jail. Sure I take time off and I'm not there every time that they open the doors, but I take membership very seriously. The dollars have changed so much. Artists today can make more in one weekend than we made in a year when I first came to Nashville. But a lot of younger artists are very rooted in the Opry and what it means because they've taken the time to study where country music comes from. Some of the newer artists, of course, could care less and came into country music from other areas. So you can't say that all the young artists appreciate the Opry, but a lot of them have heard from their parents or

grandparents what the Opry's all about and they want to be a part of it. The other thing is that these young artists are selling a lot of records and drawing a lot of crowds right now, but there will come a time when that slows down for them, and hopefully when it does, they will come and spend more time at the Opry. We all owe a debt to the Opry, and we all ought to be willing to make payments on that.

HAL KETCHUM, Opry star:

I've just started to realize the true meaning of the Opry. The community backstage is as important as the time onstage. It's an opportunity to wander through and hear Ralph Stanley and his band warm up, and feel the energy of this music. There are apprentices and there are masters. If you are interested in any way, shape, or form in this great American art form, the Grand Ole Opry is the source. To me, country music is poetry and polyester. Simplicity is a very hard thing to achieve. Anyone can be clever.

Marty Stuart surprises Dierks Bentley at a Los Angeles concert appearance with an invitation to join the Grand Ole Opry on July 26, 2005.

Alan Jackson chose the Grand Ole Opry for the location of his video for the song, "Too Much of a Good Thing."

PETE FISHER:

You look out at the audience and you literally see a three-year-old and a ninety-three-year-old. Then the Opry is a celebration of the generations. It's diversity sharing the same stage, and it's so rare today.

STEVE BUCHANAN:

The average age of our audience varies from night to night. We feel that we are seeing more young patrons as we bring in more new and developing artists. It adds to the diversity of our programming and to the diversity of the audience. Ed Clark took some famous photos when the Opry was at the Ryman in the 1940s. There's a shot of a flatbed truck with three generations coming off the back. We still have that today with three generations sitting together enjoying the show as a family. To me, a really great night at the Grand Ole Opry reflects the diversity in style and genres and age groups. You'll have comedy, bluegrass, western music, legends, and some of the brightest new stars. A great night at the Opry really shows the world the breadth and depth of country music. Those shows are just magical. Things take place here that can't take place anywhere else, and those are the times that will give you chills.

BILL ANDERSON:

Sometimes there's just the right mixture of the old and the new. It's not possible to get that every night, but there are nights when that perfect mix just seems to be there. The younger fans get tuned in to some of the older artists, and the older fans accept some of the younger acts. When that happens, the Opry is the most electric place in the world. The eightieth anniversary show is a case in point. I got a call from Pete Fisher on the Thursday before the Saturday show. He said he'd called Garth to ask him what he was going to sing, and he said, "I want to do a medley with Jimmy Dickens, Porter Wagoner, and Bill Anderson." I think it was his way of saying that those of us who've been here a while should be honored. It was a very generous, kind, and giving thing for him to do because he

could have come out there and taken over the stage with his own hits. He said, "I'm coming out of retirement to honor the Opry," and the way he did it by performing with us was a wonderful way to honor the Opry. I'd always liked Garth and my admiration for him went up tenfold.

DOUG GREEN *of Riders in the Sky:*

The experience is so rich. In one evening, you can hear Jimmy C. Newman do Cajun music, and you can see the hottest young belly button do her thing, followed by a legend like Billy Walker or Jack Greene, and then great bluegrass like the Osborne Brothers. I love it when Ray Pillow comes on and does those two-step shuffles. Nobody else is doing that anymore. But the real magic of the

Garth Brooks, Porter Wagoner, Bill Anderson, and Little Jimmy Dickens perform at the Opry's eightieth birthday bash.

Opry is when someone like Vince Gill will come out and sing a tune with us. Once, we sang with Roy Rogers on the Opry stage. We call those Grand Ole Opry moments. Often completely unplanned.

JEANNIE SEELY:

They open the doors and raise the curtain and say, "This is the Grand Ole Opry," and we all know anything can happen. It's the freedom, I guess. The freedom allows spontaneity, and encourages people to work together.

Some music—punk comes to mind—made a conscious rejection of all that went before, but country music has always been rooted in tradition. The Grand Ole Opry embodies that tradition, and remains one of the premier stages in popular music. For instance, on January 22, 2005, Marty Stuart brought African American gospel star Mavis Staples of the Staple Singers onto the Opry, and the music they performed together not only showed the deep kinship between the rural music of white and black America, but created a spontaneous musical event that could not have happened anywhere else but at the Grand Ole Opry.

DOUG GREEN:

When the Opry started, there was little else in the way of entertainment. Now, of course, there's so much more. So many things compete for your attention, but the Opry is still a viable part of the American music scene. Look, the music that Riders in the Sky play—it went out of fashion fifty years ago, but we're out there next to the hottest young act. There's nothing comparable anywhere in the world. People come up to me all the time and complain about current country music. Okay, so you don't like it, but there's such an incredible variety of music out there now on digital radio, satellite radio, Internet, and so on, and the Opry brings this variety together on one stage. That's why it's a legendary institution and a vital institution.

ANCIENT TONES AT CARNEGIE HALL:
NOVEMBER 14, 2005

As part of its eightieth birthday celebrations, the Grand Ole Opry played Carnegie Hall for the third time in its history. As on the other two occasions, cowboy hats outnumbered pearl necklaces, but this time the gossip columnists kept their barbs to themselves. The fact that the Country Music Association Awards were being held at Madison Square Garden the following night silenced everyone. Vince Gill hosted the show with his customary low-key humor, and the first act, Trace Adkins, pointedly chose "Songs About Me" as a way of preparing the New York audience for what it was about to hear.

The house lights were up for the entire show, and every artist was visibly awed by the surroundings. Ricky Skaggs mouthed "wow" to himself before introducing klezmer clarinetist Andy Statman to play the introduction to Bill Monroe's "Walls of Time." Skaggs closed with "Black Eyed Susie," a song first recorded the year before the Opry went on-air, and just the sort of song that Judge Hay hoped to preserve.

Ricky Skaggs, with his band Kentucky Thunder, makes his mark on what is a surprisingly well-established tradition of bluegrass performances at Carnegie Hall.

Vince Gill and Little Jimmy Dickens bring a little Opry-style humor to staid Carnegie Hall.

In the media meet and greet, Trisha Yearwood explained Opry membership to *Newsday* magazine: "The Opry doesn't invite you because you're selling records or having hits. This group of people is trying to preserve the history of country music, and they've decided that you're worthy. It's an honor." Recalling her own induction, she said, "Patsy Cline's children were there, and they presented me with a necklace that had belonged to Patsy." The show built on the theme of handing it on.

JON PARELES, *journalist, the* New York Times:

The concert was a country manifesto promising unity, tradition, sincerity, and glimmers of diversity. Collaborations presented country as one big family.

Bill Anderson explained how Brad Paisley and Alison Krauss had revived his songwriting career when they recorded "Whiskey Lullaby." Alison and Ricky Skaggs joined Vince Gill on a hymn inspired by the death of Vince's brother, "Go Rest High on that Mountain." Alison also performed Patsy Cline's "She's Got You," a song that Patsy recorded one month after the previous Carnegie Hall concert in November 1961. Charley Pride did Hank Williams's "Kaw-Liga," and Martina McBride sang Tammy Wynette's " 'Til I Can Make It on My Own." And Little Jimmy Dickens, who joined the Opry just months after the 1947 Carnegie Hall show and missed the 1961 show, sang his 1965 hit "May the Bird of Paradise Fly up Your Nose."

PETER COOPER, *journalist, the* Tennessean:

*The show ended with each performer back onstage, singing cast versions of
"I'll Fly Away," "I Saw the Light," and "Will the Circle Be Unbroken." But the
enduring image from the night may be of young guitar slinger Brad Paisley*

*and Hall of Famer Bill
Anderson offering a
guitar/vocal
performance of "Too
Country," asking the
New York crowd, "Are
the biscuits too fluffy/Is
the chicken too fried?"*

*Too country? Nope, not
for Carnegie Hall.*

Brad Paisley and
Alison Krauss treat
the Carnegie Hall
audience to their
award-winning duet,
"Whiskey Lullaby."

★   ★   ★

The Opry's founder, the Solemn Old Judge, George D. Hay, had a vision of preserving the music of rural southeastern America, but that music
changed through the years. What Judge Hay heard in 1925 when he
started the Opry wasn't the music that the first songcatchers heard a generation earlier, and that wasn't the same as the music that had crossed the
Atlantic. The only constant is change, and the pace of change is acceler-
ating. But in some respects Judge Hay's vision has held true.

"If the Opry is ever permitted to go upstage," he wrote on the occasion
of the show's thirty-second anniversary in 1958, "to lose its flavor and feeling of goodwill—among the artists themselves and for their listeners—it
cannot last. But if it keeps these wonderful human qualities, the Opry is
good for another hundred years. I believe most people would like the
Opry if they would slow up long enough to 'listen it out.' "

GRAND OLE OPRY

FRIDAY NIGHT LINE-UP

March 5, 2004
7:30 p.m. – 10:00 p.m.

7:30-8:00
Sponsored by:
CRACKER BARREL OLD COUNTRY STORE

PORTER WAGONER
CONNIE SMITH
JIMMY C. NEWMAN
JESSE MCREYNOLDS
& THE VIRGINIA BOYS
DIAMOND RIO

8:00-8:30
Sponsored by:
DICKIES WORKWEAR

RICKY SKAGGS
JACK GREENE
JEANNIE SEELY
THE WHITES

8:30-9:00
Sponsored by:
JOHNNY WALKER TOURS

JIMMY DICKENS
JAN HOWARD
OSBORNE BROTHERS
SHERRIE AUSTIN

9:00-9:30
Sponsored by:
COUNTRY MUSIC HALL OF FAME

BILL ANDERSON
RALPH STANLEY
MARK WILLS

9:30-10:00
Sponsored by:
NASHVILLE STAR VACATION PACKAGES

PAM TILLIS
CHARLIE WALKER
MIKE SNIDER
DEL MCCOURY BAND

ANNOUNCERS:

HAIRL HENSLEY
EDDIE STUBBS
KEITH BILBREY

Artists & schedule subject to change.

GRAND OLE OPRY

Coming Soon to the Opry Stage:

March 13: Pam Tillis, Keith Urban, Terri Clark, Montgomery Gentry, Ricky Skaggs
March 20: Jeff Bates, Andy Griggs
March 27: Steve Wariner, Hal Ketchum
April 3: Jeff Bates
April 17: Trace Adkins, Travis Tritt
April 24: Terri Clark

Artists and schedule subject to change

The Grand Ole Opry proudly uses the following musical equipment:
Yamaha Pianos & Drums, Peavey, Rivera and Ampeg Amplification, Sabian Cymbals, and Pro-Mark Drum Sticks, Brushes and Mallets.

Official Speaker of the Grand Ole Opry House

GRAND OLE OPRY

SATURDAY NIGHT LINE-UP

March 6, 2004
6:30 p.m. – 9:00 p.m.

6:30-7:00
Sponsored by:
ODOM'S TENNESSEE PRIDE

JIMMY DICKENS
CONNIE SMITH
OSBORNE BROTHERS
MARK WILLS

7:00-7:30
Sponsored by:
TOOTSIE'S ORCHID LOUNGE

PAM TILLIS
MIKE SNIDER
JEANNIE SEELY
RALPH STANLEY

7:30-8:00
Sponsored by:
STANDARD CANDY

RICKY SKAGGS
BILLY WALKER
JIMMY C. NEWMAN
THE WHITES

8:00-8:30
Sponsored by:
MARTHA WHITE

PORTER WAGONER
DEL MCCOURY BAND
CRAIG MORGAN
OPRY SQUARE DANCE BAND
WITH THE
OPRY SQUARE DANCERS

8:30-9:00
Sponsored by:
RESORT QUEST

BILL ANDERSON
JULIE ROBERTS
JIM ED BROWN
ALISON KRAUSS
+ UNION STATION
FEATURING JERRY DOUGL...

ANNOUNCERS:

HAIRL HENSLEY
EDDIE STUBBS
KEITH BILBREY

Artists & schedule subject to change.

March 6, 2004
9:30 p.m. – 12:00 a.m.

9:30-10:00
Sponsored by:
COCA-COLA

JIMMY DICKENS
CONNIE SMITH
ALISON KRAUSS
+ UNION STATION
FEATURING JERRY DOUGLAS

10:00-10:30
Sponsored by:
DREAMWORKS/ TRACY LAWRENCE

PORTER WAGONER
JESSE MCREYNOLDS
& THE VIRGINIA BOYS
MIKE SNIDER
MARK WILLS

10:30-11:00
Sponsored by:
RESORTQUEST

PAM TILLIS
BILLY WALKER
JACK GREENE
RALPH STANLEY
OPRY SQUARE DANCE BAND
WITH THE
OPRY SQUARE DANCERS

11:00-11:30
Sponsored by:
WSMONLINE.COM

RICKY SKAGGS
JULIE ROBERTS
THE WHITES

11:30-12:00
Sponsored by:
NASHVILLE STAR VACATION PACKAGES

JIM ED BROWN
DEL MCCOURY BAND
CRAIG MORGAN

TRACE ADKINS

DIERKS BENTLEY

TERRI CLARK

DEL McCOURY

BRAD PAISLEY

RALPH STANLEY

PAM TILLIS

☆ ☆ ☆

BIBLIOGRAPHY

Unless cited here, all interviews are by the author or are Grand Ole Opry file interviews.

Chapter 1

DeFord Bailey in *A Black Star in Early Country Music* by David Morton and Charles Wolfe. Nashville: University of Tennessee Press, 1993.

Edwin Craig, *Tennessean*, October 15, 1967.

Margaret Hay Daugherty, *Bluegrass Unlimited*, July 1982.

Fiddlin' Sid Harkreader, *Fiddlin' Sid's Memoirs*. JEMF, 1976.

George D. Hay, *Tennessean*, August 17, 1952; *Nashville Banner*, November 10, 1958; *A Story of the Grand Ole Opry*, self-published, 1945; *The Grand Ole Opry Hits the Road*, unpublished manuscript, 1949.

Pete Montgomery, *Tennessean*, October 4, 1970.

Charles K. Wolfe, *A Good-Natured Riot: The Birth of the Grand Ole Opry*. Nashville: The Country Music Foundation Press and Vanderbilt Press, 1999.

Chapter 2

Alton Delmore, *Truth Is Stranger Than Publicity*. Nashville: CMF Press, 1977.

George D. Hay, *A Story of the Grand Ole Opry*.

Rufus Jarman, "Country Music Goes to Town," *Nation's Business*, February 1953.

Uncle Dave Macon, *Brunswick Topics*, 1928.

Sam McGee in *A Good-Natured Riot* by Charles K. Wolfe.

Bashful Brother Oswald, *That's the Truth If I've Ever Told It*, self-published, 1994.

Vito Pellettieri in Jack Hurst, *Nashville's Grand Ole Opry: The First 50 Years*. NY: Abrams, 1975; *Tennessean*, June 12, 1960, October 4, 1970, and April 15, 1977.

David Stone interviewed by John Rumble, Country Music Hall of Fame oral history program.

Grant Turner, *Grant's Corner*, WSM-AM, November 7, 1986; March 26–27, April 8, 1987.

Irving Waugh in *Nashville's Grand Ole Opry: The First 50 Years*.

Chapter 3

DeFord Bailey in *A Black Star in Early Country Music*.

Alton Delmore in *Truth Is Stranger Than Publicity*.

Jim Denny in *Tennessean*, March 3, 1963.

George D. Hay, *The Grand Ole Opry Hits the Road*, unpublished, 1949.

Pee Wee King in *Hell Bent for Music*. Lexington: University of Kentucky Press, 1996.

Chapter 4

Roy Acuff in *Country & Western Classics*, Time-Life Music; "Roy Acuff Celebrates 26th Year with Opry," *Nashville Banner*, November 5, 1964; "Acuff, King of Country Music, Now Mostly Counts His Money," by Larry Rohter, *Milwaukee Journal*, June 24, 1977.

DeFord Bailey in *A Black Star in Early Country Music*.

Cleo Davis interviewed by Wayne Erbsen, *Bluegrass Unlimited*, February/March, 1982.

Alton Delmore in *Truth Is Stranger Than Publicity*.

George D. Hay in *A Story of the Grand Ole Opry*.

Pee Wee King in *Hell Bent for Music*.

Pee Wee King interviewed by Otto Kitsinger in *Pee Wee King & His Golden West Cowboys*, Bear Family Records, 1996.

Jake Lambert, *Biography of Lester Flatt*. Hendersonville, TN: Jay-Lyn Pub., 1982.

Edward Linn, "Country Singer: The Ernest Tubb Story," by Edward Linn, *Saga*, May 1957.

Bill Monroe interviewed by Alanna Nash in *Behind Closed Doors* and by Charles K. Wolfe, *Old Time Music*, Spring 1975.

Hank Williams interviewed by Ralph J. Gleason.

Chapter 5

Roy Acuff in *Nashville's Grand Ole Opry*.

George Barker in *Tennessean*, March 3, 1963.

Don Eddy, "Hillbilly Heaven," *American Magazine*, March 1952.

George D. Hay in *A Story of the Grand Ole Opry*, and undated 1960s radio broadcast.

Vince Hines in Albert Cunniff, "Muscle Behind the Music: The Life and Times of Jim Denny." *Journal of Country Music*, Vol. 11, Nos. 1–2, 1986.

Pee Wee King, *Hell Bent for Music*.

Pee Wee King interviewed by Otto Kitsinger in *Pee Wee King & His Golden West Cowboys*.

William R. McDaniel & Harold Seligman, *The Grand Ole Opry*. Greenberg Press, NY, 1952.

Sam McGee in *Tennessee Traditional Singers*. Knoxville, TN: UT Press, 1981.

Minnie Pearl in *Grinder's Switch Gazette*, March 1945, May 1945.

Harry Stone in *Tennessean*, October 4, 1970.

Grant Turner on *Grant's Corner*, WSM–AM, March 31, 1987.

Maurice Zolotow, "Hillbilly Boom," *Saturday Evening Post*, February 12, 1944.

Chapter 6

Chet Atkins interviewed by Alanna Nash in *Behind Closed Doors*.

Marie Claire interviewed by Albert Cunniff in "Muscle Behind the Music: The Life and Times of Jim Denny," *Journal of Country Music*, Vol. 11, Nos. 1–2, 1986.

Jim Denny in "Big Wheel on the Bandwagon," *Tennessean*, March 3, 1963.

Little Jimmy Dickens interviewed by Eddie Stubbs in *Country Boy*, Bear Family George D. Hay, radio broadcast, 1960s.

Rufus Jarman, "Country Music Goes to Town," *Nation's Business*, February 1953.

Hank Snow, *The Hank Snow Story*. Champaign: University of Illinois Press, 1994.

Jack Stapp interviewed by Bill Ivey, August 8, 1972.

Ernest Tubb interviewed in Ashboro, NC, *Courier-Tribune*, September 20, 1981.

Chapter 7

Roy Acuff in *Billboard*, February 3, 1968; "Acuff, King of Country Music Now Mostly Counts His Money" by Larry Rohter in *Milwaukee Journal*, June 24, 1977.

David Cobb in *Nashville! Magazine*, July 1986.

George D. Hay, *A Story of the Grand Ole Opry*.

Wesley Rose in *Billboard*, February 3, 1968; *Record World*, September 8, 1973.

Jack Stapp interviewed in *Nashville Banner*, October 9, 1977.

Chapter 8

Mae Axton in *Nashville Banner*, July 14, 1956.

Johnny Cash and Patrick Carr, *Cash*. NY: HarperCollins, 1997.

Marie Claire and Ken Marvin quoted in Cunniff, Albert, "Muscle Behind the Music: The Life and Times of Jim Denny."

Jim Denny in *Country Music Reporter*, October 6, 1956.

Little Jimmy Dickens interviewed by Eddie Stubbs in liner notes to *Out Behind the Barn*, Bear Family Records, 1997.

Ben A. Green, "Johnny Cash Achieves Life's Ambition, Wins Opry Hearts." *Nashville Banner*, July 14, 1956.

Stonewall Jackson and Hal Smith in Ronnie Pugh, *Ernest Tubb—The Texas Troubadour*. Durham, NC: Duke University Press, 1998.

Buddy Killen in *By the Seat of My Pants*. NY: Simon & Schuster, 1993.

Bill Monroe interviewed by Alanna Nash in *Behind Closed Doors*.

Scotty Moore in *That's Alright Elvis*. NY: Schirmer Books, 1997.

Dolly Parton, *My Life and Other Unfinished Business*. NY: HarperCollins, 1994.

Wesley Rose in *Record World*, September 8, 1973.

Chapter 9

Kenny Baker and Ralph Rinzler in *Bossmen*, by James Rooney. NY: Dial Press, 1971.

Jake Lambert, *Lester Flatt: A Biography*. Nashville, TN: Jay-Lyn Publications, 1982.

Bill Maples, "Marty, the Opry Together Again," *Tennessean*, March 1958.

Chapter 10

Ott Devine letter to Earl Scruggs, February 15, 1966.

David Hall, "National Life Buys Ryman," *Tennessean*, September 6, 1963.

Clara Hieronymous, *Tennessean*, December 6, 1964.

Ernest Tubb, *Music City News*, October 1971.

Johnnie Wright to Eddie Stubbs, *Johnnie & Jack: The Tennessee Mountain Boys*, Bear Family Records, 1994.

Chapter 11

Ralph Emery in *Nashville Tennessean*, October 14, 1973.

D. Kilpatrick in Jack Hurst, *The Grand Ole Opry: The First 50 Years.*

Ralph Rinzler, "A Man and His Music," *Pickin'*, December 1976.

Kathy Sawyer, "Lester & Earl," *Tennessean*, October 16, 1966.

Marty Stuart, "Flatt & Scruggs," *The Journal*, December 1991.

Ernest Tubb in *Music City News*, October 1971.

Pat Welch, "Flatt's Temperament Blamed by Scruggs," *Tennessean*, April 17, 1969.

Chapter 12

Randy Brooks, *Vanderbilt Hustler*, March 19, 1968.

Bill Hance, "Stringbean Would Have Been Vexed," *Nashville Banner*, November 12, 1975.

Grandpa Jones and Charles Wolfe, *Everybody's Grandpa*. Knoxville: University of Tennessee Press, 1984.

Rose Maddox and Jonnie Whiteside, *Ramblin' Rosie*. Nashville: Vanderbilt University Press, 1997.

Roger McGuinn quoted in Bud Scoppa, *The Byrds*. NY: Scholastic, 1971.

Chapter 13

Jack Hurst, "Opry Already Out to Surpass Last Year's Record Attendance," *Tennessean*, February 21, 1972.

Ada Louise Huxtable, "Only the Phony Is Real," *New York Times*, May 13, 1973.

Garrison Keillor, "At the Opry," *New Yorker*, May 1974.

Sam McGee in *Tennessee Traditional Singers.*

Uncredited report, "Acuff Says Ryman Should Go Before It Falls," *Tennessean*, March 15, 1974.

Uncredited report, "Opry Center Gets Under Way," *Tennessean*, July 1, 1970.

Uncredited report, "Stars Say No to Razing Ryman," *Tennessean*, December 9, 1976.

Uncredited report, "Tear Down Ryman, Acuff Recommends," *Tennessean*, December 18, 1976.

Del Wood in *Tennessean*, December 9, 1976.

Chapter 14

Roy Acuff quoted by Red O'Donnell, "Roy Acuff 'Lifetime Tenant' at Opryland," *Nashville Banner*, April 22, 1983; Sandy Neese, "New Opryland Home Is Fit for King of Country," *Tennessean*, April 22, 1983.

Hal Durham in Paul Kingsbury, *The Grand Ole Opry History of Country Music.* NY: Villard, 1995.

Porter Wagoner quoted in Steve Eng, *A Satisfied Mind.* Nashville, TN: Rutledge Hill Press, 1992.

Chapter 15

Bill Fletcher, *Nashville Banner*, July 2, 1983.

Michael McCall, *Nashville Banner*, February 16, 1987.

Sonia L. Nazario, *Wall Street Journal*, undated clip.

Jim O'Hara and Ed Cromer, "Upbeat Reagan Mixes Opry with Politicking," *Tennessean*, September 14, 1985.

Jay Orr, *Nashville Banner*, November 30, 1992.

Margaret Ann Robinson in "Nashvillian of the Year," *Nashville Scene*, December 27, 2001.

Chapter 16

Peter Cooper, *Tennessean*, November 15, 2005.

Mary Hance, undated clip in *Nashville Banner* archives.

Emmylou Harris, liner notes to *At the Ryman*, Warner Bros. Records, 1992.

Jon Pareles, *New York Times*, November 15, 2005.

＊ ＊ ＊

PHOTOGRAPHER CREDITS

From the Grand Ole Opry Archives:

John E. Hood Photos: pp. ii, 2, 54, 57, 58, 65, 79, 81, 83, 86, 88, 92, 99, 102, 114; Commercial Photograph Co.: pp. 15, 25; Elmer Williams: p. 31; Wiles: p. 32; Gordon Gillingham: pp. 63, 95, 103, 104, 109, 115, 116, 118, 121–124, 126, 128, 129, 132–134, 136, 140, 142, 143, 148, 166, 169, 183; Ken Spain: pp. 44, 66, 101, 117; Henry Schofield Studio: pp. 84, 100; Charles Renegar: pp. 88, 102, 112; Walden S. Fabry: pp. 95, 106; John Faber: p. 99; Photographic Arts, Inc.: p. 99; Sid O'Berry: pp. 123, 185; Les Leverett: pp. 151, 154, 155, 158, 161–165, 173, 174, 178, 185, 187, 194, 197–199, 204, 206, 209, 220, 221; Donnie Beauchamp: pp. 218, 221, 222, 224, 230; Chris Hollo: pp. xi, 228, 233, 234, 237, 239–241; Annamaria DiSanto: p. 235.

Additional Sources:

Minnie Pearl Collection: p. 5; Nashville Public Library, The Nashville Room: pp. 17, 156, 212; Bear Family Records: p. 24; Tennessee State Library and Archives: p. 81; William P. Gottlieb © Copyright 1979: p. 97; © The Tennessee Historical Society: p. 106; Colin Escott: pp. 121, 139; Showtime Music Archives: p. 148; Les Leverett: pp. 158, 180, 209; *Tennessean*: p. 201.

All other illustrations and photographs are unattributed and from the Grand Ole Opry Archives.